Flats, families and
the under-fives

International Library of Social Policy

General Editor Kathleen Jones
Professor of Social Administration
University of York

A catalogue of the books available in the **International Library of Social Policy** and other series of Social Science books published by Routledge & Kegan Paul will be found at the end of this volume.

Flats, families and the under-fives

Elizabeth Gittus
Department of Social Studies
University of Newcastle upon Tyne

Routledge & Kegan Paul
London, Henley and Boston

First published in 1976
by Routledge & Kegan Paul Ltd
39 Store Street,
London WC1E 7DD,
Broadway House,
Newtown Road,
Henley-on-Thames,
Oxon RG9 1EN and
9 Park Street,
Boston, Mass. 02108, USA
Manuscript typed by Reba Lawless
Printed in Great Britain by
Morrison & Gibb Ltd,
London and Edinburgh

ISBN 0 7100 8284 3

for Karen, Geoffrey and John

Contents

Illustrations

Flats, families and
the under-fives

Preface

The addition of this book to the now considerable literature on the problems of young families in high-rise housing may briefly be explained as follows. It is the outcome of an inevitably protracted attempt, both to dis-
charge an obligation to the Northumberland and Tyneside
Council of Social Service, whose initiative prompted the
survey described in Part one, and to comply with the late
Professor Sprott's recommendation that the content and
conclusions of Part one should be placed in a wide
setting. In Parts two and three this has been done.

Despite the time-gap, the Tyneside survey is offered as
a contribution, methodical and substantive, to the current
debate. Methodologically, it is centred on the ways in
which the mothers with young children in various forms of
local authority housing on Tyneside perceived their situation. Substantively, it was among the first empirical
studies to suggest that many of the problems that are
commonly ascribed to high-rise housing may be no less real
to young families in the lower-rise high-density development which, as shown in Part two, has proliferated following the demise of the fashion for high flats in the late
1960s. Part three introduces another general issue. Here
the provision of opportunities for play for those children
whose home conditions may be limiting are considered in
the context of the expansion of nursery education and
other forms of pre-schooling and day-care. The whole discussion is focused on the government's declared concern
about the plight of young children in local authority
flats, whatever their elevation. The most recent halt in
the pre-school programme clearly enhances the urgency of
this central theme. The responsibility for any in-
accuracies or omissions in the treatment of these complex
matters is entirely mine.

I am indebted to many people, first of all to Mr J.D.

Long, Organising Secretary of the Northumberland and Tyneside Council of Social Service and to Miss W. Smith, Head of the Council's Training Unit, for their forbearance throughout the various evolutionary stages of this document; also to the students, as they were at the time, who shared in the design of the survey, studied each area in detail, conducted the interviews, and helped in the preliminary stages of the analysis. Their names appear below.

Among my professional colleagues, in Newcastle and elsewhere, I have benefited from the encouragement of Professor Kathleen Jones, Professor Peter Collison and Professor Kathleen Bell, and from many communications with Dr Vere Hole, of the Building Research Establishment, Department of the Environment, Miss A. Watson, who chaired the working party mentioned above, Miss Pearl Jephcott, the University of Glasgow, John Darwin, Newcastle Community Development Project, Peter Malpass, Architectural Research Unit, University of Edinburgh, and with my colleagues Jon Davies, Norman Dennis, Dave Green and Peter Selman. Ann McClurkin, Chris Stephens and Sue Webber also helped with the analysis of the survey and other data. I am also most grateful to the Warden and Fellows of Nuffield College, Oxford, for enabling me to visit the College for a sabbatical term, and especially to Dr A.H. Halsey, Dr Keith Hope and Patrick Dunleavy for their injections of interest and enthusiasm. It remains to thank Mrs A. Rule, who typed the original document with her customary speed and efficiency and Mrs R. Lawless for her meticulous work in producing the final copy and, on a personal note, to record my indebtedness to my Mother. To the memory of her indomitable energy and resilience I owe more than I can say.

E.G.

THE SURVEY TEAM: D. Byrne, P. Crimmins, L. Eastop, J. Fairbairn, E. Gubbins, V. Jupp, P. Mawson, A. McNair, N. Nugent, C. Ogier, R. Payne, J. Peacock, J. Pizzey, S. Slater and E. Stewart.

Part one

The Tyneside survey

1   Background to the survey

The survey was the outcome of discussions, among social
workers of the Northumberland and Tyneside Council of
Social Service, about the conditions in which young children housed in multi-storey accommodation might be growing
up.

It was already commonly supposed that the restrictions
of flat life could be harmful to the development of the
child's personality and, if not to his own health, to that
of his mother. Several research projects had set out to
test these assumptions. Their findings, though tentative
and limited, did reveal states of loneliness, isolation
and frustration that appeared to bear some relation to
this kind of housing experience. (1) It could not be
claimed however that the association was either strong or
direct.

In January 1967 the Regional Family Casework Committee
set up a working party to consider the extent of such
problems on Tyneside. The working party was initially
motivated towards remedial action but it was evident, as
their discussions progressed, that members were interested
in certain questions that would require careful
investigation.

It is still maintained that children who are housed in
the upper floors of multi-storey blocks are at risk of becoming anti-social, backward, shy, of being unable to play
or to take enough physical exercise. The difficulty of
bringing up children in these conditions has been a matter
for concern ever since high buildings became a common
feature of local authority housing. (2)

The needs of children in three contrasting areas of
high-density development had been studied, some years
previously, by the sociological research section of the
Ministry of Housing. (3) Fundamental to their inquiry was
the principle that plans to house families at high density

3

should include some measures to compensate for the adverse
features of their environment, and especially for the lack
of free space where children could play in safety. 'The
higher the densities, the more complete the communal
amenities should be.' (4) The official manual 'Flats and
Houses' included this recommendation: (5)

The provision of play space must be one of the first
calls on the available space around dwellings in multi-
storey development which do not have gardens of their
own.... The important thing is to recognise that the
beneficial social effects of good housing conditions
can be largely cancelled out if there is nowhere immediately near their homes where children find it enjoy-
able to play.

It was generally agreed that, of all age-groups, the
'under-fives' were most likely to be affected by these restrictions, for the first five years of life are considered crucial for the development of personality. The young
child, especially between 2 and 5 years, needs to explore,
to discover and to try out his own physical abilities. He
also needs companionship with children of his own age and
with adults, beyond the special protective relationships
within his own family. Much of this experience comes to
him through play. For this he needs 'space, space that is
safe and space where he can make a mess. He needs the
company of other children, for while he may not play with
others when very young, he plays alongside them.' (6) He
also needs variety in play, for even the most absorbing
object or activity seldom holds the interest for very
long.

These fundamental needs would apply to all children of
this age, regardless of the social position of their
parents. But it is clear that there are disparities, especially within our modern urban society, both in the
awareness of these needs and in the ability to meet them.

The 1944 Education Act included the statement that sufficient places should be available in nursery schools to
cater for all children whose mothers wished to make use of
them. In these schools, in a 'rich' environment, with an
inventive teacher, the child was to learn by doing. (7)

Nursery schools and nursery classes have been proved
over and over again to be not only convenient for the
working mothers of young children, ... but also im-
mensely helpful to the mental health and growth of
ordinary children who get bored at home and want company in a calm atmosphere, free from strain, which only
a trained teacher can engender.

The chronic shortage and uneven distribution of opportunities for nursery education, during most of the 1960s,

gave increasing importance to voluntary efforts to provide
opportunities for play. Prominent in this field were the
Pre-School Playgroups Association and the Save the Children Fund. The former, staffed by a volunteer band of enthusiastic mothers, possibly made more impact, in the
early days, in middle-class areas. The latter had already, by 1967, some eighty playgrounds for children in
the large cities. Developments from 1967 to date are outlined in Chapter 9. (8)

But apart from these organised services, which are
nowadays somewhat hopefully combined under the general
heading of 'day-care', the young child also needs the
opportunity for spontaneous play in the immediate vicinity
of his home. Here the child who is housed in restricted
conditions can be at a disadvantage. Twenty years ago it
was argued that 'the provision of one or more playgrounds
must be a first call on the available space around flats,
because it is on children that the restrictions of flat
life press most readily'. (9)

Members of the working party, while accepting these
principles, were curious to know more about the families
in high-rise accommodation, in particular how mothers of
young children evaluated the situation and how they coped
with the matter of their children's play. The answers to
this and related questions were to be sought from a survey
whose design is discussed in Chapter 3. The choice of
authorities to be included was determined as follows.

A preliminary review of the distribution of multi-
storey dwellings on Tyneside had been made, by the Council
of Social Service, in the autumn of 1966. The local authorities that came within the Tyneside conurbation are
listed in Table 1, with their estimated populations and
the numbers of dwellings built by or for them up to 31
March of that year.

Information on the number of multi-storey buildings,
and especially of high blocks, was compiled from the individual housing departments. It was found that only four
out of the fourteen authorities had buildings of more than
5 storeys when the inquiry was made. These were
Newcastle, Gateshead, Wallsend and Jarrow. (10)

In South Shields, second only to Newcastle in population size and in its stock of dwellings, building high was
precluded by the danger of subsidence from extensive coal-
mining in the vicinity. By contrast, in Whitley Bay,
local authority housing catered for only a small section
of the population and for them it was possible to satisfy
the almost universal preference for a house and garden.

Longbenton included the site of some overspill housing
from Newcastle and will be considered later in that
context.

TABLE 1   Local authority housing on Tyneside (11)

Local authority		Population mid-1965	Dwellings built by or for LA to 31 March 1966
Newcastle	CB	257,460	32,109
South Shields	CB	108,540	13,463
Gateshead	CB	101,560	9,808
Tynemouth	CB	72,280	7,283
Wallsend	MB	48,720	5,952
Whitley Bay	MB	38,310	1,590
Jarrow	MB	26,450	5,664
Longbenton	UD	47,580	3,717
Felling	UD	38,710	6,971
Newburn	UD	31,630	3,057
Blaydon	UD	31,220	3,942
Gosforth	UD	27,400	2,006
Whickham	UD	26,990	2,743
Hebburn	UD	25,070	4,004

In some areas, too, there were plans to build high blocks and some were going up already. In Felling, work was beginning on 16-storey flats. In Gosforth, some of 6 storeys were due for completion in 1967, but it was intended to house families with small children on the lower floors only.

Of the four authorities with high blocks that were currently occupied, both Jarrow and Gateshead were selective in their allocation of tenancies. In Jarrow, a block of 11 storeys high had just been completed, but these were not to be let to families with children under 11, and, when a child was born, the position of the family was to be reviewed. Gateshead had fairly recently introduced a definite policy to restrict this type of accommodation to families without children, but the rehousing of young families from the older multi-storey flats was likely to take some time to complete.

On this evidence, therefore, it was decided to focus the survey within Newcastle, Gateshead and Wallsend. The localities within these boroughs that were chosen for study will be described fully in Chapter 3. In Gateshead, the choice was predetermined by the fact that young families remained in only a few high blocks near the town centre. Although it was planned to rehouse them all as soon as possible, some aspects of their experience, in regard to play and other matters, seemed to be worth recording, since they were likely to apply also to families elsewhere, in similar conditions, but with more doubtful prospects of transfer. In Wallsend, the high flats formed part of an estate of mixed development, away from the centre, and close to the very busy road from Newcastle to the coast. There were some play spaces near the flats, but the site was especially hazardous because of traffic to and from the main road and on the service roads to the estate itself.

The preliminary survey revealed that, among the 30,000 or so dwellings provided by or for Newcastle's housing department, there were 31 blocks from 10 to 20 storeys high, giving almost 3,000 tenancies. A further 8 blocks, including in all 900 flats, were being built. The largest of these was to be 28 storeys high. The 39 blocks were distributed either as isolated units, or within estates with low-rise and houses also, both within the city boundary and beyond it, as for example in Longbenton UD and in the area known as Newbiggin Hall. In all cases there was an attempt to provide space where children could play. Every block had a play area close by. In two of the newer ones there was also room indoors. One of the larger completed schemes of mixed development, known as the Cruddas Park estate, was eventually selected for its centrality, variety of building styles and for other reasons that will be discussed in Chapter 3.

Finally it must be emphasised that, in deciding to exclude from the study local authorities with no flats or maisonettes exceeding 5 storeys, it was not assumed that their tenants were likely to be free from difficulties in bringing up their children. Previous evidence and the results of this survey would suggest that their problems, while possibly of a different character, may be no less acute. It was necessary, for the purpose of this inquiry, to include at least some high blocks, and so, by definition, many authorities were eliminated. It was hoped that the findings for families in other types of dwellings, within the areas chosen, might compensate in some measure for this restriction.

2   The evidence at the time

It has been seen that, in all the areas selected for
study, some attempts had been made to meet the needs of
young children for play, in so far as their needs could be
rightly discerned from currently accepted principles of
child development. On the other hand, the observations
and experience of social workers in these areas combined
to suggest that the facilities for play were in some cases
inadequate and in others unappreciated and virtually
unused.

Faced with these apparent disparities between 'needs',
'provision' and 'demands', the working party decided,
first of all, to study the families in each area, their
reactions to their situation, the relevant problems, if
any, that they experienced and to invite their suggestions
for change.

This might appear to require just a straightforward
exercise in fact-finding. It was true that the subject-
matter and the objectives were clearly defined. But it
seemed inevitable that difficulties would arise in attemp-
ting to ascertain the 'facts', to understand the attitudes
and to assess the reality of any interest that respondents
might declare in, for example, the use of a new play room
or play area or in help with its supervision.

There was also the familiar problem of making recommendations for a whole group of residents, on evidence obtained from its individual members, with all their variety
of disposition, awareness of need, past experience,
ability to adjust, and willingness and capacity to com-
municate these subtleties in an interview situation. This
leads one, further, to question the prospect of ascertain-
ing the 'truth' on a subject of considerable local debate
and one that was at the same time likely to touch on normative issues, with the tendency for respondents to dis-
close what they considered to be acceptable practices and

opinions, rather than those to which they themselves subscribed.

Guidance at the planning stage of the survey was sought therefore from the record of previous investigations, recognising that, in this context, the reservations attached to their findings might be as instructive as their firm conclusions.

In this chapter, the surveys in this field that were available and known to the investigators at the planning stage of the Tyneside study and that had some influence on its design will therefore be reviewed. (1)

Considering the amount of publicity given already to the difficulties of families in high flats there had been surprisingly little systematic field research among them. Press, radio and television had highlighted some of the main issues, but the sum total of objective evidence remained small.

Many of the criticisms of this type of housing had been well taken. Some housing authorities, as in the case of many on Tyneside, were able to avoid this type of construction altogether, or to be selective in their allocation of tenancies. (2) For others, however, including some of the authorities with persistent housing needs, it seemed that, while the present situation was regretted, little could be done to improve conditions for the high flat dwellers, except by the intervention of some voluntary body. Moreover, since young families were usually in the minority among those housed in this way, it was easy to assume that their recreational needs might be exaggerated or were satisfied already by the routine inclusion of a play area on the site plan. The latter assumption is still made to some extent today. (3)

Few authorities had actually taken stock of the preferences of their existing tenants before planning a new estate, as had been done for instance for Liverpool, by the firm of consultants commissioned to design the Belle-Vale estate on the outskirts of the city. (4) Their inquiry, among tenants on an adjoining estate which had been completed in 1958, was said to have uncovered formidable grievances, including the shortage of spaces for play and complaints about noise and the lack of privacy. Some frustrations were more prevalent in the 3-storey flats and 4-storey maisonettes than in the tower blocks. This was thought to be partly due to the higher percentage of children among families in the lower buildings. (5) The consultants did not therefore recommend the abolition of tower blocks altogether in favour of high-density low-rise blocks of 4 or 5 storeys, but stressed the need to watch

the size-distribution of families within each dwelling
type, with an eye also on the overall number of children
per acre. They emphasised the importance of the 'threshold', or means of access to the private quarters of each
family, whether by common entrance, stairs, landing or
balcony. (6) The quality of the siting and lay-out of the
whole estate were also related to the tenants' general
satisfaction. Similar comments were frequently made or
implied by respondents in the present survey. (7)

The results of an inquiry into the play provision for
young children living in high flats in the London area
were published in 1961. (8) The inquiry was commissioned
because of concern for the well-being of these young children and their mothers that had been expressed by health
visitors working among them. The aim of the study was to
establish the facts of the situation and to indicate the
extent and nature of the problem in hopes of influencing
future building design. There was some provision already
for children on these estates, but this seemed, to the organisers of the survey, to have been based on unrealistic
assumptions about the allocation of tenancies and the
siting of play facilities.

The intention, then, was 'to discover, primarily from
mothers of young children, something about play activities
and needs, the extent to which the needs of those living
high (taken to be above the fifth floor), differed from
those on lower floors ...' and further, to study the
actual provision of play facilities and the use that was
made of them. (9)

The inquiry covered twelve municipal estates, most of
which had been built in the preceding ten years, and included other types of building besides high flats. In the
high blocks it was hoped to contact families with at least
one child aged 2 and under 5. In all, 210 interviews were
completed.

There were, in these families, 227 children aged between 2 and 5. These represented about one-quarter of all
London children, in that age group, who were living in
high flats. (10) At the time only a small proportion (0·5
per cent) of the whole 2- to 5-year-old population in the
London Administrative County were housed in this way, but
their numbers were likely to increase and the question of
providing for them to become more urgent. (11)

Interviews followed a standard set of questions. Their
form and content were agreed after discussion, with a
group of parents, on the problems of child-rearing in
these conditions. During the interviews mothers were
questioned directly, or invited to comment, on the following topics: their experience of bringing up children in

that accommodation, the children's needs for play, restrictions in their activity due to noise or fear of
neighbours' complaints, matters of health and safety, and
the general effect of these factors on themselves and on
their children. They were also asked to suggest how
things could be made easier.

On the first topic, there was a good deal of spontaneous comment which was directly or indirectly related
to difficulties over play. Direct references were made
more often by those living above the fifth floor. Adding
to the spontaneous response those who mentioned such difficulties after further prompting, it seemed that children's play was a genuine problem for a large proportion
of the sample.

Among their children's needs, that for playing freely
elsewhere than in the flat, and especially outside, with
other children and without obvious adult supervision, was
felt most acutely by mothers at all levels.

The frequency of comment about play was studied in relation to family size and structure and to the age of the
mother. Overt concern was more commonly expressed among
those aged 35 or more than among younger respondents. (12)

The majority of mothers said that their children were
not particularly restricted in their play because of noise
or the fear of disturbing the neighbours. This might have
been due to a fortunate combination of circumstances (not
disclosed), in that most of the neighbours had children
themselves and that the buildings were effectively sound-
proofed. When these conditions do not apply, the situation may be very different. (13)

Fears for their children's safety were expressed by the
majority of mothers and especially by those living 'high'.
Windows, lifts, stairs and balconies were mentioned as
sources of danger, both here and in a supplementary pilot
survey among families living on the eighth floor and above
on three housing estates. (14) It was argued that the
issues of play and safety could not clearly be separated
and that adequate opportunities for keeping the children
occupied would do much to alleviate other forms of
anxiety. (15)

In assessing the effect of these various aspects of
their situation on their families and on themselves, many
mothers referred to their children's lack of freedom and
need for the companionship of other youngsters and to
their own anxiety, tension and depression. The report was
rightly cautious about the directness of the link between
the mothers' feelings and the problems encountered by them
and their children in that type of housing. The strains
experienced by mothers in this situation might have been

due to delay in settling down in a new estate, the physical structure and amenities of the whole site, or other factors in the 'total emotional environment', that were not included in the research design, or they may be the lot of such young urban families however they are housed. These points will be taken up later. (16)

Mothers were also asked whether their children played on their own and whether the location of play caused difficulties for them. Just over 50 per cent of the children played only in the flat, and living 'high' or 'low' made little difference, except for the 4-year-olds. Mothers living on the lower floors were more inclined to allow their 4-year-old children to play outside on their own, in playgrounds or in the estate grounds, but still there was often the fear that they would wander away. Access and private balconies were used by only a minority of the sample. Mothers were worried about having to keep their children quiet, to restrict their type of play or to cope with the disorder.

Visits, usually with mother, to shops, relatives and friends or to the park or playground all went to make up the 'toddler's day'. In all, however, the impression remained that a good deal of the child's time was spent indoors and seldom away from his mother. (17)

For four of the twelve estates, the actual play facilities were studied more closely, in order to appreciate the mothers' usually adverse comments about them. In one estate, the provision for toddlers was ample and of a high standard and mothers were less critical, but elsewhere, even where some provision was made, this was often described as inadequate or unsuitable, or as affording insufficient protection from roads or from other children.

Against this discouraging picture, mothers were asked to state their preference for four alternative facilities and to say how far they would use them. A supervised playground, playroom or nursery school were equally popular (few went to nursery school already). In these choices, the element of supervision was the determining factor. The fourth option of an enclosed playground with no supervision was preferred by only a small minority.

Some of the recommendations from this inquiry have helped to formulate the general conclusions in Chapter 9. Interest at this point lay in the research plan, the topics covered, and the main results. Later surveys, including the Tyneside one, have supported some of the findings, but it was recognised that any evaluation of the relative and subjective aspects of 'satisfaction' and 'awareness of need' was precluded by the narrowness of the research design.

In 1963 the sociological research section of the Ministry
of Housing and Local Government reported on a study among
'Families Living at High Density' which was made in pre-
paration for the redevelopment of a slum area in an industrial town. (18) The object of the survey was to
    examine the design issues for the redevelopment of a
    central urban industrial area ... through the experien-
    ces of tenants living in such recently developed areas,
    ... in particular, to distinguish any special problems
    connected with living in multi-storey dwellings and to
    assess the relative merits of high and low blocks and
    of flats and maisonettes.
In order to minimise differences in environment and
design, the study was confined to three central urban
estates, two in the north and one in London, all with densities of at least 100 persons per acre and with the
necessary variety of building types.
    The study was concerned with other aspects of family
life besides the needs of younger children, and so the
basic 'population' was defined as families with children
aged under 16. Fortunately for the present purpose, the
estate with most variety of building types also housed the
greatest percentage of families with the youngest child
aged under 5. For convenience, this estate will be called
'A', the other northern one 'B' and the London estate 'C'.
(19)
    The basic population was also restricted to those who
had lived at the same address for at least a year. This
was done in order to allow some time for families to
settle down and begin to establish a circle of friends and
acquaintances, although in estate A, at least, it is pro-
bable that many of the families were known to each other
before they were rehoused. (20)
    It was hoped to select from each estate a sample of
families that were matched as far as possible, in each
type of dwelling, by size and by the age of the children.
In all, 65 interviews were completed in estate A, 53 in B
and 72 in C. In A the distribution of families by dwelling type was as follows: 11-storey flats: 18; 11-storey
maisonettes: 11; 3-storey flats: 12; 4-storey maisonettes: 12; houses: 12. The numbers of families with
children aged under 5 within each dwelling type were
likely even here to be small, nor could they usually be
separated out from the analysis.
    The survey was interesting, however, for the compari-
sons that were made between families in different types of
housing and for its concentration on three specific
estates in the hope of obtaining, in each of them, an
overall picture of the relation of households to their new

environment. As in the survey previously described,
topics covered by the questionnaire included general attitudes to the estate, problems encountered by living there,
noise and neighbours, privacy and isolation, play facilities and other aspects of estate design.

At the end of the interview, each housewife was asked
to sum up her general reaction to her present home. More
dissatisfaction was found among those with children under
5. It could not be known, without analysis of the comments supporting this general statement, whether these
feelings were due to attitudes to the locality, the accommodation, the local amenities, including play, or to the
general siting and lay-out of the estate. The report commented specifically on the importance of landscaping and
design in promoting residents' happiness. (21) On estate
A, the tenants' self-respect seemed to be eroded by the
social and physical characteristics of the area, and their
resentment coloured their attitude to their living conditions. The report suggested that in industrial slum
areas, a lift into a better environment could only be
achieved by a large-scale comprehensive redevelopment.
This should have clearly defined boundaries, and should
include some grass, trees and planting.

Among the items mentioned by housewives as main problems, children's play came high on the list and especially so in multi-storey blocks. On restriction and disturbance because of noise and neighbours, the London findings
confirmed those of the previous survey in that multi-
storey tenants were not particularly troubled by noise.
On estate A, however, these two factors caused more
trouble in multi-storey dwellings than in houses. The
greatest annoyance was found in maisonettes, where living-
rooms were placed over bedrooms and where young families
were living above the quarters of elderly tenants. (22)

Complaints about feeling 'shut off' were more common
than those about the lack of privacy. This applied to
housewives in all dwellings, except houses where the emphasis was reversed, but even here some felt isolated. On
estate A as a whole these feelings were most acute. This
was partly attributed to the respondents' previous housing
situation, where their social life was likely to have been
concentrated in the street just outside the house. Feelings of isolation were more prevalent in the multi-storey
blocks than in the houses. But no consistent differences
were found between respondents on the upper and lower
floors within the blocks.

However, as in the previous survey, it was recognised
that the design of the building, that might facilitate or
impede social contact among its residents, was just one of

a complex of factors that could have a bearing on the housewife's adjustment to her situation. These factors would include length of residence (for loneliness seemed to decrease as time went by), the age of the respondent and whether or not she had even a part-time job, also whether moving had entailed a break from the company of relatives and friends. (23) Apart from these influences, the mother's happiness would depend very much on her own resilience and adaptability and the strength of the relationships within the family.

Turning to the needs of the children, the project group were interested in studying the relation of site, lay-out and density to the children's play problems, and in comparing the opportunities for play in block dwellings with those in houses on the same estates. It was hoped that the results would provide guidance on the design of future estates so as to accommodate the recreational needs of children, and on the most suitable arrangements for families with young children in a high-density scheme.

The special facilities for young children included, near the high flats in estate A, a large, equipped, children's playground, which was inevitably 'out of bounds' for most youngsters because of danger from traffic on a near-by road. On estate B, there were a toddlers' playground and another small playground, but these were insufficient (and to some mothers unknown) and older children often chased the younger ones away. Children were not allowed to play on grassed areas. Estate C had open grassed areas and a little park adjoining it, but no special provision for the very young.

When asked directly about children's play, 80 per cent of mothers on estates A and B, and slightly fewer on estate C, referred to difficulties, and these were more often mentioned by those whose youngest child was under 5. Among families in the high flats and maisonettes, it was the children in this age group whose freedom to play was most limited by their living above the ground.

But there were more factors to consider, one being, for instance, the pattern of other activities that, of necessity or choice, made up the young child's day. (24) Also significant then (as now) was the extent to which the mother had the time and regarded it as part of her duty to take the child out to play herself. 'When mothers are used to assuming continuous care of their children, whether they live "high" or "low" makes little difference to their play opportunities.' (25)

The report recommended the provision of safe play spaces near home, for in helping to meet the children's needs for leisure, these would also alleviate the mothers' concern for their safety. (26)

Respondents in multi-storey dwellings were asked if, given a limited choice, they would prefer a flat to a maisonette. The reason most often given in favour of the latter was the possibility of keeping bedrooms just for sleeping and confining children's play to the living-rooms. The use of bedrooms for young children's play, often unavoidable in flats, was rarely considered desirable. Maisonettes had other disadvantages, however, especially if tenancies were unsuitably allocated. In general, in response to another question, mothers voiced an overwhelming preference for a house and garden. (27)

Finally it was considered that the housewife's overall satisfaction with her home could be affected by other aspects of the social environment than the type of dwelling or its height above the ground. The siting, social and physical characteristics of the whole estate, the design and amenities of the home and its proximity to work, entertainment, shopping centres and to the homes of relatives and friends all might have a bearing on individual happiness and even on the specific matter of children's play. (28) In this regard, too, the mother's assessment of her own responsibilities, though too elusive to define and observe systematically, did appear to identify a minority of contented families, even in the higher flats. (29)

However, the survey results, and especially those from estate A, illustrated some of the difficulties of family life in high blocks and it was claimed that they 'did not contradict the general conviction that houses are better for families with young children than block dwellings, but they did show that urban living conditions present many problems to families other than those associated with living off the ground'. (30)

In this respect, by virtue of its wider terms of reference and more comprehensive design and though necessarily guarded in some of its conclusions, the survey was able to go further than the previous one in suggesting some suitable background variables for the Tyneside study. Before turning to the detail, there are two further studies, in rather a different context, to mention briefly at this stage.

The findings of further research into children's play on housing estates, undertaken by the Building Research Station, were published in 1966. (31) These surveys were prompted by the need, in designing new estates, to reconcile the conflicting demands for space around buildings and to integrate play spaces within the estate design. (32)

The first study was concerned with children's play in a number of high-density estates, mainly in inner London. The second examined various problems of lay-out in a series of estates of lower densities. Some of the high-density estates were large, though some were quite small and typical of the small sites that are a common feature of inner city areas.

The techniques that were applied in this form of users' research included detailed inspection of the various sites, interviews with residents, informal discussions with housing managers and caretakers, and systematic observation of children at play throughout the estates.

The assumptions that governed the provision of play facilities seemed to include the following: that play was a greater problem at higher densities and where some families lived in high flats, that if there were play facilities in a near-by park, for example, or if residents had private gardens, special provision on the estate was unimportant or unnecessary and that the existence of traffic-free communal areas between the buildings could go some way towards solving the problem of children's play.

In order to assess the use of the varying opportunities and places for play, observers walked round the estates at regular intervals over a period of four days. It was estimated that 40 per cent of children seen to be playing outside were under 5 years old. It was noted too that much of the play for this age-group was inactive - just standing, sitting, talking and watching.

The choice of alternative places for play on high- and low-density estates seemed to follow much the same pattern. Except for private gardens, where play could obviously not be studied, the highest percentage of children in both types of estate tended to prefer the paved areas, i.e. footpaths and other spaces reserved for pedestrians. (33) A detailed study of playgrounds showed that many children used these for a very short time and that their main function was often as a place for children just to meet, not necessarily to play formally at all. Interviews with parents revealed some concern about dangers from playground equipment. (34) The advantages of open grassed areas in front of the houses where children could play, within their parents' view, were counterbalanced by the noise, damage and violation of others' privacy that sometimes resulted.

The authors recommended, among their general conclusions, that while adventure playgrounds might be provided, ideally with trained supervision, to serve whole districts, each estate should have its own facilities for play, especially for shorter playtimes and to match the

spontaneity and variety enjoyed by children under 10.
There was no separate mention of the very young. The
authors were also emphatic that the existence of ample
communal space, of itself, would not solve these problems,
that variety of provision was more essential than the
extent of play space, and that, in costing, allowance
should be made for equipment, maintenance, caretaking and
trained supervision.

It was not feasible to use similar methods of recording
in the Tyneside survey. But some of the points made here
will be referred to again when observed patterns of play
are discussed and also in the conclusions. (35)

The surveys described so far are those that were con-
sulted at the planning stage of the present inquiry.
Though tied to their own localities, they were helpful in
suggesting the main questions to include and other background information to gather in the Tyneside study, and
there was enough agreement in some of their findings to
justify looking for confirmation here also. (36) These
uses will be apparent in the following chapters.

It was also known, at the planning stage, that research
into the implications of living in flats for a variety of
households was being initiated by the University of
Glasgow. (37) When the Tyneside interviews had been completed, a comprehensive account was published of family
life in high flats in an Australian city. (38)

While the social setting of the Australian study provided some intriguing contrasts to that of the Tyneside
inquiry, some aspects of flat life that were disclosed
were similar to those obtaining here. Moreover, some of
the measures, applied already or recommended, to provide
for children's leisure, proved of special interest. These
will be discussed in their particular contexts, but it is
appropriate, at this stage, to summarise the reasoning
that prompted the Melbourne survey and to outline its
design.

The advent of high-density flatted estates in the inner
areas of Australian cities had been criticised by some as
'a denial of the accepted way of life (the "suburban"
ethos), and ... one which would create insuperable social
problems'. (39) These estates were built by the Housing
Commission of Victoria to provide homes for families on
low incomes. This type of development was chosen for the
following reasons: flats were a better economic proposition than houses in areas where land was costly, the
estates could be landscaped, with a generous allowance of
space for recreation, and, since relatively high densities
could be achieved, the population of the inner city areas
could be built up.

There was, however, considerable adverse public reaction to the flats. It was realised that their tenants
were among the least vocal members of the community and it
was assumed that protests, if any were called for, would
need to be made for them. Newspaper publicity underlined
the need for a systematic inquiry. This matter evoked the
interest and concern of the Victoria Council of Churches,
and so the Brotherhood of St Laurence, a Church of England
social service organisation, agreed to initiate the appropriate research.

The authors summarised their purpose as 'an attempt to
arrive at some understanding of what the official housing
policy means in terms of the day-to-day activities of
those people most directly affected by it, that is, the
tenants themselves'. (40) These activities naturally included children's play.

For the research, one estate was chosen in an old
working-class area of inner Melbourne. Comparisons could
thus be made between households in the 20-storey 'high-
rise', and those in several 4-storey 'walk-up' blocks.
The households were not restricted to those with children
and there were in fact no children aged under 5 in the
high-rise blocks. The families in the walk-up blocks were
larger and the parents younger. Random samples were taken
within each building type, yielding 41 households in the
former and 43 in the latter, i.e. approximately one-third
of all households in each case.

It is interesting here to note, by way of contrast with
this aspect of housing policy in Gateshead, as mentioned
in Chapter 1, that in Melbourne the provision of walk-up,
4-storey accommodation for families with children was to
be discontinued. The report suggested, with some reservations, that such families might in future be housed in
high-rise blocks, as long as ampler accommodation and
suitable facilities could be guaranteed. (41)

There are other contrasts too that will be mentioned
later. Meanwhile, as would apply to the other studies
that have been reviewed here, the authors described their
research as 'an attempt to find mass solutions to mass
problems without ignoring the particular needs of particular people and ... faced with all the dogged individualism
of their reactions'. (42)

The methods used on Tyneside to study the individuals
in this situation, and to elicit their reactions to it,
will now be described.

3   The survey design

Mannheim has said that 'a human situation is characteriz-
able only when one has taken into account those concep-
tions that the participants have of it, how they experience the tensions in this situation and how they react to
the tensions so conceived'. (1) It was agreed that, in
the study of this particular human situation, interviews
with the parents of young children should form a major
part of the research design.

Students of the Department of Social Studies were invited to take part and fifteen of them who were especially
interested in this problem and in the prospect of field
research in this context, formed the interviewing team.
(2)

The choice of Newcastle, Gateshead and Wallsend as the
areas for study has been explained briefly already in
Chapter 1. After discussions with housing officials in
the three boroughs, the research design for each locality
was worked out as follows: (3)

NEWCASTLE

When the survey was being planned, there were already over
thirty high blocks built by or for the local authority and
situated either within the city boundary or just outside.
These provided, in all, almost 3,000 tenancies, but it was
not known, at the time, how many of these were families
with children under 5. The task of identifying these
young families in all the high blocks would have been substantial and the prospect of selecting a random sample of
them for interview was rejected anyway for the following
reasons.

Earlier studies had noted the contribution, to tenants'

satisfaction and adjustment, of the quality of the immediate environment, whether the lay-out and design of the
whole estate or the character of the immediate vicinity of
a single block dwelling. (4) It was thought that these
factors might also have some bearing on the extent to
which special facilities for play were used, for it would
be necessary to be able to set against the latter the alternative opportunities, however informal, or maybe unde-
sirable, that the neighbourhood might provide. These
various influences could hardly be evaluated for a widely
distributed sample made up of small groups of families
dispersed throughout the city.

Moreover, the Ministry's study had supported the impression gained from the preliminary survey on Tyneside,
that in focusing attention on the problems of families in
high blocks, these should be compared with the difficulties experienced in other multi-storey dwellings and even
in houses. (5) This kind of 'control' would be impossible
to arrange satisfactorily if the main group were widely
dispersed.

Given that families in a number of dwelling types were
to be included and that, for some of the other 'background' variables, their experience should be comparable,
the first idea for Newcastle was to follow up all families, currently with children under 5, who had been rehoused under the same clearance scheme from one particular
area. Lists were made of all families with children under
10, who had been rehoused from part of Byker, not far to
the east of the city centre, under the same compulsory
purchase order, whose operative period extended roughly
from mid-1964 to mid-1967. By this means, it was hoped to
ensure similarity in some aspects of the previous experience of the families chosen for study. They would all
have moved from the same kind of environment and have been
exposed, at least, to the same pattern of social life and
contact - 'common-sense' categories by which one might
expect such families to appraise their present home and
its situation. (6)

It was interesting however to find that, of the 300 or
so families with children under 5, very few indeed had
actually been rehoused in high blocks. This illustrated
the housing department's practice of avoiding this kind of
allocation for young families wherever possible. A group
of families who had been transferred, under this scheme,
to houses and 2- or 3-storey flats in Longbenton UD, was
retained in the survey design.

For the main Newcastle study, it was then decided to
concentrate on one estate. Cruddas Park was chosen, as
being among the largest, recently completed, inner-city

estates. Here there were tower blocks, maisonettes, a
smaller number of lower flats and split-level houses. The
whole estate was landscaped and although, at the time, the
squalor and dereliction of its immediate surroundings detracted from the appearance of the site, there was at
least some promise of a pleasing environment.

All the families on the estate with children under 5,
who were living in the high blocks, maisonettes and
houses, were included in the survey.

GATESHEAD

As explained already, it was found to be no longer the
policy of this housing authority to allocate families with
young children to high blocks. Moreover, wherever possible, young families who were still housed in this way
were to be transferred to other accommodation. However,
in some high flats near the town centre, some young families still remained, and in some of these there were large
numbers of children. These blocks were known as Barnes
Close, Priory Court and Regent Court, and it was decided
to include all the young families found in them.

The Gateshead group provided an interesting contrast to
the Newcastle part of the study. None of the high blocks
here was part of an estate. They were all isolated units
in the midst of busy streets and car-parking areas and
their position reflected, at least during working and
shopping hours, some aspects of inner urban living at its
most precarious.

WALLSEND

Here a different approach again was suggested by the local
housing situation. The high flats in the Willington
Square estate were to form the focal point of the study.
In this development, there were also some lower-rise
buildings, including maisonettes. But the site was much
smaller than Cruddas Park, and the survey would have
needed to cover a wider area if adequate numbers were to
be obtained. This extension would inevitably have introduced variety among the families included, in terms, for
example, of the duration of their tenancy and the type of
area where they lived before.

It seemed, from the preliminary discussions, that the
local authority encouraged an element of fluidity in its
housing situation and that transfers between tenants were
not infrequent. It appeared, too, that lists could be

most conveniently supplied of those who had moved to their present address within each calendar year. In order to achieve relative homogeneity, at least in terms of the length of current tenure, it was therefore agreed that lists should be compiled of those who had moved to their present home in 1964, 1965 and 1966, indicating, in each case, the type of dwelling currently occupied. From these lists, after the students had visited the area, those addresses were chosen that were in the vicinity of the Willington Square development, or to the south of it.

Given the lists of families in each locality, most of those with children under 5 were identified by the appropriate health department, from the records of the health visitors, by permission, in each area, of the Medical Officer of Health. (7) For Gateshead, these families were already known. For parts of Cruddas Park, other than the high blocks, the young families were identified by the students' preliminary door-to-door inquiry.

The resulting numbers in each locality and in each type of dwelling are given in Table 2. Interviews were sought with all of them, except for the occupants of houses in Wallsend. Here a sample, yielding 37 possible units for the final analysis, was selected by random numbers from the total of 60. (8)

The great majority of the families who were approached co-operated readily in the survey. There were very few direct refusals. Most of the discrepancies between the numbers listed originally and those that were interviewed, were due to such uncontrollable factors as a change of tenancy where the new family had no children under 5. These changes were allowed for in calculating the 'effective' totals. Sometimes, however, a family could still not be contacted, after repeated calls at various times and often by different interviewers. These circumstances accounted for the non-contact rates as given at the foot of Table 2.

Before the interviewing began, the students, who had divided themselves into groups already to work in each of the survey areas, made between them a study of their chosen locality, noting the provision for play and other amenities. Their reports formed the content of the descriptions of these areas, as given in the next chapter.

Here it remains to consider the questions that were included in the interviewing schedule and the implications of the research design.

TABLE 2 Number of interviews completed

Locality and type of dwelling	No. of families with under-fives	No. of interviews completed	non-contact rate %
CRUDDAS PARK, NEWCASTLE			
high flats	94	84	
maisonettes	19*	19*	
split-level houses	39	36	
	152	139	
LONGBENTON			
2/3-storey flats	20	19	
houses	14	13	
	34	32	
GATESHEAD			
high flats	47	44	
WALLSEND			
high flats	24	20	
4-storey flats	11	10	
2/3-storey flats	45	42	
maisonettes	25	23	
houses	37**	36	
	142	131	
TOTAL			
high flats	165	148	10·3
2/3/4-storey flats	76	71	6·6
maisonettes	44	42	4·5
houses	90	85	5·6
	375	346	7·7

* including two 2-storey flats kept separate in the
   analysis
**sample from a total of 60

The questionnaire or interview schedule is reproduced in
Appendix A. The schedule was drawn up in a series of
group discussions in which all members of the research
team took part. The topics covered by the previous studies, as described in Chapter 2, were included as far as
possible, in order that the various findings might be compared. Also included were some of the general 'background' variables. It was hoped that these would reflect,
for each family, some relevant features of their previous
experience and present way of life, such as were referred
to, in the earlier studies, as other unrecorded aspects of
the 'social or total emotional environment'. (9)

The sequence of items in the questionnaire was arranged
so as to follow the natural flow of conversation. It was
not possible to organise a pilot study and inevitably
there was some ambiguity and apparent repetition to clear
up. This was reported early in the interviewing programme
and so could be dealt with by further instructions to the
interviewers. It was possible, in the analysis, to look
for inconsistencies in the responses, but in the end there
was very little evidence of misunderstanding or lack of
clarity.

The questions may be considered under the following
headings:

A Basic information about the family, including size,
   age, employment.
B Previous housing experience, past and present attitudes
   to the home and locality.
C Present patterns of living with a bearing on children's
   play.
D Reactions to the present situation with reference
   specifically to matters affecting the play habits and
   general adjustment of the children under 5.

This classification represents the framework both for
the analysis and for the arrangement of later chapters.
The various items, under each heading, are summarised
below, with an indication of the chapters in which they
will be mainly discussed.

A Basic information (see Chapter 5)

   items
     1-3   family composition
      4   age
      5   employment   for head and/or wife
   6,7,8   hours of work
      9   occupation
     10   place of work

B   Previous housing experience, attitude to home and
locality (see Chapter 5)

> items
> 12a   duration of present tenure
>   b,c,d   previous accommodation: ownership, type,
>   location
>   e   reasons for moving
>   f   choices available
>   g   satisfactions at the time
> 13a   wife's attitude to present accommodation
>   husband's attitude to present accommodation
>   b   wife's attitude to present locality
>   husband's attitude to present locality

C   Present patterns of living

> items
> 14a   number of rooms (see Chapter 5)
>   b,c   patterns of use
>   d   use of the balcony
> 26   prams and storage space
> 17a,b   help with children, regularly and in times of
>   illness (see Chapter 6)
>   c   help of this kind in previous home
> 19   where children under 5 play; outside, inside
>   the home, elsewhere indoors if relevant
> 20a,b   neighbours with children
> 21a,b   companions and toys
> 18   knowledge and use of local organisations for
>   looking after children
> 24a,b   knowledge and use of local facilities for re-
>   creation, etc.
>   c   visits to relatives and friends
>   d   journeys to school
> 25   'the toddler's day'

D   Reactions to the present situation (see Chapter 7)

> items
> 15   difficulties in bringing up children here
> 16   opinions on facilities for play
> 27   local facilities for play compared with those
>   in previous situation
> 22a,b   restrictions on play because of noise and
>   neighbours
> 23a,b   restrictions on play because of accident risk,
>   suggestions for reducing the danger
> 29   mother's assessment of youngster's health, now
>   and before moving

One or two points need to be made concerning the plan and methods that were used in the research.

It is evident from Table 2, and from the preceding discussion, that the design was essentially locally based. The families with young children in high flats in Cruddas Park, Gateshead and Wallsend, must be seen in their own distinct and contrasting local settings. It would be inappropriate to combine them into one group, without first investigating their possible differences. It would also be quite wrong to suggest that they were a 'representative' sample of all young families housed in this way.

Nevertheless, the results confirmed that, in some respects, the families in high flats in Cruddas Park were more similar to those in equivalent accommodation in Gateshead and in Wallsend than to young families in maisonettes and houses on the same estate. Moreover, for certain questions, but not all, the various groups that were distinguished in the survey did display, on each topic, a recognisable pattern of response, and one that was in line with the findings of previous studies.

The kind of statement that is valid and useful, and that one would hope to be able to make on the evidence of such local studies, is that, given one set of circumstances, there is a probability that certain attitudes or patterns of behaviour will obtain. The onus is on the investigator correctly and clearly to specify the basic circumstances, and this is not always simple or even possible.

Reference has been made to the importance of the background variables, such as those included in sets A, B and even C, above, in relation to the appraisal of the reactions and attitudes that comprised set D. For some of the groups of families in the survey, the numbers were too small for these relationships to be assessed. But it was sometimes possible to confine the analysis, in an exploratory way, to one or two of the larger groups. For instance, the group of high-flat families in Cruddas Park divided equally into those with under-fives only and those with older children as well. For this group again, and for those in Gateshead, it was possible to distinguish sufficient numbers of mothers who went out to work.

The local character of the survey was dictated partly by differences among the authorities, both in their housing situations and in their official policies. However, so long as these local features were understood, the inherent flexibility of the design did enable some interesting comparisons to be made.

Finally, there was the problem of obtaining an unbiased response on a matter that was already of some discussion among the people who were approached, and in a situation where, as in Cruddas Park, the families selected were often neighbours, who spread news of the survey around, although it was restricted to as brief a period as possible. In such circumstances, much depends on the interviewer's approach, his adherence to the form of the interview, despite the pressure to digress, and on his awareness of the situation and ability to record it.

Moreover, the students who were the interviewers here, were concerned themselves about the needs for children's play in these localities. They realised, however, that these personal considerations should not be allowed to intrude on their fieldwork. They were willing to accept the discipline of the investigator, which Elton Mayo has described as 'the subordination of oneself, of one's opinions and ideas, of the very human desire to give gratuitous advice, and the subordination of all these to an intelligent effort to help another convey ideas and feelings that he cannot easily express'. (10) The measure of their success must be judged by the results.

4   The local settings

Of all the areas studied, (1) the Newcastle estate at
Cruddas Park came closest to the recommendation, quoted
earlier, that slum clearance should be followed by 'large-
scale, comprehensive redevelopment, with clearly defined
boundaries ... some grass, trees and planting'. (2) (See
Figure 1.)

As viewed from the railway approaching the centre of
Newcastle from the west, both the boundaries and the potential attractiveness of the site could be recognised.
From this distance the appearance of the estate was en-
hanced by the slope of the ground, which had been utilised
in the split-level design of the houses, and in the posi-
tioning of the high blocks. Closer to, the grassed areas
often seemed to be spoiled by broken glass and rubbish and
the inevitable grime from near-by industry and demolition.
But some effort had clearly been made to create here, just
a short way out from the city centre, an overall environment in which the residents might take some pride. (3)

The estate was bounded, to the south, by Scotswood
Road. (4) A barrier had been erected, at one point, to
safeguard young children from running down on to this busy
thoroughfare. The site, as it was at the time of the
fieldwork, extended from Clumber Street in the west, to
Maple Street in the east, both of which fed into Scotswood
Road. The land to the north was still being developed,
and a neighbourhood centre was being built. The new
centre was to include shops and other amenities, the
shortage of which was felt very strongly at the time of
the survey.

Park Road, which also joined Scotswood Road, divided
the site into two distinct parts. To the west were all
but one of the 15-storey blocks, while one high block, the

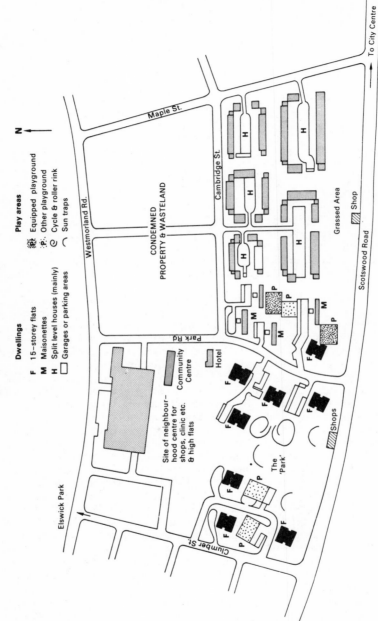

Figure 1. CRUDDAS PARK, 1967

Dwellings

F 15–storey flats
M Maisonettes
H Split level houses (mainly)
☐ Garages or parking areas

Play areas

🏀 Equipped playground
:P: Other playground
© Cycle & roller rink
⌒ Sun traps

maisonettes and split-level houses lay progressively to
the east.

The seven high blocks to the west of Park Road were
arranged in two groups. The Pines, the Sycamores and the
Larches mounted the slope fairly close to the road, with
the Hawthorns offset to the rear of the last two. Each
block could be reached, by car, from Park Road, and each
was provided with garages and parking space. Play facilities here included two cycle or roller-skating rings,
below the Hawthorns, and some sun-traps, facing south,
with concrete seats. These features were probably the
most popular of all the facilities on the estate and, on
fine days, seemed to be well used.

Between this group of high blocks and those at the far
western end of the estate was a sloping area of grass and
trees, known to some of the residents as 'the Park'. (5)
There were no through roads. Play was discouraged here,
at the time, because the grass was not yet grown.

The most westerly group included the Poplars first,
then the Beeches and the Willows close to Clumber Street,
the boundary road, to which all three gave access. Within
this complex there were two enclosed playgrounds, surfaced
with tarmacadam, and with protective walls on the sides
where there was a considerable drop to the sloping ground.
There was no special equipment, but seats had been provided so that mothers could watch their children at play.
These playgrounds were intended to be solely for the use
of children under 12, but this restriction proved difficult to enforce.

To the east of Park Road and fairly close to its junc-
tion with Scotswood Road, was the remaining high block,
the Cedars, and, further up the hill, four 4-storey
blocks, each of which included sixteen 2-storey maisonettes. Two of these blocks, with the Cedars, had access
to Park Road. The other two had outlets to Cambridge
Street on the north side. Garages were provided, as
before. In this part of the estate there was an enclosed
playground, similar to those already described, but there
were no seats here. There were also two play areas, with
some attempt at landscaping, and equipped with climbing
frames and a castle turret. These spaces for play partly
compensated for the shortage of open land between the
buildings here, as compared with the more generous landscaping of the western section of the estate.

The rest of the development, eastwards to Maple Street,
comprised five rectangular arrays of split-level houses,
and a few 2-storey flats and bungalows. Each of these
arrays had an interior close, with access, for cars, from
Maple Street to the east or Cambridge Street to the north.

There were garages in each close. Each house had a small
garden, which was fenced, although the original scheme had
been for an open plan design. There were no playgrounds
in this part of the estate, but there was much grass. The
wide expanse between the houses and Scotswood Road was
open and unprotected from the road. Ball games were prohibited and there were no swings.

Despite the overall impression of spaciousness, Cruddas
Park was without question a high-density estate. Children
and young people were very much in evidence. (6)

The high blocks, which were the first to be built, were
designed on the assumption that their tenants would include families with children. On each floor there were
six dwellings, two for smaller households, of single or
elderly persons, in the centre and the rest, for families,
or larger households, in the four corners. The eight 15-
storey blocks might therefore house some 480 families. At
the time of the survey, 94 of this total, i.e. nearly 20
per cent, were found to include children of pre-school
age. In the maisonettes, which came next in order of construction, the 64 tenancies included 17 families with
children in this age group, while the 180 or so split-
level houses, and 2-storey flats, the most recent part of
the estate, yielded 39 families for the survey. The overall proportion of homes with children aged under 5 was
therefore 150/724 or just over 20 per cent, with the highest percentage in the maisonettes.

At the time of the survey, the Save the Children Fund
ran a nursery school in the local community centre, which
was situated to the west of Park Road, and north of the
Hawthorns and the Larches. This school was open daily,
but it only catered for a small number of children, and
there was a waiting list. In addition to this, one
afternoon a week was set aside, at the centre, for mothers
on the estate. They could leave their children to play in
one of the rooms while they themselves attended lectures
and debates in the hall. The mothers would take turns to
be with the children. The popularity of this venture
seemed to have waned since its inception, and it was
thought that a less formal and demanding arrangement might
have had a more lasting appeal. It was hoped that the new
centre, when completed, would help to meet the special
needs of children in this age-group.

The nearest open space to the estate was Elswick Park,
which, though some little distance away, seemed to be
regularly visited by Cruddas Park families. (7) Here
there were swings, roundabouts and ample space for ball
games.

The lack of shops on the estate at the time of the

survey has been mentioned already. It was expected that the new shops that were planned would remedy this situation. However, for those who preferred, as many seemed to do, to travel for shopping or other social purposes to the city centre or beyond, there was a frequent bus service along the Scotswood Road.

The quality of 'community spirit' or even 'sense of belonging to a locality', however one may define these concepts operationally, could scarcely be assessed from preliminary visits to the estate or from responses to the set questions included in the formal interviews. However, some of the general comments proffered by respondents gave more than a hint of certain social divisions among them.

Some mothers from the houses remarked that they did not allow their children to use the adventure playgrounds near the maisonettes, because they imagined, incorrectly, that these were exclusively for the maisonette families, of whom they seemed to disapprove. Among the tenants of the high blocks, some respondents volunteered the information that the 'block' was the dominant social unit. They belonged, they said, to the Cedars, to the Larches etc. rather than to the whole estate. This attachment, if genuine, would have implications for the success of any venture that required co-operation or the sharing of responsibility among families from several parts of the estate. While these observations were tentative, it was possible that divisions of this kind could have resulted from the phasing of the construction of the estate with each group of newcomers being 'labelled' as different from those who were already established. Moreover, it seemed likely that attempts to provide for the 'whole community' (as it was hoped to do, for example, within the new centre), if introduced after these prejudices had taken root, might be greeted with apathy. In fact, when two years later a member of the research team made a visit of observation to the estate, he found that this had been the case. (8)

LONGBENTON

The families included in the survey who had moved from Byker, near the centre of Newcastle, to Longbenton, just beyond the city boundary, found themselves in a very different kind of environment from the one from which they had come. Of those interviewed, thirteen were accommodated in houses and nineteen in 3-storey flats. The buildings within the estate formed two broad groups, with houses to the east and multi-storey development, including many 3-storey and two 14-storey blocks, to the west. The survey families being few in number, were fairly scattered throughout each section of the estate.

In the west, there was plenty of grass where children could play around the buildings. But in some parts, brick walls, which enclosed the drying yards, had broken the continuity of this open space. There was an equipped play area beside each of the high blocks, but these were understood to be just for the use of the children-living there.

In East Longbenton, each house had its own garden, which provided a safe place for the younger children to play. Older children played frequently on the roads, some of which were quite busy. The only swings here were in an open space known as the 'back field'. The swings were not boxed in, and so mothers were reluctant to allow their very young children to go on them. The 'back field' was, incidentally, the only public open space of any size. The nearest park was a bus-ride away.

The Community and Welfare Centre was fairly centrally placed, and accessible from both parts of the estate. Here a playroom with slides, toys and other attractions, was open for two mornings each week. There was no super-vision, so mothers stayed with their children. Each week, at the centre, there was a young wives' club. Members could also attend a sewing meeting, on one afternoon a week, and bring their children who were cared for by girls from a local school.

There were adequate shopping facilities in both parts of the estate, especially in the western part, where the shopping centre included a supermarket and a laundrette.

There were frequent bus services to and from Newcastle. Many mothers made regular journeys into the city to main-tain their links with their old neighbourhood.

Conditions in Longbenton, especially in regard to the opportunities for play, were similar to those observed by Hole and Miller in the lower-density estates that were in-cluded in their study. (9)

GATESHEAD

Conditions in Gateshead differed strikingly from those in either of the areas described so far.

Barnes Close, Regent Court and Priory Court, that were covered by the survey, were all very close to the town centre, the town hall and the river. They stood near the north-west, south-west and south-east corners respectively

of a rectangle, that was bounded at the time, to the east
and west, by the main, one-way thoroughfares for north to
south traffic passing through the town. Most of the space
within this rectangle was due for comprehensive development. Plans included a new shopping centre and multi-
storey car park. The main road system was also to be
radically changed. (10)

Barnes Close, Regent Court and Priory Court were not
the only high blocks in the centre of Gateshead, but they
were, at the time, the only ones still housing families
with children under 5. Barnes Close occupied a triangular
site among roads that were made especially hazardous, at
certain times of day, by the one-way flow of traffic.
Here there were four 10-storey blocks, accommodating 245
households, of which 24 had children under 5. Regent
Court, to the south, was a single 10-storey block. Here,
among 160 households, 15 were found to have children of
pre-school age, a similar percentage to that in Barnes
Close. Priory Court comprised three 8-storey blocks, with
138 households. Among these, only 8 remained with youngsters under 5. Much higher proportions of households with
children under 16 were found, of course, in each case.

While 50 per cent of Gateshead respondents came from
Barnes Close, the living conditions of all the families,
and the external hazards to which they were exposed, were
similar enough for them to be regarded as a homogeneous
group.

Nevertheless, Barnes Close, Regent Court and Priory
Court were physically distinct from each other. They were
isolated units amidst all the rush of inner urban life.
Although here, in the evening, when the shops were closed
and the traffic had subsided, conditions might be relatively peaceful, living in this situation was on the whole
precarious, especially for young children.

The amount of space available for play close to the
base of the flats, a feature that previous studies had
specially advocated for young children, was inevitably restricted. Each block comprising Barnes Close was surrounded by a narrow grass verge. Children were not allowed to play here. Had they done so, they would have been
in danger from the fast-flowing traffic only yards away.
At the front of all four blocks there was a large tarmac
play area, intended for the use of young children. The
area was surrounded by inadequate wire netting, some of
which seemed, to the observers, to have been pulled down
to make a short cut to the bus stop.

At the front of Regent Court, some twenty yards of un-
enclosed grass separated the flats from the main road. At
the back, a large, enclosed, semi-circular area did

provide some opportunity for youngsters to burn off their excess energy. Only when the gate was left open was there a danger of children running on to the car park at the back.

Priory Court was similarly placed, close to a busy road, and separated from it by a small grass verge with no adequate protection for children. Behind the three blocks that made up Priory Court, there was a fenced area for the older children. The under-fives, as has been seen, were very much in the minority already in Priory Court, although almost one household in three had at least one member under 16.

There was no equipment for play in any of the areas. The janitors each exercised some degree of supervision, especially in preventing older children from using areas that had been set aside for the very young.

The recreational needs of the older children, in these surroundings, seemed to be even more problematic than those of the under-fives. The nearest open space where they could play freely was a distance away, across dangerous roads. However, parents often expected them to stay near home so as to take care of their younger brothers and sisters.

Living near the centre of the town, the families in all these high flats were able to share in the local amenities. Shops and frequent bus services were available to them. There were some nursery facilities in the town but, as was so often the case, these had long waiting lists and could be expected to provide very few places for the children here.

The situation of the Gateshead flats is unlikely to have been unique. There still are families in similar conditions elsewhere, with little expectation of removal. It was understood that, by the time the survey was completed, most if not all the families involved would have been rehoused. However, their inclusion in the survey provided both a useful comparison with the other areas and a salutary reminder of what this kind of development and allocation can entail, especially for the very young.

WALLSEND

The remaining locality, within Wallsend, was typical of areas of predominantly local authority housing that have been developed over a period, rather than, as in the case of Cruddas Park, as part of one specific plan. Like Cruddas Park, it included several types of building, high

14-storey blocks, 2-, 3- and 4-storey flats, maisonettes and houses. Except for some of the maisonettes in the south of the survey area, the surroundings, for the most part, were not unlike those in Longbenton. They were sufficiently far from industry, and from the older, more crowded parts of the borough, for the air to be clean and free from smoke. Most of the area was in fact a smokeless zone.

The study area came broadly within the north-east corner of the borough, well to the north of the Tyne and just south of the Newcastle to Tynemouth coast road. It included part of Rosehill and High Howdon. The old town of Wallsend, which was the nucleus of the borough for administration and services, and from which many of the respondents originated, lay some two miles to the south-west.

The 14-storey and 4-storey blocks stood in the north of the area within which interviewing took place. They were immediately to the south of the coast road, from which a ditch and high fence gave adequate and necessary protection. In between the high flats were the 4-storey blocks, with lower flats and houses facing them to the south. These were all part of a separate, recent development. There was plenty of grass surrounding the flats, and it seemed that virtually all of this was available as play space. There were also, between the high blocks, some tarmac playgrounds whose low fences were in some need of repair. Equipment was confined to swings and concrete pipes for boys to crawl through. There was also a field near by. All the dwellings of 4 storeys or more covered by the survey were located here.

Of the lower flats, the 3-storey blocks were more recent, while the 2-storey blocks which had gardens were of older vintage. Very few of the latter were included in the survey.

The 3-storey flats, where families were interviewed, were mostly to the south, and in a few cases to the west, of the new development just described. Around the 3-storey blocks there were no playgrounds or play areas, but expanses of green of varying extent. Traffic was a hazard to the many children, who, having been accustomed to playing freely in the back lanes near their former homes, could not easily be restrained from playing on the roads with which the whole area was interlaced. The verges were supposedly not for play. They were in some places too narrow and close to the roads for safety, and some were strewn with glass and litter.

The maisonettes and houses were similarly scattered throughout the whole study area. The maisonettes were

arranged either in rows, along the streets, or in
'courts'. Each block, for the most part, contained four
dwellings, two up and two down. There were no gardens,
but strips of grass at the front and rear of each block.
The houses, of course, had their own gardens, which provided the best play situation for the very young. Older
children here also played frequently on the roads.

There was a playground a little distance away in Howdon
Park. Indoor arrangements for play were very limited.
There was a play centre in the borough, but this was a
bus-ride away. One local church provided a play group for
the under-fives, on one afternoon a week, where mothers
were expected to remain with their children. The group
did not seem to be very well known. There was a large
clinic in the area and many schools, since there was a
predominance of children in the population. There were
few shops within walking distance from any part of the
survey area, and many mothers travelled frequently into
the older parts of Wallsend, to combine shopping with
visits to relatives and friends.

With the possible exception of the little estate which
included the higher blocks, the most striking feature of
the area covered by the survey was its lack of social co-
hesion. There was certainly no evidence of a 'sense of
belonging'. One respondent apathetically described the
area as 'just somewhere to live'. Perhaps the feeling was
best conveyed by one of the interviewers who commented,
sadly, 'nobody knew whether there was a community centre
and nobody wanted to know.'

These descriptions of the local settings for the various
parts of the survey have deliberately been made as far as
possible without reference to the results from the questionnaire. They are the background against which the reactions and concerns of the mothers may be appreciated.
There were sharp contrasts between the areas, but there
were some common features too, as will be seen.

Nevertheless, in considering the patterns of response
that do emerge, it is important that these aspects of the
home situation of the various families involved should be
kept in mind.

5   The families

This chapter covers some basic characteristics of the
survey families, including the size and composition of the
family group, the employment position of the parents, the
type of dwelling and locality where they lived previously,
their satisfaction with their present home and how they
used the rooms.(1) All of these may have some bearing on the
present habits and potential needs of their children with
regard to play. (2)

FAMILY SIZE AND COMPOSITION

One would expect variations in family size to be associated with variations in the size of the accommodation and
especially in the number of bedrooms. Table 3 part (a)
shows, for each locality and type of dwelling, the number
of families with two and with three bedrooms, and in each
of two size groups.
    It is evident from the summary, in Table 3 part (b),
that family size in these terms was more closely related
to the number of bedrooms than to the type of structure.
Except for some in Gateshead, the high flats had two bedrooms, and apart from some in Cruddas Park, the houses had
three. Families resident in the flats were on the whole
smaller than those living elsewhere.
    In the high blocks in Cruddas Park, there were more of
the smaller families on the upper floors - a point that is
taken up later. (3) In all the 2-bedroomed flats together, almost 30 per cent of families had five or more
members. Since they had only a kitchen and living room
besides, the shortage of space could be limiting, especially for the children. But the larger families in the
more ample Gateshead flats and in the maisonettes in
Wallsend were by no means exempt from problems of this
kind. (4)

TABLE 3 Family size by size and type of dwelling

(a)

Locality and type of dwelling	Number of families with				All
	2 bedrooms		3 bedrooms		
	under 5 members	5 members or more	under 5 members	5 members or more	
CRUDDAS PARK (5)					
high flats*	44	8	–	–	52
high flats**	22	10	–	–	32
maisonettes	9	2	1	5	17
houses	9	4	2	21	36
LONGBENTON					
3-storey flats	15	4	–	–	19
houses	–	–	2	11	13
GATESHEAD					
high flats	7	10	2	25	44
WALLSEND					
high flats	14	6	–	–	20
4-storey flats	7	3	–	–	10
2/3-storey flats	19	10	–	13	42
maisonettes	–	–	–	23	23
houses	2	1	2	31	36

(b) summary

Number of members	2 bedrooms under 5 %	5 or more %	all %	all no.	3 bedrooms under 5 %	5 or more %	all %	all no.	All under 5 %	5 or more %	all %	all no.
High flats	72	28	100	121	5	95	100	40	60	40	100	148
Lower flats	71	29	100	58	} (5, 95, 100 → 40)				58	42	100	71
Maisonettes and houses	74	26	100	27	7	93	100	98	22	78	100	125
All dwellings	72	28	100	206	7	93	100	138	46	54	100	344

* 6th floor or above
**below 6th floor; this distinction is made to facilitate comparison with the first London
Survey, see p.10.

The total number of persons in each family is, however, less informative than those aspects of its structure that reflect the position of the child who is under 5. It is pertinent to ask, for example, whether he may enjoy, within the home, the companionship of others in his age-group, or a little older, and whether he is still too young for active play to have become a practical issue. The families were therefore classified as follows:

Families, with children under 5 only, having
    a   only one child
    b   more than one child
Families, with some older children, having
    c   only one child under 5
    d   more than one child under 5

(For some purposes the categories have been subdivided to distinguish those families where no child under 5 was beyond the toddling stage)

Table 4 gives the numbers of families in each of the categories a to d. Except for some of the smaller groups, Cruddas Park high blocks housed the largest percentage of families with all their children under 5, and most of them were above the fifth floor. In 20 of the 52 families in these upper flats the child under 5 was an only child, a much higher proportion than was found elsewhere. Omitting the 8 only children who were still under 2 years of age, there remained 12 of the 52 families where a lone 2- to 5-year-old would need to find companions outside the home.

In the 8 high blocks in Cruddas Park, there could be some 288 families above the fifth floor. One might be tempted to dismiss the plight of the solitary youngster as a minority problem, since it applied here to 12/288 or less than one family in twenty. But one cannot ignore the dilemma inherent in a policy of housing management which, by limiting the allocation of flats to those married couples who are at the beginning of the family cycle may exacerbate, if only for a time, the problem of isolation for those children who do arrive.

It could be argued, further, that, even in the larger families, the most difficult time during the day for the children between 2 and 5 and their mothers is when the older children are at school, for it is mostly then that the younger ones need to play. Disregarding the presence of all children of school age, it is possible to classify all the survey families as in Table 5. It is evident that, in many sections of the survey, almost 50 per cent of families included one 2- to 5-year-old, who was liable to be on his own, at least during normal school hours. For nearly 30 per cent of Cruddas Park families, the problems of leisure for the under-fives appeared at the time

TABLE 4   Family composition

Locality and type of dwelling	a	b	c	d	a + b %	c + d %	All no.	%
CRUDDAS PARK					***			
high flats*	20	10	20	2	58	42	52	100
high flats**	6	6	18	2	38	62	32	100
maisonettes	1	3	8	5 }	25	75	53	100
houses	4	5	16	11 }				
LONGBENTON								
3-storey flats	3	9	6	1	(12)	(7)	19	
houses	–	2	8	3	(2)	(11)	13	
GATESHEAD								
high flats	6	2	27	9	18	82	44	100
WALLSEND								
high flats	1	6	7	6	(7)	(13)	20	
4-storey flats	2	4	2	2	(6)	(4)	10	
2/3-storey flats	2	14	12	14	38	62	42	100
maisonettes	–	–	15	8	–	100	23	100
houses	1	2	19	14	8	92	36	100

* 6th floor or above
** below 6th floor
***where the groups are too small for the results to be
    percentaged, the actual numbers included are given in
    brackets. This convention will be adopted throughout

to be less urgent, for the children were still very young.
    But, from the mother's standpoint, the presence of more
than one infant in the family, though good for the children, could be nerve-racking in circumstances where the
youngsters were unable to play outside on their own, and
where space inside the home was limited. From the sum of
categories b and d in Table 4, it follows that mothers
with more than one child aged under 5 comprised over 20
per cent of respondents in the high flats and considerably
more of those in the lower flats in Longbenton and Wallsend. The numbers who had more than one 2- to 5-year-old
on their hands are shown in the fourth column of Table 5.
In fact, as will be seen, it was this whole group of
mothers with more than one child of pre-school age who
were most vocal about the practical difficulties of living
above the ground with a young family and the effects on
their own health. The report of the Seebohm committee has
subsequently drawn attention to their needs. (6)

TABLE 5 Family composition: under-fives only

Locality and type of dwelling	all under 2	Families with (children): one aged 2 and under 5		more than one aged 2 and under 5	All	
		alone	with some under 2			
	%	%	%	%	%	no.
CRUDDAS PARK						
high flats*	31	46	13	10	100	52
high flats**	28	47	12	12	100	32
maisonettes	-	(9)	(3)	(5)		17
houses	25	31	14	31	100	36
LONGBENTON						
3-storey flats	(3)	(6)	(5)	(5)		19
houses	-	(8)	(3)	(2)		13
GATESHEAD						
high flats	18	57	11	14	100	44
WALLSEND						
high flats	(3)	(5)	(8)	(4)		20
4-storey flats	(1)	(3)	(4)	(2)		10
2/3-storey flats	24	14	40	21	100	42
maisonettes	13	52	13	22	100	23
houses	8	47	19	25	100	36

* 6th floor or above
**below 6th floor

These various distinctions will be referred to again in later chapters. They represent two different ways both of anticipating the difficulties that might arise and of evaluating the reactions of mothers to their situation.

AGE OF PARENTS

In all but a very small number of the families visited, both husband and wife were living at home, and therefore the husband was regarded as the 'head of the household'. In the few exceptions the head was a widowed or separated mother, or one who assumed the role of head as the husband was working away from home for a long period. Information was obtained, for each family, on the ages of the head and wife. The results, as summarised in Table 6, reflect the variations in family size and structure that have been noted above.

TABLE 6   Ages of husband and wife: summary

Type of dwelling	Age of husband (or head)			Age of wife			All families	
	under 30	30+	40+	under 30	30+	40+		
	%	%	%	%	%	%	%	no.
HIGH FLATS Cruddas Park and Wallsend	47	41	13	58	36	6	100	104
Gateshead	11	43	45	18	59	23	100	44
LOW FLATS	52	45	3	72	27	1	100	71
MAISONETTES	31	50	19	44	44	11	100	40
HOUSES Cruddas Park and Longbenton	17	75	8	42	52	6	100	49
Wallsend	6	59	35	14*	44	31	100	36

*for 4/36, i.e. 11% of respondents here, the age was not disclosed

It will suffice to comment here that, among mothers in the high flats, those in Gateshead were older on average than the rest, while the highest percentage of mothers under 30 was found in Longbenton.

In two of the previous studies the mother's age

appeared to have some bearing on certain aspects of her adjustment to the home and environment. The London survey found that the degree of concern over their children's play was greater for the older mothers than for those under 35, whereas, surprisingly, no such relationship was found with the size and age structure of the family. (7) On two of the estates in the survey of 'Families at High Density', it was the younger housewives who, like those in Longbenton, felt most lonely and isolated. (8) These findings relate of course to different aspects of adjustment, and the results from the two surveys are not necessarily conflicting. In the present study, however, family structure will be used as an independent variable more often than the mother's age.

EMPLOYMENT

In all sections of the survey, the great majority of family heads were employed full-time. Very few were unemployed and it was only the minority of female heads who were not working. Shift work or regular night duty was the pattern for 40 per cent of heads in Wallsend and Gateshead and for 20 per cent of those elsewhere. This routine could involve the strain of keeping the youngsters quiet during the day while their father was asleep. On the other hand, the father might be available for part of the day to help with the children. The frequency of night working among the neighbours of families in multi-storey dwellings could only be inferred from comments on the restrictions on children's play, because of the noise and disturbance that they might create. It will be discussed under that heading. (9)

The classes of occupation followed differed between one locality and another, rather than between the types of accommodation. The classification for occupied heads is shown in Table 7.

The classification of each job in terms of the degree of skill involved was often difficult, for the description of the head's occupation was given by the wife and only rarely was the husband present. No economic or class differences between the various groups of the survey families are therefore implied.

The question of the mother's employment seemed to be of greater interest. In England and Wales as a whole the employment or 'activity' rate among wives, aged under 55, who had children of pre-school age, had increased from 11 per cent in 1961 to 18 per cent in 1966. (10) The percentage rates for mothers in paid work in the survey were

TABLE 7   Occupation of head

Locality and type of dwelling	Class of occupation non-manual	manual skilled or semi-skilled	unskilled	All occupied heads	
	%	%	%	%	no.
CRUDDAS PARK					
high flats	9	73	18	100	82
rest	10	71	19	100	52
LONGBENTON	–	81	19	100	32
GATESHEAD	–	73	27	100	41
WALLSEND					
high flats 4-storey flats }	7	90	3	100	29
2/3-storey flats	10	79	12	100	41
maisonettes houses }	12	77	12	100	52

as follows (as in the national figures, part-time and
full-time employment are combined): Cruddas Park: 21
(high flats: 18, rest: 27); Longbenton: 9; Gateshead:
36; Wallsend: 12.

Again the figures reflect variations in the local
labour markets - as well as in individuals' freedom or in-
clination to take a job. In Wallsend, for example,
mothers not infrequently deplored the shortage of employment for them sufficiently near home. The actual numbers
of working mothers were only sufficient for further analysis in Cruddas Park and in Gateshead. In these areas, the
mother's employment position seemed to be related to the
structure of the family. In Cruddas Park, just over 10
per cent (4/33) of mothers with one child under 2 years
old (and no others under 5) were employed, as compared
with nearly 25 per cent (25/103) of the rest. In Gateshead, the number of mothers with only very young children
was too small for this comparison, although there was evidence of a similar pattern here also.

The detailed comments recorded by the interviewers suggested a more subtle distinction between respondents in
the two areas. The majority of working mothers in Gateshead were part-time cleaners in local offices. A few
worked as assistants in the near-by shops, cafés and

cinemas. These were the usual occupations for women
living close to the town centre. The hours were convenient and involved little disruption of the pattern of
family living. For mothers with older or larger families
it was relatively easy for them to take this kind of work.
By doing so they were conforming to the local way of life
and, among those interviewed, there was no evidence of any
underlying social ambition.

In Cruddas Park, however, there were no such opportunities close by. The decision to take a job involved a
greater effort on the mother's part, even if only because
of the travelling time. A greater variety of occupations
was reported here than in Gateshead. Very few in Cruddas
Park were cleaners. Those here, who were employed in
shops and canteens, often had longer hours, which obliged
them to make some regular arrangements for the care of
their children. Not a few seemed to be socially aspirant.
They had taken a job to increase the family income, either
so as to improve their present home, which they liked, or
to enhance their prospects of moving elsewhere. But, in
the meantime, most of them seemed to be content with their
situation or to have come to terms with it. Moreover, because of their success in arranging for the care of their
children, with relatives, sometimes with neighbours, or in
the nursery at the community centre or elsewhere, they
would be less inclined to be dissatisfied with the run of
local provision for children of this age. For the Gateshead mothers, whose orientation to work was less 'instru-
mental', these connections with other attitudes were
thought to be unlikely. (11)

Among the previous studies reviewed in Chapter 2, only
the Australian one discussed the mothers' employment. For
the walk-up sample in Melbourne (which included families
with children under school age), it was found that 8 per
cent of married women went out to work, over half of them
on a part-time basis. As was the case in Gateshead, the
main occupation was office cleaning in the city centre,
conveniently near to home. Also as in Gateshead, few of
the Australian working mothers mentioned any definite
arrangements for the care of their children while they
were at work. But the authors suspected that in fact they
did rely on neighbourly assistance to a degree that the
interviewers failed to elicit. (12) For this reason, differences between working mothers and others, in their
attitudes to the home and to the locality, were not
discussed.

PREVIOUS HOUSING EXPERIENCE

Only five respondents in the Tyneside survey had lived in
their present home since marriage. For the rest, the
length of residence varied between the areas, as in Table
8. In Wallsend, however, the survey was deliberately confined to families who had moved to their present address
in 1964, 1965 and 1966 (though here some inaccurate recol-
lection of their length of stay is evident for the few who
gave this, in 1967, as four years or more).

   In Cruddas Park and more particularly in Gateshead, a
large number of families had lived in their present home
since the days when the buildings (and the whole site in
Cruddas Park), were relatively new. Another large group
had been there for two or three years, which was long
enough for them to have settled down and for the longer-
term advantages and disadvantages of their situation to
have become apparent. The Longbenton families who were
included in the survey had all moved in within the previous three years. In Wallsend, families in the
maisonettes were distinguished from the rest by the small
number of comparative newcomers among them.

TABLE 8   Time at present address

| Locality and type of dwelling | Time at present address | | | | All | |
	under 2 years	2-4 years	4 years or more	since marriage		
	%	%	%	%	%	no.
CRUDDAS PARK						
high flats	16	38	46	1	100	84
rest	17	74	8	2	100	53
LONGBENTON	31	69	–	–	100	32
GATESHEAD	–	18	75	7	100	44
WALLSEND						
high flats	(8)	(11)	(1)	–		20
lower flats	43	56	2	–	100	52
maisonettes	9	87	4	–	100	23
houses	39	58	3	–	100	36

   It has been seen above that the survey families in the
flats in Cruddas Park and in Wallsend were almost equally
divided between those with all their children under 5 and
those with older children as well. (13) In each locality,

family structure, defined in this way, seemed to be associated with length of residence. In the Cruddas Park
flats, the younger families were a larger proportion of
those with less than four years' residence (30/45) than
of those with four years' residence or more (11/38). In
the Wallsend flats, among families who had been there for
less than two years, 18/30 had all their children under 5,
compared with 11/42 of the rest.

In each of these localities, therefore, for 25 per cent
or more of all respondents, the difficulties commonly experienced by mothers in adjusting to a new environment
might have been exacerbated by those of caring, in these
unfamiliar surroundings, for their very young children.
The association of these circumstances with satisfaction
with the home will be examined later, but first it is relevant to consider the localities and types of dwelling
from which the families came and their reasons for moving.

It is necessary to distinguish, in this context, between families currently living close to the central area,
as in Cruddas Park and in Gateshead, and those at some
distance away, as in Longbenton and in most of the survey
area of Wallsend. A broad classification of the localities from which they had moved, as in Table 9, shows that
around 70 per cent of respondents in the more central
areas were already familiar with some aspects of inner
urban living.

TABLE 9   Locality of previous residence

Present locality and type of dwelling	Previous locality				All	
	inner/ older areas	inter- mediate newer areas	else- where	none		
	%	%	%	%	%	no.
Inner:						
CRUDDAS PARK						
high flats	69	11	18	1	100	84
rest	66	9	23	2	100	53
GATESHEAD	75	7	11	7	100	44
Outer:						
LONGBENTON	100	–	–	–	100	32
WALLSEND						
high flats	(15)	–	(5)	–		20
other flats	78	20	2	–	100	52
maisonettes	69	30	–	–	100	23
houses	28	59	14	–	100	36

Most of the Cruddas Park families had moved from densely populated inner areas ranging, west to east, from Scotswood to Byker and Walker. Those from the most outlying districts ('elsewhere' in the table) came from Denton or from Westerhope, beyond the city boundary. The rest came from areas to the north or north-west of the city centre. Many Gateshead families had been rehoused within the same locality, as was the case for those in estate A of the Ministry of Housing's survey. (14) There were also some, as in Cruddas Park, who had moved in, or returned, from further out.

The Longbenton families were a deliberately selected group of those moved out from Byker. Many of those in the flats and maisonettes in Wallsend had come from the older parts of the borough. Those in the houses who had come from the newer or less central parts of Wallsend, would have reached the last stage in their housing experience, since their homes were now sufficiently spacious, and a further removal would be unlikely.

Reference has been made already to the attachment of the Longbenton and Wallsend families to their former homes or to the central areas, which they visited frequently and regularly. Some of those who were interviewed in Cruddas Park and in Gateshead had actually come back into the more central areas where they had lived some time before. But their numbers were not large enough for any generalisations to be based on their experience.

Mothers in all areas were also asked about the type of accommodation that they occupied previously and their reasons for moving. Except for those in the maisonettes and houses in Wallsend, the majority of families had previously been tenants (or sub-tenants) of private landlords or had been living with relatives. Removal brought them into the housing class of local authority tenants. (15) Their perception of their new status and their expectations from it may have affected their response to some of the main questions in the survey.

Table 11, which includes both former housing status and previous locality, and Table 12, which gives the reasons for moving, combine to suggest that, in terms of the concept of housing classes, two main patterns of experience may be distinguished.

There were, first, a group of families, the majority just mentioned, who had been rehoused from decaying or otherwise inadequate property in the inner areas. Whether their move resulted from slum clearance or compulsory purchase, or whether it was on their own application, it was recognised by many to have been to their overall advantage in terms of the space and amenities within the home. In

TABLE 10   Former housing status

Present locality and type of dwelling	Tenants of				With rela-tives	None	All	
	LA flat	other	private flat or rooms	other				
	%	%	%	%	%	%	%	no.
Inner:								
CRUDDAS PARK								
high flats	15	11	57	4	11	1	100	84
rest	6	13	53	17	9	2	100	53
GATESHEAD	5	14	52	14	9	7	100	44
Outer:								
LONGBENTON	3	–	94	3	–	–	100	32
WALLSEND								
high flats	(1)	(2)	(12)	(2)	(2)	(1)		20
other flats	6	13	56	12	13	–	100	52
maisonettes	39	22	35	–	4	–	100	23
houses	44	31	19	3	3	–	100	36

TABLE 11   Former housing status and previous locality*

Present locality and type of dwelling	Tenants of				With relatives		None	All	
	LA		private landlord						
	a	b	a	b	a	b			
	%	%	%	%	%	%	%	%	no.
Inner:									
CRUDDAS PARK	12	11	60	4	7	4	1	100	137
GATESHEAD	9	9	64	2	9	–	7	100	44
Outer:									
LONGBENTON	3	–	97	–	–	–	–	100	32
WALLSEND									
flats	8	10	64	4	6	7	1	100	72
maisonettes	43	17	22	13	4	–	–	100	23
houses	11	64	14	8	3	–	–	100	36

*a   including inner, intermediate and older areas
 b   including outer and newer areas

TABLE 12 Reasons for moving

Present locality and type of dwelling	Reasons for moving* and previous locality**						Others	All	
	1		2		3				
	a	b	a	b	a	b			
	%	%	%	%	%	%	%	%	no.
Inner:									
CRUDDAS PARK	39	1	32	12	7	7	2	100	137
GATESHEAD	32	-	43	-	7	11	7	100	44
Outer:									
LONGBENTON	100	-	-	-	-	-	-	100	32
WALLSEND									
flats	10	-	64	12	4	6	4	100	72
maisonettes	-	-	61	30	9	-	-	100	23
houses	3	-	19	58	6	14	-	100	36

* reasons for moving:
  1 slum-clearance, compulsory purchase, demolition
  2 'to get own house, more space, more amenities', 'on waiting list' or 'exchange' (very few)
  3 'to be more central, nearer work' for reasons of finance or health or for the sake of the children
**previous locality: as in Table 11

all areas except Longbenton, there was a second group who had moved within the class of local authority tenants. These families had either, as in Cruddas Park and in Gateshead, returned to the centre from more outlying areas, because of their general desire to be more central or to economise on the journey to work, or else, as for many of those occupying houses in the newer parts of Wallsend, they had moved from smaller local authority dwellings within the same locality.

When these various categories of families were examined, in relation to respondents' satisfaction with their move at the time and currently, no clear distinction emerged. Those, for example, whose removal seemed to have resulted from their own initiative or preference, were not always enthusiastic about the new home that was offered to them.

Clearly, within each housing class or type of housing experience, families differ for various reasons, administrative and personal, in their actual freedom to move and in the alternatives that are open to them. (16)

Individuals differ, too, in their perception of these
choices, and indeed, of what 'choice' in this context im-
plies. (17)   Table 13 shows the element of choice, if any,
that the respondents here associated with the move to
their present home and their reaction to it, in
retrospect.

Those, in all parts of the survey, who considered that
they had been free to choose both locality and type of
accommodation, were almost unanimous in recording that
they had been satisfied at the time with the outcome of
their decision.   For the rest, among those who moved to
Longbenton, to houses and maisonettes in Cruddas Park and
to houses in Wallsend, the majority had been satisfied at
the time of removal, whereas more misgivings were recalled
by those who had been rehoused in flats in Cruddas Park
and Gateshead and in flats and maisonettes in Wallsend.

This perception of choice appeared to have been an important factor in respondents' initial satisfaction or
displeasure with their new home. (18)

PRESENT SATISFACTION WITH HOME

Table 14 shows the respondents' current reaction to their
accommodation and to the locality, and how they rated each
of these with their former home.

The results are interesting when one considers the previous experience of the people involved.   They illustrate,
too, the various ways in which people may assess 'satisfaction' and the futility of seeking valid judgments in
response to one or two simple questions alone. (19)

The husbands' opinions were mostly conveyed by their
wives, hence they were generally consistent.   More differences of opinion were found in Gateshead, where notably
more of the husbands were said to be satisfied with the
flats.   They seemed to have been less directly affected
than their wives by the stresses of coping with young
children!

Unqualified approval of their accommodation was most
frequent among wives in Longbenton and in the Wallsend
houses, and most infrequent among those in the high blocks
in Cruddas Park and Gateshead and in all the flats in
Wallsend.   Throughout the whole survey area, however, many
respondents, whether generally satisfied or not, acknowledged the improvement on their previous accommodation,
usually because of the greater space or better amenities
that they now enjoyed.   In those sections where dissatisfaction was more general, there was also some spontaneously adverse comment on the facilities for children and on

TABLE 13 Choice associated with removal and satisfaction with new home at the time

Present locality and type of dwelling	Choice of*				Complete choice		Partial or no choice		All**	
	L and A	L only	A only	none	satisfied	rest	satisfied	rest		
	%	%	%	%	%	%	%	%	%	no.
Inner:										
CRUDDAS PARK										
flats	21	27	–	52	16	5	34	45	100	82
rest	58	17	2	23	54	4	25	17	100	52
GATESHEAD	22	2	–	75	22	–	37	41	100	41
Outer:										
LONGBENTON	41	47	3	9	34	6	56	3	100	32
WALLSEND										
flats	6	19	3	72	4	1	31	64	100	72
maisonettes	4	9	–	87	4	–	26	70	100	23
houses	25	8	3	64	25	–	72	3	100	36

* L locality
  A type of accommodation
**omitting those with no previous residence since marriage

TABLE 14   Current satisfaction with home and comparison
with previous one

(a) accommodation

Present locality and type of dwelling	Satisfied		Comparison with previous home			All	
	wives	husbands	better	worse	others		
	%	%	%	%	%	%	no.
Inner: CRUDDAS PARK							
flats	35	39	66	27	7	100	84
rest	53	49	89	5	5	100	55
GATESHEAD	37	64	70	20	9	100	44
Outer: LONGBENTON	94	94	100	-	-	100	32
WALLSEND							
high flats	(5)	(8)	(12)	(7)	(1)		20
other flats	27	25	54	33	13	100	52
maisonettes	52	57	74	9	17	100	23
houses	97	81	78	6	17	100	36

(b) locality

Present locality and type of dwelling	Satisfied		Comparison with previous home			All	
	wives	husbands	better	worse	others		
	%	%	%	%	%	%	no.
Inner: CRUDDAS PARK							
flats	71	63	25	31	44	100	84
rest	67	58	36	17	46	100	53
GATESHEAD	86	75	30	7	64	100	44
Outer: LONGBENTON	72	81	75	22	3	100	32
WALLSEND							
high flats	(15)	(13)	(10)	(6)	(4)		20
other flats	73	56	54	21	25	100	52
maisonettes	57	65	52	22	26	100	23
houses	75	89	31	11	59	100	36

the noise and lack of privacy in the present home as compared with the previous one.

For the locality, the overall picture was reversed. Gateshead respondents were more satisfied with an environment with which they were already familiar. In other areas, notably Cruddas Park, while many were generally satisfied with the locality, they still compared it unfavourably with where they lived before, on grounds of inconvenience, lack of shops, or class of neighbours. Overall, however, the locality seemed to be more readily tolerated than the type of accommodation, and its drawbacks, even when mentioned, seemed to be more often submerged beneath a general, if unenthusiastic, acceptance.

It appears, from Tables 13 and 14, that both initial and current reactions to their accommodation were most divided for mothers in the high flats in Cruddas Park and Gateshead and in the flats and maisonettes in Wallsend. For respondents in the first two areas, present reactions were independent of those at the time of removal. For instance, one mother in three in these areas was currently satisfied with her flat, whatever she had thought of it on moving in. In Wallsend, however, more of those who were initially pleased with their new home retained their favourable attitude, while distinctly more of the rest still had misgivings about it. This persistent dissatisfaction, voiced by the tenants of flats and maisonettes in Wallsend, underlined their attitude to other issues raised in the survey and reflected their general concern for their children. In all three areas, virtually all of those who expressed continued satisfaction with their home, and even 50 per cent of those who were ambivalent or critical, acknowledged that it was an improvement on their former living conditions.

Among the families in Cruddas Park high blocks and in all the flats in Wallsend there was enough variety in duration of tenure and in family structure to permit the analysis of present reaction to the home by these two factors. In neither area was there evidence of a simple process of settling-in. If anything, more of those in Cruddas Park with less than 2 years' residence were satisfied with their flat, while in Wallsend more of the relative newcomers had reservations about their home, definite approval or disapproval being more common among those with the longest stay. Family structure, distinguishing those with all the children aged under 5 from those with older children as well, was more consistently related to definite approval or disapproval of the home. In both areas, fewer of the mothers in the former group were satisfied. Also, in Wallsend, more of them were distinctly dissatisfied.

For the comparative newcomers in each area, mothers
with young children only were more often critical of their
home than other respondents with similar length of residence, and less often unreservedly approving of it. Their
special problems of adjustment, as anticipated in the
earlier discussion, seemed to have some bearing on their
attitude here.

The main threads in this complex pattern of housing experience and individual reactions to it will be picked up
again in later chapters.

USE OF ROOMS

Apart from some houses in Wallsend, all the dwellings in
the survey had a kitchen and one living-room. (20)   The
majority of families, in most areas, confined their meals
to the kitchen.   Where the numbers permitted more detailed
analysis, there was an even greater tendency among the
larger families to keep the only living-room free of
formal meals.   In Wallsend, however, nearly 70 per cent of
those in the lower flats and smaller houses took their
meals in their one living-room, while all but one of the
families who were provided with a separate dining-room
used it as such.

Three questions were asked as to where the children
played inside the home. (21)   These gave consistent results.   Those based on the rooms used by the younger children are summarised in Table 15.   The sharpest distinction, in the general pattern of use was found between the
high flats in Cruddas Park and the maisonettes and houses
in Wallsend.

An earlier survey reported that many housewives would
prefer a maisonette or house to a flat partly because of
the possibility, in the former dwellings, of keeping bedrooms free of children's play. (22)   The tendency for
children to play in the bedrooms was evident for families
in flats of all kinds.   The same practice was followed,
though to a lesser extent, by those in the maisonettes and
houses in Cruddas Park.   In Cruddas Park as a whole and in
Wallsend, this use of the accommodation was partly related
to family size and structure.   In the larger families and
in those with some older children, indoor play of the
under-fives was more often confined to the living-room.
Such families seemed to be obliged, by the demands of
space, to conform to a more traditional pattern of use,
confining meals to the kitchen (as above) and play to the
living-room.   Some of the older children needed to do
their homework in the bedrooms. (23)   In these

circumstances, free and undisturbed play for the younger members was virtually impossible. In fact many of the mothers of the larger families in Gateshead stated explicitly that the younger children were not allowed to play inside the flat at all. (24) In the smaller families, in all the flats, they tended more often to use the bedrooms.

TABLE 15   Rooms where younger children played

Locality and type of dwelling	Younger children played in: living-room	bed-room	both or anywhere	nowhere inside	All families	
	%	%	%	%	%	no.
HIGH FLATS						
Cruddas Park	26	24	38	11	100	84
Gateshead	41	18	23	18	100	44
Wallsend	(8)	(4)	(4)	(4)		20
LOWER FLATS						
Longbenton	(4)	(5)	(10)	(-)		19
Wallsend	35	31	25	8	100	52
MAISONETTES						
Cruddas Park	(7)	(3)	(6)	(1)		17
Wallsend	65	-	20	4	100	23
HOUSES						
Cruddas Park	39	14	41	6	100	36
Longbenton	(8)	(2)	(3)	(-)		13
Wallsend	61	8	30	-	100	36

The expected difficulties of providing play-space for young children within the limited area of flats of all kinds, as compared with maisonettes and houses, were illustrated by these results.

USE OF BALCONY

Respondents were asked whether they used the balcony, if they had one. Later they were given the opportunity of mentioning the balcony as a place where their children played and the dangers, if any, that they associated with this practice.

The question applied only to those in high flats in Cruddas Park and Wallsend, in some lower flats in

Longbenton and in the maisonettes in Cruddas Park.   The
balconies in the high blocks in Cruddas Park were small,
recessed and private, while those in Wallsend, often referred to as 'the veranda', protruded from the building
for its whole length, and gave access to each flat.   In
each locality, those who professed to use the balcony were
found rather less often above the fifth floor (13/52 compared with 10/32 in Cruddas Park, and 10/14 compared with
6/6 in Wallsend).

In Cruddas Park, however, only one mother allowed her
children to play there, and many of the rest said that the
practice was officially prohibited, or mentioned their own
precaution of keeping the balcony locked.   Other uses of
the balcony here included clothes-drying (though this also
was discouraged, since it might spoil the appearance of
the whole block), putting the baby in the fresh air, or
just sitting out.   Dangers to young children were recognised by over 20 per cent of respondents above the fifth
floor, but were not explicitly mentioned by any of those
living closer to ground level.   The actual fears associated with the balcony were no doubt more prevalent than
this, as evidenced by the majority decision, among the
families in the flats here, to make no use at all of this
potential access to fresh air.

In Wallsend, some use of balconies or verandas was inevitable, by virtue of the construction of the buildings.
In 12 of the 20 families the under-fives regularly played
there.   There was, in these flats also, a general sense of
the danger to venturesome children of all ages.   One
mother was alarmed by the fact that some older boys
climbed on their bicycles to look over!   The very few
mothers in the high blocks who put their babies outside at
all put them on the veranda.   In general, the lack of privacy detracted from the use of the veranda as a place for
the older members of the family to sit out of doors.

The Cruddas Park maisonettes and some flats in Longbenton had small private balconies, which were generally
used but seldom for children's play.   One of the fears expressed by mothers in the maisonettes was that small children might try to squeeze through the narrow gap between
the front panel of the balcony and the floor.   Of the 10
Longbenton families with a balcony, 6 made some use of it,
3 of them for children's play, while 5 of the 10 mentioned
its hazards for their younger children.

A sample survey involving 258 tenants of flats and
maisonettes in different parts of London found evidence of
this general fear of balconies, especially in the younger
families. (25)   On the other hand, two-thirds of the
sample appreciated the balcony, as it helped to counteract

the feeling of being closed-in, and partly replaced the
garden or backyard as somewhere to grow plants, to put out
the pram, to keep birds, to do odd jobs, or simply for
storage. The survey also found that 40 per cent of the
under-fives played regularly on the balcony, a high result
in view of parents' general unease. The report, which was
restricted to private balconies, suggested certain safeguards that might be incorporated in their design. These
included a wire mesh front with no gaps, an opening to the
balcony from the kitchen so that the mother could easily
watch the children, and the absence of any protrusion that
might give a foothold for climbing.

The Melbourne study revealed a similar mixture of appreciation and apprehension and commented that, with certain precautions, a generous balcony could overcome some
of the problems of supervising the more passive recreation
of the very young. (26) The Ministry of Housing survey
found that 75 per cent of housewives with private balconies would rather have them than more space inside the
home, despite their present cramped living conditions.
(27)

The earlier discussion of the use of space from the
present survey findings would underline the need for
serious attention to be given to this feature of flat and
maisonette design.

BABIES AND PRAMS

Tyneside mothers were asked if they had a pram for the
baby and, if so, whether they put the child outside in it.
They were also asked where they stored the pram. These
topics may present a main source of difficulty for flat-
dwellers with the youngest children. Unfortunately for
the purpose of the analysis, it was not always possible to
distinguish perambulators from push-chairs. (28) One interviewer, speaking from his experience as a family man,
was impressed by the use of push-chairs for children of an
unusually early age.

In the high flats in Cruddas Park and Gateshead, only 5
of over 70 mothers to whom the question applied put their
babies outside. The few in the upper floors at Cruddas
Park used the balcony for this purpose. This use was more
feasible in the high flats at Wallsend, but here only 4
out of 15 mothers put their babies out on the veranda.

In the lower flats and maisonettes there was less
general reluctance to put the baby outside on his own (22
out of 57 respondents actually did so and usually on the
grass immediately below). Mothers in the houses at

Cruddas Park appreciated their gardens for this purpose
and 2 mothers in 3 put the baby there.

The storage of the pram evoked more comment, especially
in the flats at Wallsend, where lock-up sheds were provided at ground level. Some mothers here complained that
the sheds were unsuitable for pram storage because of damp
and dirt or that the locks were unsafe. Some felt obliged
to use the pram store for coal, as tradesmen refused to
carry fuel upstairs to the coal cupboard.

Because of the patterns of use adopted by previous
tenants, some respondents were unaware that there was an
'official' pram store. Table 16 illustrates the contrast
in this matter between families in flats and those in
maisonettes and houses. While it was common practice, in
all types of dwelling, to keep the pram within the actual
living space, this tendency was greatest in the flats,
where space already was likely to be at a premium.

TABLE 16   Place where pram was stored

Type of dwelling	Pram store or shed	Inside flat, etc.	Under stairs or in passage	Else-where	All families with prams	
	%	%	%	%	%	no.
High flats	12	62	22	5	100	87
Lower flats	19	62	15	5	100	47
Maisonettes	(-)	(6)	(9)	(3)		18
Houses	12	46	29	12	100	48

This chapter has set out to examine certain tangible
and interrelated aspects of what has been described elsewhere as the whole 'social and emotional environment' of
the survey families. Some have been discussed at length,
being of interest on their own. For most of them, differences were found that might have a bearing on the specific topic of children's play and, with these in mind,
attention will now be directed to the youngsters
themselves.

6   The under-fives

This chapter will examine some of the ways in which the
children passed their time, where they usually played and
who their companions were.

The London survey of children in high flats commented
that 'visits to shops, relatives and friends, parks and
playgrounds went to make up the toddler's day'. (1) These
activities will be considered in that order, for the Tyneside children.

VISITS TO SHOPS AND TO RELATIVES OR FRIENDS (TABLE 17)

Mothers were asked, 'Do you have any shops near here, and
if so, how often do you take your children to them?'

In all areas except Cruddas Park, the great majority of
mothers said that they went every day, even where, as in
Wallsend, the nearest shops were at some distance from
home. In Cruddas Park, at the time of the survey, local
shops were few. The shopping centre was not yet completed
and the few remaining general stores were dotted around
the edge of the estate. This situation evoked many spontaneous complaints, especially from respondents in the
houses (21/36), who referred to the inconvenience of
having to take their children with them up the hill to the
shops in Elswick Road, or even 'into town'. On the other
hand, mothers in the high flats were less complaining.
Many of them said that they shopped every day 'to give the
children some fresh air' and also to make their own informal social contacts.

In all areas, mothers took their children frequently to
the homes of relatives or friends. The comments showed
that these visits were not just to 'gran's', but to other
families with children with whom their own youngsters
could play.

TABLE 17   Visits with children to shops and to relatives or friends

(a) to the shops

Locality and type of dwelling	Frequency of visits			All respondents	
	daily	less often	never (or none near)		
	%	%	%	%	no.
CRUDDAS PARK					
high flats	38	24	38	100	84
maisonettes	(1)	(1)	(15)		17
houses	8	22	69	100	36
LONGBENTON	88	12	–	100	32
GATESHEAD	92	2	5	100	44
WALLSEND					
high flats	(16)	(4)	(–)		20
other flats	71	23	6	100	52
maisonettes	78	22	–	100	23
houses	67	33	–	100	36

(b) to relatives or friends

Locality and type of dwelling	Frequency of visits				All respondents	
	daily	several a week	less often	never		
	%	%	%	%	%	no.
CRUDDAS PARK						
high flats	13	40	39	7	100	84
maisonettes	(2)	(8)	(7)	(–)		17
houses	11	36	44	8	100	36
LONGBENTON	3	34	59	3	100	32
GATESHEAD	20	20	39	20	100	44
WALLSEND						
high flats	(3)	(7)	(9)	(1)		20
other flats	12	46	38	4	100	52
maisonettes	4	43	48	4	100	23
houses	11	36	41	11	100	36

Some variation was apparent in Gateshead. Here, while 20 per cent of mothers made such visits every day, just as many reported no contacts of this kind. In each of these groups, the majority of respondents had previously lived in the central area, and many would have relatives and friends close by. Patterns of visiting in Gateshead were related to the age of the mother and to her employment. More of the first group, the 'visitors', were under 40 and none of them went out to work, whereas more of the second group were over 40 and nearly half of them had a job.

Table 17 shows that, in all sections of the survey, some 40 to 50 per cent of respondents took their children to visit relatives or friends more than once a week. It is consistent with this finding that there was no general shortage of help with the children, especially, for example, when the mother was ill.

Apart from such emergencies, relatively more of the respondents in Gateshead and in the maisonettes and houses in Wallsend stated or implied that they needed no help with their children. Mothers in these sections of the survey were older, on average, and had more children than was found elsewhere, and they often relied on the older children to take care of the younger ones. (2) Only in Longbenton did some mothers complain that they had no help of this kind, whereas in Byker, where they lived previously, they had been able to turn to parents, other relatives or neighbours.

There was no evidence that the survey families in high blocks were particularly short of help when it was needed.

VISITS TO PARKS AND PLAYGROUNDS

The situation of the nearest park and the local provision of playgrounds or play areas has been described in Chapter 4 for each section of the survey. Mothers' awareness of these facilities and the frequency with which they visited them with their young children are shown in Table 18.

Families on the Cruddas Park estate were the most fortunate in having Elswick Park within fairly easy walking distance. For those in the Gateshead flats, a visit to Windmill Hills, the most popular open space, involved crossing some of the town's busiest streets. For most of the survey families in Wallsend, the nearest park was more distant. In Longbenton there was no park at all. These differences are reflected in Table 18 part (a).

Among the families in high blocks at Cruddas Park, one mother in four said that she took her children to Elswick Park every day. The proportion was higher (one in three)

TABLE 18   Children's visits to the local park and to the play area or playground

(a) to the park

Locality and type of dwelling	daily	Frequency of visits			All respondents	
		several a week	less often	never or none near		
	%	%	%	%	%	no.
CRUDDAS PARK						
high flats*	33	17	23	27	100	52
high flats**	12	22	31	35	100	32
maisonettes	(2)	(4)	(9)	(2)		17
houses	3	6	39	53	100	32
LONGBENTON	-	-	3	97	100	32
GATESHEAD	5	20	34	41	100	44
WALLSEND						
high flats 4-storey flats }	3	13	33	50	100	30
lower flats	2	24	24	50	100	42
maisonettes	-	13	61	26	100	23
houses	-	8	56	36	100	32

(b) to the play area or playground

Locality and type of dwelling	daily	Frequency of visits			All respondents	
		several a week	less often	never or none near		
	%	%	%	%	%	no.
CRUDDAS PARK						
high flats*	37	13	12	38	100	52
high flats**	47	6	16	31	100	32
maisonettes	(6)	(2)	(2)	(7)		17
houses	12	3	22	62	100	32
LONGBENTON	-	-	6	94	100	32
GATESHEAD	32	11	9	47	100	44
WALLSEND						
high flats 4-storey flats }	33	20	20	27	100	30
lower flats	2	2	12	84	100	42
maisonettes	-	-	4	96	100	23
houses	6	6	22	66	100	32

* 6th floor or above
**below 6th floor

for families in the upper floors. Elswick Park was well
provided with swings (from comments throughout the survey
the most popular piece of play equipment), and with roundabouts. There was ample space for ball-games and for
everyone to follow his own pursuits without upsetting
other people. Children from the Cedars, an isolated block
to the east of Park Road, and from the houses, went to the
Park least often, partly because they were farthest away
from it.

In Gateshead, almost all the survey families with all
the children under 5 were taken to Windmill Hills from
time to time, so that the children could have some freedom. But for 50 per cent of families with older children,
such visits were rare. In these larger families, the
older ones were used to minding their younger brothers and
sisters while they played in the available space around
the flats.

Mothers in Wallsend tended to confuse the park and the
playground in replying to these questions. Apart from the
estate with the high and 4-storey flats, the only playground was in the nearest park. Visits to the park were
therefore sometimes described as visits to the playground,
and vice versa. Occasional visits of this kind were reported by the majority of families, regardless of whether
they had gardens of their own.

The results for Cruddas Park, in Table 18 part (a), do
actually refer to Elswick Park (the High Park as some
mothers called it), and not to the 'park', the name that
was often used for the grassed area between the two main
groups of high blocks. Some mothers referred to the
latter open space as the play area, even though its use
for active play was officially discouraged at the time of
the survey. There were suntraps in the area where mothers
could sit and watch their children. Visits, whether to
these or to the 'park' generally, were often mentioned.
It was not always possible to distinguish in the analysis
between visits of this kind and those to the actual playgrounds on the estate. Table 18 part (b) therefore includes both.

Following the description of the areas in Chapter 4,
Table 18 part (b) applies mainly to children in the high
flats in Cruddas Park, Gateshead and Wallsend. It is interesting to note that, in each case, some 30 or 40 per
cent of mothers said that they took their youngsters every
day to one or other of the play spaces that had been provided (the 'park' at Cruddas Park included). The results
for the three areas were still more consistent when families with all the children under 2 years old were omitted.
In this case too, the differences between the upper and

lower floors in Cruddas Park virtually disappeared.

There was no evidence, in Cruddas Park or elsewhere, that the use of playgrounds (or their equivalent) differed between families with only one 2- to 5-year-old and those with more than one child in this age group. This was to be expected for the reasons advanced already in Chapter 5. (3)   Similarly, it was found that whether or not there were other children at school made no difference to this aspect of the daily routine for the under-fives. (4)

It appeared too, that a substantial minority among families in the high blocks in Cruddas Park, Gateshead and Wallsend never used the estate play areas at all. Moreover, the fact that a child was said to visit the 'playground' every day did not imply that he played there most often, or for very long. The most popular places for children's play, out of doors and elsewhere, were the subject of separate questions and will be discussed later.

It remains to consider, in this section, mothers' knowledge and use of the local nursery facilities.

NURSERY FACILITIES

Two sets of questions were included to discover mothers' awareness of nursery facilities in their locality and the use that they made of them. (5)   Respondents were also invited to comment on the existing provision and to suggest how it might be improved.

The formal distinctions between nursery schools, nursery classes and play centres were not stressed. In fact, mothers used a variety of terms for the same service. The second set of questions attempted to deal with these items separately, but it was necessary to combine the replies in the analysis in order to give a more realistic picture of the use of such facilities in general. (6)

In Longbenton and Wallsend the great majority of mothers (at least 90 per cent), said that, so far as they knew, there were no organisations in their locality for looking after young children. More of those in Cruddas Park and Gateshead mentioned some local service. Those who said that they did not know of any (20 per cent in Cruddas Park and 60 per cent in Gateshead), did not appear to differ systematically on any of the background variables from the more informed respondents. There was no evidence, for example, that awareness of local nursery facilities was related to the families' length of residence in the area. Nor was it connected with the potential needs of the family as evidenced by the number and ages of the children.

The actual provision in each area at the time of the survey has been described in Chapter 4. (7)   Cruddas Park appeared to be the best served.   There was a daily nursery school at the community centre (though this could only take eighteen children), and a crèche on one afternoon a week for children of mothers attending meetings there. Another nursery school was fairly near, in Elswick Road, and yet another, further out, in Scotswood.   There were also day nurseries, though at some distance from the estate.   All of these services catered for a densely populated area and, apart from the provision in the community centre, were in great demand from families off the estate.

At the time of the survey, there were in all some 200 children under 5 in Cruddas Park.   Not surprisingly, only a minority had the benefit of these nursery and play facilities.   Many respondents on the estate knew of some local organisation of this kind.   Most of them referred to the nursery at the community centre or the school in Elswick Road.   But only one mother in seven from the high blocks and elsewhere on the estate took her children regularly to some such organisation, a few of them going to more distant parts of the city.   A further 8 per cent of mothers in the high blocks were on the community centre's waiting list which, from general comments, seemed to be lengthy.

All but two of mothers in Cruddas Park who used these facilities did so every day.   Almost 50 per cent of them were working mothers, as compared with 21 per cent of all respondents in Cruddas Park.   That the under-fives in Cruddas Park had rather greater use of these various services than would be expected from the current rate in the country as a whole, is a reflection of the widespread shortage of them rather than the adequacy of the local provision. (8)

In Longbenton, Gateshead and Wallsend there were fewer such arrangements within the vicinity.   Only eight respondents, in the three areas together, reported that they used them at all.

The comments volunteered by mothers on nursery facilities in general are summarised in Table 19.   In all areas, especially in Cruddas Park, Gateshead and the flats in Wallsend, around 40 per cent of mothers had nothing to say on this matter or admitted that they had never thought about it.   Over 10 per cent, in all areas, said that these facilities were unnecessary, that each mother should look after her own children or that she was best able to do this, and that, on this principle, they themselves were content to go on as they were.   The remainder, at least 40 per cent in all areas, made specific comments or suggestions.   Mothers in Cruddas Park were the most critical of

TABLE 19 Comments* on nursery and play organisations

Locality and type of dwelling	No comment 1	No need 2	Need for nursery			Playground, etc. 6	Supervised play 7	Other	All respondents	
			3	4	5					
	%	%	%	%	%	%	%	%	%	no.
CRUDDAS PARK										
high flats	33	10	11	14	20	7	7	4	100	84
maisonettes } houses	37	17	4	13	13	4	6	6	100	53
LONGBENTON	25	16	–	–	47	–	12	–	100	32
GATESHEAD	45	11	2	5	11	2	18	5	100	44
WALLSEND										
high flats } 4-storey flats	40	17	7	3	23	3	7	3	100	30
other flats	37	16	7	2	24	12	2	–	100	43
maisonettes	17	17	–	–	43	13	9	–	100	23
houses	28	11	3	6	22	6	25	–	100	36

*1 'don't know' or 'never thought about it'
2 'happy as we are', 'mother's responsibility'
3 concern about waiting list or age of admission
4 concern about expense
5 just 'need a nursery'
6 'need a special playground or room for the under-fives'
7 'need an informal arrangement, with supervision' or 'just need somewhere safe to leave the children for a short time'

N.B. in a few cases mothers made comments under more than one heading.

the existing services. Elsewhere, apart from simple expressions of the need 'just for a nursery', mothers referred to the need for a special playground or playroom
for the children under 5, or for some arrangement for
supervised play.

One might expect the younger mothers to be more directly concerned with nursery or play facilities and more
aware than the older generation of their potential value.
There was some evidence of this. In Gateshead, more of
those who were under 40, including all but two of the
under 30s, had some definite comments to make. All but
two of the small but distinctive group of respondents from
the houses in Wallsend, who advocated a child-minding service with voluntary or paid supervision, were under 40
(7/9 compared with 14/23 of the rest whose age was known).
However awareness of these matters, as evidenced by the
tendency to comment, seemed to be less clearly associated
with the age of the mother, than with the ages and number
of her children.

In Cruddas Park, the number of facilies was sufficient
to be analysed in these terms. Among those in the high
flats, 40 per cent of those who made no comment had all
their children under 2 years of age, compared with 25 per
cent of the rest. All but one of the few who said 'we're
happy as we are' or 'the children are our responsibility'
had just one 2- to 5-year-old. On the other hand, all but
one of the group of mothers with more than one child in
this age-group had some suggestion to make or criticised
the existing services. Mothers in the maisonettes and
split-level houses followed a similar pattern. Here a
higher proportion of those who made no comment, or who
were content as they were, had only one child between 2
and 5 (19/28 compared with 9/25 of the rest). Of those
who were more forthcoming, 12/25 had more than one child
in this age-group as compared with 4/28 of the rest.

Apart from these associations, the replies illustrated
how mothers differed in their notions of what was best for
their children and of their own responsibility for them.
They differed, too, in their assessment of the objectives
and value of nurseries and play-groups. The general run
of comments may be summarised as follows:

As mentioned already, a substantial group of mothers
felt that these services were unnecessary for them. They
could look after their own children and it was their duty
to do so. (9) Some respondents, in all areas, considered
that the child's place was in his own home, with the
people he knew. Others, again in all parts of the survey,
said that it was good for the child to have the opportunity of mixing with other children, and adults too, in

nurseries or play groups, and that this experience would
help prepare him for going to school. Such arguments,
made from the point of view of the child, were admittedly
most common among mothers in multi-storey dwellings, where
the children's contact with others might be more limited.
But there was also a general sense of the value of nursery
groups among those in the houses, where the children were
less restricted.

There was also a minority of respondents from the
houses, and those especially in Wallsend, who advocated a
less formal kind of service to meet their own needs,
rather than those of the children. They wanted somewhere
where they could confidently leave the children, either in
an emergency, or regularly, for a few hours each week,
while they went shopping. In all areas, too, there was
evidence of the opinion that nurseries were only for working mothers, or that they should be provided in order to
free mothers to take a job. Thus, the various arguments
for and against services of this kind, as spelt out in the
Plowden Report, were reproduced in the mothers' own unprompted observations. (10)

In view of the present interest in day-care for the
under-fives, some further comments are appropriate here,
in anticipation of the discussion in Chapter 9. (11) At
the time when the interviews were completed, pre-school
provision, other than in play groups, was generally very
small. The Plowden Committee had not yet reported and
the widespread expansion of these services was still a
distant prospect. Since then, the subject has become increasingly topical. More recent studies have disclosed
less ignorance about pre-school services in general than
was found here, though no greater knowledge of those that
were available locally. An inquiry in 1971 among working-
class mothers in the East End of Newcastle found 'widespread support for the provision of nurseries and no op-
position to the idea, ... though a large majority gave the
reason that nurseries help mothers who have to work as the
main point in their favour'. (12) Also in 1971 an extensive survey was conducted in Kirkby, an area of mainly
local authority housing, and among families in various
tenure groups in London. It was found that 10 per cent of
the Kirkby children and 28 per cent of those in London
were already attending nursery schools, classes or play
groups. But as many as 72 per cent of parents in Kirkby
and 62 per cent in London would have liked their children
to attend if any local provision had been made for them.
(13) Although in these more recent studies the potential
demand was rather greater than was evident in any part of
the survey here, there appeared to be a similar confusion

about the nature of the various forms of provision and their basic rationale.

VISITS TO COMMUNITY CENTRES AND CLINICS

Some 10 per cent of mothers in the high blocks at Cruddas Park, and 4 per cent of those elsewhere on the estate said that they sometimes went with their children to the community centre. These visits were usually weekly or 'occasional'. These respondents had made no mention of visiting the nursery class or crèche, and they may have gone to the community centre for that purpose. Even if they were added to the group who said that they used the nursery facilities at the centre, the total was still a small proportion of all mothers on the estate with children under 5.

Only two respondents in Longbenton said that they went to the local community and welfare centre. A playroom was open here on two mornings and there was a weekly young wives' club, with a crèche for the children. However, these were open to all families on the estate, of whom only a small minority were included in the survey. There was no community centre in Gateshead or Wallsend.

Over 50 per cent of mothers in all areas said that they took their children every week, or occasionally, to the local clinic.

TAKING OLDER CHILDREN TO SCHOOL

In all sections of the survey, a minority of mothers with older children took them to school each morning and met them afterwards. In nearly every case their younger children went along too. However this was part of the daily routine for only 10 per cent of the survey families in Cruddas Park and Longbenton and in the maisonettes and houses at Wallsend, but for rather more, 20 per cent, in Gateshead and 40 per cent in the high flats at Wallsend.

SUMMARY

The London survey of toddlers in high flats asked mothers to keep a record of how their children spent a given day. (14) This was attempted in the present survey, but the response was too incomplete for analysis.

The foregoing review of the various activities, one at a time, adds up to a familiar impression of the routine

aspects of the child's life. However, this study was
primarily concerned with the time that was not taken up by
shopping and other less frequent excursions in the company
of his parents. Some aspects of the child's own playtime
will now be considered.

WHERE THE CHILDREN PLAYED OUTSIDE

The replies to the question, 'Whereabouts do your children
(under 5) play out of doors?' are shown in Table 20. The
results are grouped in order to distinguish between the
high flats, lower flats and maisonettes, and houses.

The picture for the high flats is not inconsistent with
the earlier discussion on the use of playgrounds or play
areas. But there was a greater tendency, in all types of
multi-storey dwelling than elsewhere, for the children to
play, as their mothers said, 'just outside or close to the
entrance'.

In all the high flats, and also in the lower flats and
maisonettes in Wallsend, a distinct group of mothers said
that their children were not allowed to play outside at
all. In approximately half these cases, in each area, the
children were too young anyway. However, this still left
a number of children between 2 and 5 whose recreation out
of doors was limited to the various activities described
in the previous sections.

The patterns of play out of doors, among children in
the multi-storey dwellings, did not appear to be related
to the size and age-structure of the family, e.g. whether
or not there were older brothers and sisters to look after
them. Young children in the houses, and in some of the
lower flats, with enclosed gardens, evidently played there
in most cases. But the results also illustrate the pre-
vailing tendency to play in the street.

WHERE THE CHILDREN PLAYED INSIDE

Mothers were also asked whether their children played anywhere indoors, other than inside their own living quarters
(Table 21).

The majority of respondents in all flats and maisonettes said that children were not allowed to play inside
the building. Judging by their comments, this statement
seemed to imply 'we don't let them', 'the neighbours don't
like it', 'the caretaker prevents them', or 'it says that
they mustn't in the rent book'.

The danger and the inconvenience of allowing children

TABLE 20 Where the children played outside*

Locality and type of dwelling	Nowhere or not allowed %	Just outside near the entrance, etc. %	Playground or play area %	Own garden %	Park or field %	Street %	Elsewhere %	All respondents %	no.
HIGH FLATS									
Cruddas Park	24	48	21	–	8	2	1	100	84
Gateshead	31	36	30	–	–	–	9	100	44
Wallsend	(11)	–	(8)	–	–	–	(1)		20
LOWER FLATS, MAISONETTES									
Cruddas Park	{1}	{14}	(3)	–	{1}	(4)	–		17
Longbenton	{3}	{13}	–	(1)	{2}	–	–		19
Wallsend	14	81	5	3	3	11	2	100	75
HOUSES									
Cruddas Park	8	11	3	64	6	44	8	100	36
Longbenton	(1)	(1)	–	(9)	(3)	(2)	–		16
Wallsend	3	3	–	75	8	28	6	100	36

*more than one reply in some cases

TABLE 21 Where the children played inside*

Locality and type of dwelling	Nowhere 'too young' %	Nowhere 'not allowed' %	Passage or landing %	Entrance or hall %	Stairs %	Balcony or veranda %	All respondents %	no.
HIGH FLATS								
Cruddas Park	13	65	21	–	–	1	100	84
Gateshead	7	50	39	5	–	–	100	44
Wallsend	–	(6)	(1)	(1)	–	(12)		20
LOWER FLATS								
Longbenton	(3)	(10)	(1)	–	(1)	(4)		19
Wallsend	–	60	29	12	10	–	100	52
MAISONETTES								
Cruddas Park	(2)	(7)	(2)	–	(3)	(3)		17
Wallsend	9	65	17	–	9	–	100	23

*i.e. indoors other than in the flat, etc.

to play on the stairs, or in the entrance to multi-storey
buildings, are real enough to warrant some restrictions.
But these may be difficult to enforce. (15) Some 10 per
cent of mothers in the Wallsend flats, for example, said
that their children played on the stairs, though this
practice was explicitly forbidden, according to the rent
book.

In most multi-storey buildings there was only limited
room on the landings or in the passages and entrance
halls. The high blocks in Gateshead had more space of
this kind than those in Cruddas Park. Around 40 per cent
of mothers in Gateshead said that their children played in
the passage or corridor, whereas, in Cruddas Park, some 20
per cent mentioned the landing. Those in Gateshead whose
children played in the entrance lobby, were all living on
the lower floors. In the 3-storey flats at Wallsend, some
10 per cent of mothers said that their children played in
the hall. One mother had even put a slide there to keep
her youngsters amused on wet days!

The use of the balcony or veranda for children's play
has been described already in Chapter 5. It must be noted
that these questions about where the children played were
left open. No pre-selected answers were suggested to the
respondents and there was no probing. It has been seen in
Chapter 5 that, in flats especially, many families had
little room for play within their own private space. In
spite of the hazards and restrictions, it seems inevitable
that some children will attempt to play elsewhere inside
the buildings, if only to join their friends.

PLAYMATES

Given the difficulties of playing anywhere outside the
home and the shortage of space within it, it is reasonable
to suppose that children in multi-storey dwellings, and
especially those living 'high', may be isolated from the
company of others in their age-group, apart from members
of their own family. The empirical evidence to date was
slight, and in any event was difficult to collect. The
London investigators reported that one child in seven from
their sample of flat-dwellers never played with other
children and that such isolation was more prevalent among
those on the upper floors. On the other hand, one child
in four had some regular contact with children from other
families. (16)

The Tyneside mothers were asked, first, whether any of
their 'neighbours' had children of the same age as their
own youngsters and, second, whom the latter played with as

a rule. Neither question was of value on its own. (17)
Cross-analysis of the results showed that in all sections
of the survey, except the high flats in Cruddas Park and
Gateshead, up to 10 per cent of mothers said that their
children played on their own, although their neighbours
had youngsters of the same age. By comparison with this
general result, the under-fives in the upper floors of
Cruddas Park did appear to be more isolated. Here one
mother in four (7/28) said that her children played alone,
although there were others of the same age living near.
(18) The corresponding figures for the lower floors in
Cruddas Park and for the flats in Gateshead were one in
nine and one in seven. Children in the Wallsend flats
could play together more readily, partly because of the
different construction of the blocks and the tendency to
use the veranda. Here only one mother of the small group
of twenty families said that her child played alone, and
the majority of children had companions of their own age
on the same floor.

PLAYTHINGS

Members of the committee were interested in the kind of
toys and other playthings used by the children, especially
those in the more restrictive environments. The replies
were many and varied. But, within their limits of reli-
ability, they followed a similar pattern in all housing
types, and certainly gave no evidence that children in the
high flats were restricted in their range of toys, or type
of play. 'Bikes', cars, scooters and dolls' prams were
top favourites everywhere (especially in the flats!), followed by a range of drawing and building sets, dolls and
games.

From the analysis of the factual data on the characteristics of the survey families and the general activities of
the under-fives, several conclusions may be drawn. These
are set out in the introduction to the next chapter, which
goes on to discuss the mothers' opinions of the local
arrangements for their children's play and their suggestions for dealing with some of the problems involved.

7   The response of the mothers

INTRODUCTION

Against the background of the local settings, the chapters
so far have discussed certain features of the survey families including the number and age-distribution of the
children, especially those under 5, the employment position of the parents, the type of accommodation and the
locality in which they lived previously and their general
reaction to their new home. With some of these as independent variables, families' use of the existing arrangements for play and the various ways in which the children
passed their time have then been compared.

It is evident that mothers' daily routine included a
number of activities that were intended to compensate, in
some measure, for their children's inability to play
freely at home. These may be summarised as follows:
    Shops were visited frequently with the children;
mothers living on the upper floors of Cruddas Park often
made a special effort to do this, although the shops were
not very near.
    Relatives and friends were visited at least once a week
by many respondents. In Gateshead, this was more often
the practice of the younger mothers and those who did not
go to work.
    Parks and similar open spaces were widely appreciated
as places where the children could play without being dis-
turbed or giving annoyance. This was found to be the case
even among respondents in the Wallsend houses whose home
surroundings were least inhibiting. Among the more restricted flat-dwellers, mothers in the upper floors of
Cruddas Park went most often to the park near by, while
those, in Gateshead, whose children were all young, took
them from time to time to the more distant 'Windmill
Hills'.

Nursery or other kinds of formal provision for the under-fives were minimal in some areas. In Cruddas Park and Gateshead mothers most often knew of some such arrangement, but those who did were not distinguished from the rest by either length of residence or family structure.

In Cruddas Park, working mothers actually used some formal arrangement more frequently than the rest.

The invitation to comment on these services or to suggest improvements or innovations evoked no response from some 40 per cent of mothers in all areas. Definite opinions and suggestions were voiced more often by the younger mothers and, in Cruddas Park, most of all by those with more than one child under 5.

The pattern of play itself was not related, as some of the 'compensatory' activities were, to these family characteristics. Similar results were found in those localities and types of dwelling where the opportunities were comparable. Playgrounds and play spaces were visited daily by the children, with their mothers, in over 30 per cent of the high-flat families, but a similar number never went there at all. It was common practice here, and in the lower flats in Wallsend, for the children to play just outside, close to the entrance. A minority, in all multi-storey buildings, played inside, in the passage or hall, or on the landing, even though these were 'out of bounds'. Children from the houses used their gardens, but some also played in the street. It seemed, too, that more children in the upper floors of Cruddas Park usually played on their own, although 'neighbours' had children of the same age.

Despite the regularities that have appeared, mothers' comments on their home and on the formal provision for the under-fives displayed a mixture of acceptance and displeasure even among those, such as the high-flat dwellers, whose situation appeared to be most problematic.

These matters will now be pursued in the analysis of mothers' views on child-rearing in their particular environment, the local dangers, as they saw them, for the under-fives, the effects of their living conditions on themselves and on their children, the general run of their comments on the arrangements for play and any innovations or improvements that they had to suggest.

PROBLEMS OF CHILD-REARING (OPEN QUESTION)

Early on in the interview, mothers were asked whether they had encountered any difficulties in bringing up children

in their present home, and if so what the main problems
were. (1) Their unprompted replies are summarised in
Table 22.

TABLE 22 Difficulties in bringing up children

Locality and type of dwelling	None	Difficulties with: building, surroundings	play, health, personality	Others	All respondents	
	%	%	%	%	%	no.
HIGH FLATS						
Cruddas Park*	25	19	62	4	100	52
Cruddas Park**	34	16	53	3	100	32
Gateshead	23	39	48	–	100	44
Wallsend	(9)	(4)	(6)	(1)		20
LOWER FLATS						
Longbenton	(15)	(1)	(2)	(1)		19
Wallsend	35	58	17	–	100	52
MAISONETTES						
Cruddas Park	(10)	(7)	(2)	(2)		17
Wallsend	35	79	9	–	100	23
HOUSES						
Cruddas Park	75	25	3	–	100	36
Longbenton	(12)	–	–	(1)		13
Wallsend	92	6	3	–	100	36

* 6th floor or above
**below 6th floor

The patterns of response varied more clearly by type of
dwelling than by locality. Mothers in the houses mentioned few difficulties. Some in the houses in Cruddas
Park referred to problems associated with the building
(windows especially), and with the need to avoid disturbing the neighbours – topics that were raised specifically
in later questions.

In all multi-storey dwellings, some 25 per cent or more
(considerably more in Longbenton) admitted to no problems
in bringing up their children. Around 50 per cent of
mothers in the high flats mentioned the lack of play opportunities, the strain of having to watch the children
continually, or the adverse effects on the children's personality of their having to be kept indoors. A distinct

minority in the high blocks in Cruddas Park, and more of
the mothers in Gateshead were troubled by the dangers to
which their children were exposed, within the building or
from traffic on the estate and in the streets near by.

Hazards associated with the structure of the building
were a major worry to mothers in the lower flats at Wallsend. In the maisonettes, the main source of grievance derived from the fear of disturbing the neighbours, especially, in Wallsend, the more elderly tenants on the
ground floor.

In order to explore the bearing of family size and structure on the incidence of these problems, respondents in
the high flats at Cruddas Park were divided first of all
into those with all their children under 5 and those who
had older children as well. More of the first group (76
per cent compared with 48 per cent) mentioned problems
classed in Table 22 under the heading 'play, health and
personality', while more of the second maintained that
they had found no difficulties in bringing up their children (38 per cent compared with 21 per cent).

There was, however, a more telling relationship with
the age-grouping of the under-fives, disregarding their
older siblings (Table 23). As was found in the discussion
of local nursery facilities, it appeared that in the high
flats at Cruddas Park mothers with more than one toddler
were most harassed. The same was found in the high flats
in Gateshead and Wallsend. These variations by family
structure were not evident in other forms of multi-storey
dwellings, and the special problems encountered in the
high blocks were thereby underlined.

In Cruddas Park, the tendency discussed in Chapter 5,
for mothers who were comparative newcomers to the high
flats, and whose children were very young, to be dissatisfied with their living arrangements was further illustrated here. Among those with under four years' residence,
24/30 of mothers whose children were all under 5 said that
they had experienced difficulty in bringing them up compared with 8/15 of those who had older children as well.

As had been anticipated, the spontaneous replies of
mothers in Gateshead to this general question on child-
rearing revealed no distinction between those who were
working and the rest. But the distinction was not clear
in the formal analysis for Cruddas Park, though it was
suggested by the earlier scrutiny of the general comments
made by the working mothers there. (2)

TABLE 23 Difficulties in bringing up children - by age-
grouping of those under 5 (Cruddas Park high flats only)

Age-grouping (under-fives only)	None	Difficulties with: building, surroundings	play, health, personality	Others	All respondents	
	%	%	%	%	%	no.
All under 2	40	24	36	4	100	25
One child only and aged 2-5	23	16	62	3	100	39
More than one child under 5	15	5	85	5	100	20
All	29	17	58	4	100	84

THE FACILITIES FOR PLAY (DIRECT QUESTION)

As compared with their response to the open question,
mothers' replies when asked directly for their opinion of
play facilities were relatively consistent in all multi-
storey dwellings. (3) Here the criticism of the provision
for the under-fives was almost unanimous. Some 50 per
cent of replies were terse and of the kind that the form
and position of the question had invited, to some extent.
'Terrible', 'nothing', 'hopeless', were frequent reactions. An almost equal number of mothers however were
more specific. They mentioned sources of dissatisfaction
that have been touched on already, and that will be considered in detail later. There was less dissatisfaction
among respondents in the houses and their complaints were
of a different order. But even in the houses at Wallsend
one mother in two regarded the local facilities as unsatisfactory. Virtually all of those, in all sections of
the survey, who are shown, in Table 24, as being uncriti-
cal of the play arrangements for the under-fives, had previously replied that they had found no difficulty in
bringing up their children in their present home, although
the converse was obviously not true. A minority of
mothers in all areas had evidently found their own means
of coping with an unsatisfactory situation, or had tacitly
accepted it.

TABLE 24   Mothers' opinions of facilities for children's play

Locality and type of dwelling	Unsatisfactory for the under-fives with comment	just 'terrible', etc.	Others	All	
	%	%	%	%	no.
HIGH FLATS					
Cruddas Park*	46	46	8	100	52
Cruddas Park**	41	47	12	100	32
Gateshead	57	41	2	100	44
Wallsend	(9)	(11)	–		20
LOWER FLATS					
Longbenton	(8)	(4)	(7)		19
Wallsend	33	60	8	100	52
MAISONETTES					
Cruddas Park	(8)	(4)	(5)		17
Wallsend	48	52	–	100	23
HOUSES					
Cruddas Park	28	53	19	100	36
Longbenton	(5)	(3)	(5)		13
Wallsend	28	17	56	100	36

* 6th floor or above
**below 6th floor

Some typical complaints were found in each section of the survey. In the high flats at Cruddas Park, mothers referred to the need to be continually with the children. Those in Gateshead, and in the 14-storey blocks in Wallsend, mentioned the shortage of swings, the general inadequacy of the playgrounds or the fact that these were used by older children. Mothers in the lower flats at Longbenton referred to the general lack of facilities on the estate and to the drying yards that broke up the grassed area and detracted from its value as play space. In the maisonettes at Cruddas Park, the danger from features of the estate, and from traffic, were said to be the main deterrents to play, while mothers in the maisonettes in Wallsend, who had small gardens of their own, thought that they were unsuitable for children's play, as they were unfenced and gave no protection from the roads.

Complaints from mothers in the houses referred more generally to the lack of formal play facilities in the wider neighbourhood, especially the need for parks. Some mothers in the houses at Cruddas Park complained that the playgrounds were unsuitable or unsafe. Others here, while satisfied that the under-fives could play in their own gardens, were more concerned about the needs of the older children, and the lack of space where they could play football. Respondents in Wallsend were troubled by the lack of public facilities for recreation in their part of the borough. A typical comment was 'the children only have the street and the garden to play in, the park is too far away.'

PLAY FACILITIES COMPARED WITH THOSE IN PREVIOUS HOME

Mothers were asked later on to compare their present situation, in the matter of children's play, with their experience where they lived before (Table 25). (4)

TABLE 25 Present facilities for play compared with those in previous home

Locality and type of dwelling	bet-ter	Present facilities worse	same	mixed/ unsure	all	Not appli-cable	All respon-dents
	no.	no.	no.	no.	no.	no.	no.
HIGH FLATS							
Cruddas Park*	2	25	6	1	34	18	52
Cruddas Park**	6	15	4	-	25	7	32
Gateshead	7	18	11	-	36	8	44
Wallsend	3	12	4	-	19	1	20
LOWER FLATS							
Longbenton	14	1	4	-	19	-	19
Wallsend	20	18	10	-	48	4	52
MAISONETTES							
Cruddas Park	6	4	5	-	15	2	17
Wallsend	2	12	9	-	23	-	23
HOUSES							
Cruddas Park	25	3	2	-	30	6	36
Longbenton	11	1	1	-	13	-	13
Wallsend	20	4	10	1	35	1	36

* 6th floor or above
**below 6th floor

In all the high flats, two mothers out of three who had
young children in their previous home said that play was
now more difficult. A similar response was given by those
in the maisonettes at Wallsend. In the houses in each
area, and in the Longbenton flats, the majority view was
that the play situation had improved. In the maisonettes
at Cruddas Park, and in the lower flats at Wallsend the
response was more varied, even, so it seemed, among
mothers whose previous situation had been very much the
same.

The particular changes, in regard to play, that were
mentioned by mothers in each of these three groups are
shown in Table 26. Under the heading 'better' are those
aspects of their present home and surroundings that, in
the mothers' opinion, had made it easier now for their
children to play, and under the heading 'worse' are the
aspects that had made it more difficult for them.

Thus, a high proportion of mothers in group A (mostly
from the houses) appreciated that they now had more open
space, more protection from roads, and the benefit of
their own garden. There were a few, however, who missed
having a park within easy reach, whose gardens now were
smaller, or who were more worried about the roads.

In group B (mostly the high flats), the balance was on
the debit side. Many missed the garden, or the back-yard,
felt the lack of open space, or complained that their
children could no longer be left to play on their own. A
larger minority than in group A took the opposite view.
Play was easier now. There was more space, they had the
park, it was safer for the children and, after all, they
could only play in the back-yard and back-lane before. A
considerable number, in the high flats, thought that the
play situation for their children had not changed at all.

The third group, C (mostly from the lower flats in
Wallsend), was particularly interesting. Here, mothers
from very similar backgrounds differed in their evaluation
of their present home. Half of those who mentioned some
change in the youngsters' opportunities for play said that
these had improved. They had more space now, formal or
otherwise. Conditions were safer for the children, and
better than just having the back-yard. An almost equal
number, however, felt that their children had become more
restricted. Some, understandably, missed the garden.
Others, by contrast to those just mentioned, referred,
with some nostalgia, to the back-yard or back-lane.

There was no prompting on these questions, nor pre-
coding of possible replies. The classification was based
on the mothers' own free comments. While the general
problems of families in the high flats were brought out

TABLE 26   Changes affecting children's play (present home compared with previous one)

Aspects of change	Present dwelling type* and assessment of change**					
	A		B		C	
	b	w	b	w	b	w
PROVISION FOR PLAY						
Open space, parks, etc.	31	6	5	10	11	2
Playgrounds, etc.	2	–	4	4	3	–
Own garden	16	2	–	23	–	6
CONDITIONS FOR PLAY						
Freedom to play alone	5	–	1	26	2	–
DANGERS FROM						
Roads and traffic	17	1	7	3	7	1
Buildings and surroundings	1	–	1	3	–	2
'BACK-YARD' OR 'BACK-LANE'						
'Could only play there before'	5	–	3	–	7	–
'Could play there before'	–	–	–	20	–	9
ANY OTHER	2	–	4	–	1	2
All respondents	70	9	20	82	26	22
Conditions the same	18		35		15	
All ·where applicable	97		137		63	

* A all houses, and Longbenton flats
  B all high flats and Wallsend maisonettes
  C maisonettes in Cruddas Park, lower flats in Wallsend
**b present conditions for children better than before
  w present conditions for children worse than before

once again, even here mothers were far from unanimous. The results for the lower flats in Wallsend, especially in the rating of the back-yard, were reminiscent of the range of mothers' comments on local nursery facilities. (5) They point, as before, to mothers' varying perception of their children's needs and to their idiosyncratic assessment of the local provision for them.

For groups B and C in Table 26, the pattern of mothers' evaluation of changes affecting their children's play appeared to be independent both of their previous type of housing and of the area from which they had moved. Among

families in the high flats in Cruddas Park and, less
clearly, in the lower flats in Wallsend, the present
family structure and the number of children under 5,
rather than their former living conditions, seemed to have
coloured mothers' replies to these questions.

In the discussion of mothers' general problems in
bringing up their children in their present home, it was
the mothers of the younger families who appeared to be
most troubled. Likewise here, in Cruddas Park high flats,
14/20 of those with all the children under 5, thought that
their play situation had worsened, compared with 24/39 of
those with older children as well. Only 2 of the former
group compared with 8 of the latter said that it had improved. Similar differences were found in the Wallsend
flats. More particularly, among those in Cruddas Park, 13
mothers out of 16 with more than one child under 5 considered that the conditions for play were worse than
before, compared with 20/31 of those with only one toddler, and 7/12 of those whose children were all under 2.

NOISE

The remaining sections deal with particular aspects of the
children's play situation that are commonly supposed to
present difficulties to families in multi-storey dwellings. These have been mentioned already among mothers'
spontaneous comments. Now they are the subject of direct
questions.

First there is the problem of noise. This is likely to
be a general source of trouble in multi-storey dwellings,
unless a high standard of sound-proofing is incorporated
into their design. (6) But the particular issue here was
whether children were restricted in their play because
their mothers felt obliged to keep them quiet.

Previous research has confirmed that noise is indeed a
problem in multi-storey dwellings, but has suggested, too,
that mothers are less conscious of it than one might
expect. The first study, among young families in high
flats in the London area, noted that only one mother in
five limited her children's play on these grounds, and
that the majority were not especially bothered by noise or
by the fear that neighbours might complain. (7) The
Ministry of Housing survey reached a similar conclusion
for the London estate. However, on the northern estate,
A, where there were more young children, noise was comparatively more of a nuisance in the multi-storey dwellings, especially in the maisonettes, where young families
were housed directly above elderly tenants. (8) In

Melbourne, where children appeared to be more free to play outside on their own than is usual in this country, noise was mentioned more as a disturbance to sleep than as a reason for limiting play. The authors commented that families with young children might be expected to display both a greater tolerance of other people's noise and a greater readiness to adjust their own lives to avoid causing undue offence. (9) The extent of the problem, as families see it, will therefore partly depend on whether the neighbours have children too, and whether there are shift or night workers around who have to sleep during times when children may want to play indoors.

The results for Tyneside are shown in Table 27. (10)

TABLE 27   Restrictions on children's play because of noise and/or disturbance to neighbours

Locality and type of dwelling	Respondents mentioning		All	
	some restriction	no restriction		
	%	%	%	no.
HIGH FLATS				
Cruddas Park	54	46	100	84
Gateshead	66	34	100	44
Wallsend	(8)	(12)		20
LOWER FLATS				
Longbenton	(9)	(10)		19
Wallsend	60	40	100	52
MAISONETTES				
Cruddas Park	(3)	(14)		17
Wallsend	74	26	100	23
HOUSES				
Cruddas Park	22	78	100	36
Longbenton	(2)	(11)		13
Wallsend	8	92	100	36

Families in the Wallsend maisonettes reported most trouble on this score. This was largely due to the fact that those with children were housed on the upper floors, while the ground-level occupants were childless or elderly. As many as three mothers in four complained of this arrangement. That it presented a genuine problem in the maisonettes was evidenced by the fact that 40 per cent of mothers had spontaneously referred to it already, in answer to the open question on their difficulties in bringing up their children. (11) Moreover the strain of keeping on good terms with their more elderly neighbours, because of noise or other disturbance, seemed to be the main reason here for some mothers' persistent dissatisfaction with their home since they moved in. (12) Among families in the maisonettes at Cruddas Park, where this type of housing allocation did not apply, noise was seldom mentioned as a source of worry or disharmony.

In Gateshead, two mothers in three said that their children were restricted because of noise. In half of these instances, members of the family, or neighbours, were on night duty or shift work. This pattern of working hours was particularly common in Gateshead (and in Wallsend too). By the time of the survey, families with young children were only a small minority of those in the high flats, and it is not surprising that there was some reference to complaints from other residents. Those who said that they were not limited by noise, either had only one child under 2 years of age and no others under 5 or they had fairly large families of four children or more, whose freedom to play indoors was limited, in any event, by lack of space.

Mothers in the lower flats at Wallsend referred to complaints from the neighbours downstairs, to the high incidence of night-duty or shift work, or, more typically, to the fact that, because of noise, the children were prevented from playing in the lobby or on the stairs. In the high blocks on the Cruddas Park estate, 50 per cent of respondents told of restrictions on this score. Here the likelihood of children disturbing elderly neighbours was less than in the Wallsend maisonettes, since the structure of the blocks at Cruddas Park enabled the younger families to be housed in the corner flats on each floor, as separate as possible from those without children. Night working was less common here than in Gateshead or Wallsend, though some mothers did refer to it.

In the high flats in Cruddas Park and in the lower flats in Wallsend, noise was more often mentioned by respondents with more than one child under 5.

The large minority in the houses at Cruddas Park to whom noise was a problem were concerned about limitations on their children's freedom to play outside, and the need for open space where they could spend their energies without giving annoyance. In the houses in Wallsend, the mothers who said that they had to keep their children quiet all added that their husbands were on nights.

Table 27 shows evidence, in all sections of the survey, of an attitude of give and take. Some mothers seemed

insensitive to noise themselves. Others said, with no
sense of hardship, that of course one must consider the
neighbours. One mother kept her children quiet during the
day in the hope that the neighbours, in turn, would not
disturb their sleep in the evening.

It seems that, while noise from a variety of sources
can cause inconvenience and annoyance in high-density
housing, it is not just another 'high-flats' problem. The
general impression from the comments here was that some of
its effects might be mitigated by an appropriate distribution of various types of household within the dwelling, if
this were feasible, and by an enlargement of opportunities
for children's play outside the confines of their home.

DANGERS TO CHILDREN

Mothers were asked whether they thought that their children ran any risk of accident out of doors, inside their
living quarters and, in the case of multi-storey dwellings, anywhere else inside the building. (13)

Table 28 suggests a high degree of anxiety, among all
respondents, about the possibility of accidents to their
children while they played outside. Only in the houses at
Wallsend was there a substantial group who did not feel
that their children ran any special risk of this kind.
But, even here, nearly 60 per cent of mothers mentioned
the dangers from traffic. Elsewhere, the minorities who
said that there was nothing really to worry about, would
appear to be largely accounted for by the numbers of
mothers whose children were not yet 2 years old. (14)

However, cross-analysis for the high flats at Cruddas
Park, where the numbers were large enough to permit it,
showed that this was not necessarily so. Mothers tended
to reply positively to this question, regardless of the
ages of their children. The proportion mentioning some
risk was 60 per cent for those with only children under 2,
compared with 70 per cent for those with just one child
who had passed the toddling stage, and 90 per cent for
mothers with more than one child under 5.

The fact that most of the survey families were well
used to town life, should not lead one to belittle
mothers' concern about the roads, especially as many had
complained already that their children no longer enjoyed,
while at play, the comparative safety of their own bit of
garden, the back-yard or back-lane.

However, the other dangers that mothers perceived
within the places set aside for play, or on the estates
generally, were more directly relevant to this study.

TABLE 28 Risk of accident outside

Locality and type of dwelling	No risk %	Some risk %	Source of risk* 1 %	2 %	3 %	4 %	5 %	6 %	7 %	All respondents %	no.
HIGH FLATS											
Cruddas Park	26	74	55	20	12	–	1	–	1	100	84
Gateshead	7	93	80	14	25	–	2	–	–	100	44
Wallsend	(5)	(15)	(13)	–	–	–	–	(3)	–		20
LOWER FLATS											
Longbenton	(6)	(13)	(12)	–	–	–	–	–	(1)		19
Wallsend	21	79	62	–	2	–	8	6	4	100	52
MAISONETTES											
Cruddas Park	(3)	(14)	(12)	(4)	(2)	–	–	–	–		17
Wallsend	26	74	74	4	9	–	–	–	–	100	23
HOUSES											
Cruddas Park	22	78	56	6	8	17	3	–	–	100	36
Longbenton	(2)	(11)	(10)	–	(1)	(1)	–	–	–		13
Wallsend	42	58	58	–	–	–	3	–	–	100	36

*1 roads, traffic
2 walls, railings, concrete blocks in the playgrounds
3 garage roofs, car-parks
4 concrete steps
5 glass and rubbish
6 swings
7 others, outside

Table 28 shows that approximately one mother in three in the high flats and maisonettes at Cruddas Park, and one in seven in the houses, mentioned risks of this kind. Some complained about the spacing between the railing around the playgrounds, which, they said, was wide enough for a small child to get his head jammed. Some were unhappy about the extensive use of concrete on the estate, especially in the design of play equipment, such as blocks and turrets. Others spoke of the temptation to children to climb over walls or on to the garage roofs in their own quest for adventure. Children tended to play also in the car-parking areas and these were mentioned, in Cruddas Park and elsewhere, as a further source of danger. (15)

The survey of children's play on housing estates, described in Chapter 2, found that where playgrounds were provided, parents, on the whole, expected and wanted their children to use them, but that some were worried about the risk of accident, especially from equipment designed to encourage adventure. A study of accidents sustained by children concluded, however, that they were as likely to hurt themselves when playing around the estate as when using playground equipment. (16)

Observation on the Cruddas Park estate, and mothers' accounts of accidents to their own children, would support this. The older children, not unnaturally, seemed to relish clambering over walls, playing on the garage roofs and even jumping from them into the courts below. The dangers from this kind of activity were mentioned more often by mothers who had some older children (45 per cent compared with 19 per cent of those with under-fives only). Though some mothers could have been thinking primarily of the risks to the older children, some were also genuinely afraid that the younger ones would be tempted to copy their older brothers and sisters.

It was also found that the dangers from equipment, or other features of the play areas, were mentioned more often by parents whose under-fives actually played there several times a week than by those whose children went there less often (13/54 compared with 4/30). Similarly, in Gateshead, it was the group of mothers who said that their children actually played outside who referred most often to the possibility of accident elsewhere than on the roads. Parental anxiety was evidently not strong enough to restrain the children altogether.

Nevertheless, some respondents did express considerable alarm, adding that there was little that they could do. As reported in the first London survey, it seemed that effective supervision, while the children ran off their surplus energy, would be the only answer to their parents'

fears. According to mothers' comments in the Tyneside
survey, as in the previous ones, the guarantee of supervision would seem to carry a higher priority, in their
view, than the provision of play equipment. (17)

It must be remembered, however, that the pursuit of adventure takes up only a small part of playtime for this
age-group. Hole and Miller observed that 'although the
conventional picture of play is one of constant movement,
... a large proportion of play was physically inactive;
children were standing, sitting, walking or simply watching others.' (18) Provision for this type of play seemed
to be lacking on all the estates that they visited - high
and low density alike.

The suntraps at Cruddas Park were well used for this
purpose. There were seats where mothers could sit, and
ample space, though again concrete-based, where the children could play. Elsewhere there was no special provision
of this kind. In general, the need for sheltered, semi-
enclosed and preferably grassed areas, where young children could amuse themselves in this more passive way, as
near to home as possible, should be given at least as much
weight, in the design of play-facilities, as the youngsters' need for adventure. (19)

As the risk of accident from roads and traffic was said to
be a source of worry to many mothers, so too was the possibility of their children having a mishap indoors. Table
29 shows that some 50 per cent of respondents in all the
high flats, in the lower flats at Longbenton and in the
houses at Cruddas Park, mentioned some risk to their children while they played inside the home.

Some of the problems in all types of dwelling at
Cruddas Park derived from mothers' nervousness of the
electrical installation, especially the heating system.
Some 30 per cent in the flats and houses said that the
electric fires and wall-sockets were dangerous for children. In the flats, these comments were made more often
by mothers who had lived there for less than four years
and whose children were all under 5. A smaller number,
again both in the flats and in the houses, were worried
about the size of the kitchen and the difficulty of keeping children away from the cooker. As one would expect,
this was more of a problem in the larger families, the
great majority of whom used the kitchen, rather than the
living-room, for all their meals.

Some respondents in the houses at Cruddas Park mentioned dangers to their children from the small flights of
stairs that were part of the split-level design, or from
the bedroom windows that opened on to the sloping roof of
the single-storey section.

TABLE 29 Risk of accident inside the home

Locality and type of dwelling	No risk %	Some risk %	Source of risk 1 %	2 %	3 %	4 %	5 %	All respondents %	no.
HIGH FLATS									
Cruddas Park*	42	58	27	21	2	25	10	100	52
Cruddas Park**	50	50	19	–	–	31	9	100	32
Gateshead	41	59	52	–	–	11	2	100	44
Wallsend	(14)	(6)	(3)	(1)	–	(2)	–	100	20
LOWER FLATS									
Longbenton	(9)	(10)	(1)	(5)	(2)	(1)	(2)		19
Wallsend	65	35	29	–	4	4	–	100	52
MAISONETTES									
Cruddas Park	(14)	(3)	(1)	(1)	–	(2)	–		17
Wallsend	83	17	17	–	–	–	–	100	23
HOUSES									
Cruddas Park	53	47	8	–	14	33	6	100	36
Longbenton	(9)	(4)	–	–	(2)	(2)	–		13
Wallsend	92	8	3	–	–	3	3	100	36

* 6th floor or above
**below 6th floor
1 windows
2 balcony (but included also in Table 30)
3 stairs
4 electric fires and sockets
5 kitchen

Apart from these local features, the hazards that were mentioned in all multi-storey dwellings throughout the survey area were balconies and windows.

Parents' fears about the former have been discussed already in Chapter 5. (20) The weight of comment about windows was partly induced by an unprecedented series of accidents to Tyneside children that occurred in the few weeks covered by the survey.

Towards the end of June 1967, a 4-year-old child was killed in a fall from the window of a thirteenth-floor flat in Cruddas Park. (21) Up to that time, no respondents in the high flats on the estate had mentioned windows among the dangers to their children. Interviewing was suspended for a while, and resumed with some misgivings. One interviewer found that, afterwards, every mother seemed to have been affected by the incident and spoke of the windows at some length. Another told a different story. He was surprised to find that, even in the block where the accident happened, relatively few spontaneously referred to it. Some had only learnt about it from the newspapers. Others said 'It's strange, we didn't know the family at all' - a telling comment on the lack of communication even within the block.

Among all mothers who were interviewed in the high flats at Cruddas Park after the accident, 38 per cent of those on the sixth floor or above, and 25 per cent of the rest, mentioned the windows as being dangerous for their children (and, in almost every case, along with, rather than in place of, one or other of the hazards discussed already in this section).

In some of the flats, safety catches, which made it impossible to open the windows beyond a certain point, were still intact. In others, however, the catches had been taken off by previous tenants and not replaced, or they had been removed by the current occupants so that they could clean the windows. In both these circumstances, some mothers, while acknowledging that the situation could be dangerous for young children, were confident that they were able to take the necessary precautions themselves.

Following the 1967 accidents, the Housing Department took positive action. A letter was sent to tenants of upstairs flats throughout the city offering to fit safety catches free of charge. After a rush of applications in the first few days, the demand for catches tailed off sharply.

By August 1968, after the death of a 2-year-old child in a 22-foot fall from a window in an older block of flats, to the west of Cruddas Park, it was reported that the eventual response to the Corporation's offer had been as low as 2 or 3 per cent. (22)   The Chairman of the Housing Management Committee appealed again to tenants to have these safety devices fitted without more delay.

Perhaps the most telling observation, in the context of the present study, came from a parent living on the top floor of a block in Cruddas Park, who said, 'The windows are dangerous and you always have to remember to keep an eye on the children. Since there is nowhere really for them to play, the window is an attraction up here. They like to look out to see the ships in the river and the trains.'

It was not surprising to find that, in Gateshead, where families were larger, on average, than in Cruddas Park and where the opportunities for play outside were more limited and precarious, 50 per cent of mothers complained about the windows. The need for ventilation seemed to be a complicating factor. One mother said that she tried to cope with it by keeping the children together in one room while she left all the windows open in another.

Some references to windows by mothers in all the multi-storey dwellings in Wallsend were prompted by another fatal accident only two weeks after the child was killed in Cruddas Park. This time, a 22-month-old baby fell 60 feet to the ground from a window in the high flats within the Wallsend survey area. (23) In these flats, the balcony or veranda runs almost the full length of the building on each floor, but leaves the windows at each end of the block with a sheer drop to the ground. It was from one of these end windows that the child was killed.

Coming so soon after the Newcastle fatality, and being the fourth serious accident on Tyneside that summer, this latest tragedy changed the general tone of the response to the survey – at least in Wallsend. From then on, mothers tended to comment more freely on the dangers of housing young children in this way than on their needs for recreation. Almost every respondent who was interviewed after this event mentioned the windows, and this applied to all the multi-storey dwellings covered in Wallsend, not just to the high flats.

From the distressing events of the summer of 1967, one can only conclude that the matter of children's safety inside their multi-storey homes is a problem of a different order from that of play, and must be dealt with as such. The experience in Newcastle during the following year showed how difficult it is, even in the face of tragedy, to introduce safeguards once the buildings are occupied.

A recent press report drew attention to the fact that (24)

children ... in high-rise blocks of flats face a
hitherto unrecognised danger - falling out of windows
... these accidents happen mainly when windows are
fitted without safety catches. Toddlers in particular
are at risk from windows that swivel right round for
cleaning either side.

The report followed several such accidents to children in
Edinburgh and Glasgow and one, in Dudley, where the window
was only open five-and-a-half inches!

National statistics suggest that such accidents have
become more frequent. Figures supplied by the General Register Office to the Tyneside investigators gave the
number of children under 14 killed in falls from balconies
and windows as 12 in 1965 and 19 in 1966. On Tyneside
alone there were 4 serious accidents of this kind (2 of
them fatal) to children under 5 in June and July 1967 and
3 (of which 2 were fatal) between July and October 1968.
The press report just mentioned put the total number of
such deaths in 1971 as 20 children under the age of 10.

According to the report, some local authorities, like
Birmingham and the Greater London Council, had safety
catches as compulsory fittings from the start. Others had
spent considerable sums, as Newcastle had offered to do,
on adding them to existing buildings. The report adds
that, while the Building Research Establishment was studying this particular aspect of danger, there was nothing in
current building regulations to make safety catches
compulsory.

Though the risks that have been discussed in this section are accentuated by the fact that young children in
multi-storey dwellings do have to spend a good deal of
time indoors, even the most effective provision for their
recreation outside the home will not protect them altogether from dangers of this kind.

The remaining question applied only to families in multi-
storey dwellings. Mothers were asked whether their children were liable to have an accident anywhere in the
building outside their own home (Table 30). Many respondents considered that the means of access to their flats
or maisonettes were potentially dangerous. Lifts and
stairs in the high blocks and stairs in the lower flats
and maisonettes were often mentioned.

In Cruddas Park the lifts were more of a worry to
mothers on the upper floors, while the stairs were mentioned correspondingly more often by those living closer
to ground level. A minority in all the high flats referred to the doors, especially the swing doors in the
entrance halls. Fire-escapes were mentioned by a small

TABLE 30 Risk of accident elsewhere indoors (multi-storey dwellings only)

Locality and type of dwelling	No risk %	Some risk %	Source of risk***					All respondents	
			1 %	2 %	3 %	4 %	5 %	%	no.
HIGH FLATS									
Cruddas Park*	39	61	42	–	15	8	–	100	52
Cruddas Park**	44	56	50	3	6	3	–	100	32
Gateshead	16	84	27	41	27	5	–	100	44
Wallsend	(3)	(17)	(12)	–	(11)	(1)	–		20
LOWER FLATS									
Longbenton	(15)	(4)	(4)	–	–	–	–		19
Wallsend	31	69	60	4	2	–	6	100	52
MAISONETTES									
Cruddas Park	(5)	(12)	(6)	–	–	–	(4)		17
Wallsend	43	57	57	–	–	–	–	100	23

* 6th floor or above
** below 6th floor
1 stairs, railings on stairs
2 landing or corridor, especially windows
3 lifts
4 doors
5 fire-escape
*** the balcony (or veranda) was also mentioned, among the sources of risk elsewhere indoors by 10 respondents in Wallsend high flats and 6 respondents in Cruddas Park maisonettes

group of parents in the lower flats in Wallsend and in the maisonettes in Cruddas Park.

Over 40 per cent of mothers in the high flats in Gateshead were worried about the windows in the landings or corridors. According to the Housing Manager, these windows had already been fastened up when the survey began.

The need for such precautions in all multi-storey buildings was illustrated a year later, when a Newcastle child fell 20 feet on to a concrete floor from an open landing window in a 4-storey block, close to Cruddas Park. (25) The child had been playing on the landing with his friends. He had climbed up to the window, which was unprotected. The press report alleged that other children in the same flats had had similar, though less serious, accidents.

Many of those respondents in the Tyneside survey who complained about the stairs said that it was too easy for children to climb the banister rails. In the following July this practice led to the death of a Gateshead child, who fell 30 feet over the banister of a communal staircase in a block of maisonettes. (26)

It has been shown in Chapter 6 that, in spite of the housing authorities' attempts to shield children from these dangers, some mothers openly stated that their youngsters were in the habit of playing on the landing or stairs. (27) Paradoxically, it was this group of mothers who spoke most often of the risk of accident. In the high flats at Cruddas Park, this applied to 14 out of 18 mothers whose children were said to play inside the building, compared with 29 out of 56 who said that they were not allowed to do so. The corresponding results for the lower flats in Wallsend were 13/18 and 17/31. In Gateshead, the overall mention of potential risks was the same, whether or not the children played indoors. But more of the mothers whose children played on the landings said that the practice was dangerous (11/17 compared with 5/24 of the rest).

Some respondents, in all areas of the survey, told of mishaps, to their own or neighbours' children, from one or other of the communal features of the buildings that have been discussed in this section. In this complex matter, the evidence would confirm that the possible dangers to children, in all multi-storey dwellings, are real enough. While adequate play facilities elsewhere would obviously help, the risks will not be effectively reduced unless official precautions and restrictions are coupled with a greater degree of parental vigilance and responsibility.

EFFECTS OF DANGERS ON PLAY, AND MOTHERS' SUGGESTIONS

Mothers were asked whether the various dangers that they
had mentioned had in fact limited their children's play
and, if so, whether they themselves had any ideas for improving the situation. Table 31 shows that, in most
multi-storey dwellings, more than 50 per cent of respondents said that their children were restricted on these
grounds. In the high flats, this applied to at least two
mothers in three, while in the other flats (especially
Longbenton), and in the maisonettes, the response was
rather lower. The smaller group of mothers in the houses
at Cruddas Park, who referred to dangers elsewhere than on
the roads, were concerned about features in the design of
their homes that have been discussed already.
     When Table 31 is compared with Table 27, (28) it ap-
pears that, on the whole, the children in high flats were
rather more restricted by danger than by noise, while, for
those in other multi-storey dwellings, the emphasis was
reversed.
     In all areas, except Gateshead, relatively few mothers
made definite suggestions. Some 10 per cent had no ideas
to offer, or replied bluntly that nothing could be done.
A rather higher proportion (in Cruddas Park high blocks
and in the Wallsend maisonettes), retorted, 'Change the
policy - don't put young families here.' Another 10 per
cent, or less, considered that definite safety precautions
should be taken, or the existing ones made more effective.
The comments covered railings on the garage roofs, catches
on the windows, speed limits on estate roads, and other
measures that have been mentioned already in the previous
section.
     Most interesting, for the purpose of the survey, are
mothers' own ideas for some specific arrangements whereby
the under-fives might play in safety (see columns headed 4
and 5 in Table 31).
     Although these proposals came from a small minority
(except in Gateshead), they are worth examining more
closely. One mother in ten in the high flats in Cruddas
Park advocated a playground outside, especially for the
younger children. The greatest demand was simply for a
small area of the grass (which they said was good), to be
fenced off, and for some supervision to be ensured, either
by 'the corporation' or by a rota of volunteers drawn from
the parents themselves. Rather more (about 20 per cent of
those on the upper floors and 10 per cent of the rest),
suggested a playroom inside their block, possibly on the
ground floor. Others thought that the roof might be used
for play space. Again the need for some form of supervision was recognised.

TABLE 31 Children's risk of accident outside, indoors or elsewhere, restrictions on their play and mothers' suggestions for improving the situation

Locality and type of dwelling	Risk of accident			Restrictions on play*		suggestions**					All respondents	
	no risk	just 'roads'	any others	none	some	1	2	3	4	5	%	no.
	%	%	%	%	%	%	%	%	%	%	%	no.
HIGH FLATS												
Cruddas Park	6	7	87	21	66	12	26	6	10	13	100	84
Gateshead	–	2	98	25	73	11	5	16	41	2	100	44
Wallsend	(1)	–	(19)	(6)	(13)	(2)	(7)	–	(2)	(2)		20
LOWER FLATS												
Longbenton	(2)	(6)	(11)	(7)	(4)	(4)	–	–	–	–		19
Wallsend	6	8	87	35	52	12	13	10	15	2	100	52
MAISONETTES												
Cruddas Park	–	(2)	(15)	(7)	(8)	(2)	(1)	(2)	(3)	–		17
Wallsend	9	17	74	13	61	17	26	9	9	–	100	23
HOUSES												
Cruddas Park	11	19	69	33	36	11	–	25	–	–	100	36
Longbenton	(1)	(6)	(6)	(3)	(3)	–	–	(3)	–	–		13
Wallsend	42	53	6	3	3	–	–	3	–	–	100	36

* for those mentioning any risks of accident other than 'roads'
**as *, but for those also mentioning some restriction on children's play
1 no suggestions
2 'change the policy', 'keep children out of (flats)', etc.
3 improved safety precautions
4 playground or play area outside
5 playroom or other play space indoors

Some 40 per cent of parents in Gateshead asked for a
'suitable' playground or play area. Apart from one request for sandpits and slides and another for seats,
mothers did not specify what they would regard as suitable
for the younger ones. Only two mentioned supervision. In
the lower flats and maisonettes in Wallsend, as in the
high blocks at Cruddas Park, one mother in ten suggested a
play area, or just an enclosed stretch of grass, to be reserved for the under-fives.

While the ideas put forward by mothers were modest and
not particularly novel, they might be taken to indicate a
central core of demand which should not be ignored, especially if they were found to represent the needs of a particular group of families.

In order to pursue this last point, the results, as
summarised in Table 31, were first divided between mothers
who had a job (full- or part-time) and the rest. No differences were found however between the two groups.
Neither, except for one area, was there any marked variation in the response according to the specific ages of the
under-fives or the presence or absence of other siblings.
The high flats in Cruddas Park provided the exception.
Here, the proportion of mothers who said that their children's play was limited for reasons of safety was 50 per
cent for those with children under 2 only, 70 per cent for
those with one child between 2 and 5 (and no others under
5) and 95 per cent for those with more than one child of
pre-school age. Suggestions for a playroom or playground
came most often from those with just one child beyond the
toddling stage. The majority of mothers with more than
one child under 5 replied that things were unlikely to improve for them until the family was able to move to a
house with a garden.

Among families in the upper floors at Cruddas Park, the
requests for play space came rather more from mothers
whose children already made some use of the existing playground (10/32 compared with 4/20 of the rest). Elsewhere
the figures were too small for analysis.

Here, too, mothers' replies to this question bore some
relation to their earlier comments on nursery facilities,
and the innovations that they would welcome. One mother
in three of those who had previously advocated more nursery schools or supervised play space, made specific suggestions for play facilities in the present context. This
compared with one mother in ten of all other respondents
to the nursery facilities question. Thus just under 20
per cent of mothers in the high flats at Cruddas Park,
replying to these two distinct questions, consistently advocated an enlargement or extension of the present

arrangements for their under-fives.

One conclusion from the analysis, with regard to
'social action', is that the initiative in improving or
extending arrangements for the children's play must come
from outside. The parents will not readily take it themselves. But is there likely to be any support for such
measures, and from whom, and what strategy, if any, might
the initiator usefully employ? In examining the survey
data, here and under previous headings, for a reply to
these questions, it must be remembered that the weight and
tenor of mothers' comments on a situation that the majority regarded as static and unalterable are only partial
indicators, if they give any clue at all, as to the support that they were likely to give to a definite attempt
to improve matters for them. Given this understanding,
and in the light of the experience of the Young Volunteer
Force on the Delaval estate (described in the notes to
Chapter 4), and of some recent student ventures in this
field, the prospects are not wholly discouraging. (29)

Some mothers, as has just been indicated for those in
the high flats at Cruddas Park, made thoughtful, consistent and constructive suggestions. The whole analysis so
far has shown that, among these respondents, a higher proportion had more than one child of pre-school age, or just
one youngster between 2 and 5 with no older siblings for
companionship. The preliminary canvassing that would seem
to be essential to the success of any innovation for children's play might usefully be directed towards families in
one or both of these categories. The extent of their
willingness to be involved might turn out to be greater
than has been indicated here.

EFFECTS OF LIVING IN PRESENT HOME

Towards the end of the interview, mothers were asked
whether living in their present home had had any effect on
them and on their children. They were also invited to
comment on the health of their under-fives and on any
change that they had noticed since moving. (30)

Subjective assessments of health or morbidity are no-
toriously difficult to evaluate. The questions included
here were deliberately kept brief, and the answers must be
considered solely in the light of what has gone before. A
more precise form of questioning, together with comparative data for a wider 'population', would be needed if the
results were to stand on their own.

The incidence of neurosis among high-flat dwellers is
now a well aired if poorly documented theme. Several

interviewers remarked that their respondents seemed to know about the 'high-flats syndrome' - or words to that effect. Previous researchers have noted, too, that there are undeniable tensions associated with the experience of being uprooted from a close network of relatives and friends, however the families are rehoused. Moreover, the rearing of young children in a busy urban environment is seldom devoid of strain. These points must be borne in mind in assessing the results given here.

Tables 32 and 33 do show, within their limits, that problems of this kind are not confined to young families in high flats. The emphasis was broadly consistent for respondents in all multi-storey dwellings, and still more so for those in flats, whatever their elevation. Here,

TABLE 32   Effect on mothers of living in present home

Locality and type of dwelling	No reply or no effect	Better now	Worse now***					All respondents	
			1	2	3	4	all		
	%	%	%	%	%	%	%	%	no.
HIGH FLATS									
Cruddas Park*	27	8	44	4	13	4	65	100	52
Cruddas Park**	44	9	31	3	12	-	47	100	32
Gateshead	48	5	32	9	7	5	47	100	44
Wallsend	(6)	(2)	(8)	(3)	(1)	-	(12)		20
LOWER FLATS									
Longbenton	(9)	(3)	(2)	(1)	(4)	-	(7)		19
Wallsend	29	13	37	10	6	6	58	100	52
MAISONETTES									
Cruddas Park	(11)	(4)	(1)	(1)	-	-	(2)		17
Wallsend	39	26	26	9	-	-	35	100	23
HOUSES									
Cruddas Park	25	58	11	-	3	3	17	100	36
Longbenton	(6)	(7)	-	-	-	-	-		13
Wallsend	50	42	3	3	-	3	9	100	36

*   6th floor or above
** below 6th floor
***worse now:
    1   more nervy, irritable, etc.
    2   more colds
    3   lonely, can't get out
    4   in other ways, or just 'worse'

TABLE 33   Effect on the under-fives of living in present home

Locality and type of dwelling	Not applicable 'born here' %	No reply or no effect %	Better now %	Worse now***					All respondents	
				1 %	2 %	3 %	4 %	all %	%	no.
HIGH FLATS										
Cruddas Park*	10	38	2	4	10	33	4	50	100	52
Cruddas Park**	7	66	–	16	–	12	–	27	100	32
Gateshead	7	52	2	14	7	7	12	39	100	44
Wallsend	–	(10)	(1)	(3)	–	(6)	–	(9)		20
LOWER FLATS										
Longbenton	(1)	(14)	(3)	–	–	–	(1)	(1)		19
Wallsend	6	56	15	10	2	8	4	23	100	52
MAISONETTES										
Cruddas Park	(1)	(11)	(3)	(1)	–	(1)	–	(2)		17
Wallsend	–	83	9	–	4	–	4	9	100	23
HOUSES										
Cruddas Park	11	47	42	–	–	–	–	–	100	36
Longbenton	(3)	(3)	(7)	–	–	–	–	–		13
Wallsend	8	64	28	–	–	–	–	–	100	36

* 6th floor or above

** below 6th floor

***worse now:

1 more nervy, irritable etc.
2 more colds
3 lonely, can't get out
4 in other ways or just 'worse'

between 50 per cent and two-thirds of mothers felt ad-
versely affected, around one in ten said that they had improved, usually in health, while the remainder were unable
or disinclined to specify any noticeable change. Respondents in the maisonettes, especially in Wallsend, were
more evenly divided on this issue. Among those in the
houses, the majority opinion was that the effect of the
change had if anything been beneficial.

The minority, in all multi-storey dwellings, who said
that they, or their children, had been better since
moving, mentioned some improvement in their accommodation
or, especially in parts of Wallsend, the benefit of a less
polluted atmosphere. The detrimental effects are subdivided in the tables. For the mothers, the results repeated the findings of previous studies in suggesting a
high incidence of 'nerves', irritability, depression and
loneliness. (31) For the children, isolation and lack of
companionship were most often mentioned in the high
blocks. (32) In all types of multi-storey dwellings some
of the mothers and children were said to be more prone to
colds or bronchial troubles, which most respondents put
down to their having to spend too much time in a centrally
heated atmosphere.

In all this, there were no consistent differences by
length of residence, either as a single variable or along
with family structure. Nevertheless, some mothers volunteered that while flat life had been difficult at first,
they had become used to it.

Some respondents in the lower flats in Wallsend were
particularly irritated by the poor standard of upkeep of
the communal staircases and entrance halls. As shown already, general dissatisfaction with the living conditions
was voiced more often here than in any other section of
the survey. (33) In the Wallsend maisonettes, noise was a
recurrent problem. (34) Clearly there were a number of
factors operating here, of which the children's play was
only one.

But, as has been found in many other contexts, mothers'
assessment of the effects, on themselves, of their present
housing situation was most consistently related to the age
and number of the younger children. Pooling the results
for all multi-storey dwellings (and disregarding children
of school-age), the proportion of respondents who felt
that the effect was deleterious was 43 per cent for those
with children under 2 only, 56 per cent for those with
just one child between 2 and 5, and 64 per cent for those
with more than one youngster of pre-school age. This
overall pattern was found, in all the relevant sections of
the survey, where the numbers were large enough for
analysis.

The presence or absence of older children seemed to make no difference to the results here. In fact, from the individual remarks, it seemed that many of the children who were at school had settled down well and that they actually enjoyed living in the flat or maisonette.

The great majority - over 80 per cent - of mothers in all sections of the survey said that the health of their under-fives was good or 'all right'. No one in the houses, and very few elsewhere, went so far as to claim that their children had definitely become unfit since moving.

In answering these questions, some mothers were clearly giving vent to frustrations and tensions stemming from the isolation and lack of privacy, either of which may be associated with life in a flat or maisonette. Others, no doubt, were reacting to the experience of being uprooted from the proximity of family and friends. Even in the houses in Cruddas Park, and to a lesser extent in Wallsend, there were complaints of tension and loneliness. (35) Several mothers added that, since moving, they had been receiving medical or psychiatric treatment. But it was obviously beyond the scope of the survey to assess the extent or the degree of ill-health among the respondents or their children.

Some medical evidence on the comparatively high morbidity rates among flat-dwellers has been presented by D.M. Fanning. (36) This was derived from general practitioners' records for two groups of families of members of the armed services stationed in Germany. One group was living in 3- or 4-storey flats and the other in houses - both from choice. The greatest differences between the two groups were found in the incidence of respiratory infections among young women and children, and of psychoneurotic disorders among women. The highest sickness rates of all were found among the children under 5, living in flats, and this result was largely attributed, by Fanning, to their lack of freedom to play out of doors. Fanning considered that some mothers in the flats, especially those who were in their 20s or over 40, were feeling the effects of a double social disturbance in the severance of ties with their family of origin and in their attempt to adjust to the restricting environment of flat life.

The Tyneside findings, for the mothers, were, in a very general way, in line with his conclusions, though here, the number and age-grouping in each family of the children not yet at school seemed to be more discriminating than the age of the mother herself. Few specific references

were made to poor or deteriorating health among the Tyneside children. Medical evidence would be needed to test
Fanning's conclusions, especially for this age-group.

The great majority of respondents in the Tyneside
survey, as one would expect, were accustomed to taking
their under-fives to the local doctor. (37) Fanning suggested that doctors working in general practice, or in
public health, might usefully help to evaluate the incidence of morbidity, of one kind and another, among families in different types of housing. This idea would seem
to be feasible and worth pursuing, both for the pre-school
children and their mothers, even within specific areas
such as those that have been studied here.

PREFERENCE FOR SOMEWHERE ELSE TO LIVE (38)

Respondents in all multi-storey dwellings were nearly unanimous in their preference for a house - given the (then)
unlikely situation of their being free to make the choice
(Table 34). Only 8 mothers out of the 259 interviewed
here had no wish to change. A further two in the upper
floors at Cruddas Park and one in the high blocks at
Wallsend said that they would be content with a flat, but
one nearer to ground-level.

In the houses, 52/85 mothers were happy with their
accommodation. The rest, most of whom were from Cruddas
Park, expressed a desire for a larger, detached house.
More of those with larger families replied in this way (9/
13 with 6 members or more, compared with 10/23 of the
rest). (39)

The reasons given for preferring a house (or occasionally a bungalow) are summarised in Table 34. They show a
difference in emphasis between the results for the high
flats and those for the lower flats and maisonettes taken
together (Table 34a).

In the high flats the main reasons given were the
desire for a garden, or just somewhere that would be
better for the children. By contrast, in the lower flats
and maisonettes, the need for more space and the desire
for greater privacy were mentioned almost as often. The
general dislike of communal living expressed by mothers in
the lower flats and maisonettes, especially in Wallsend,
has been referred to already in several contexts. It
seems to have accounted for much of the tension and irritability discussed in the previous section. (40)

The earlier studies also discussed a compelling, though
not unanimous, preference for living in a house. In a
follow-up to Joan Maizels's London survey, Peter Townsend

TABLE 34   Preference for other accommodation

Locality and type of dwelling	No change	Preference if free to choose house or bungalow***								Flat near ground	No reply	All	
	%	1 %	2 %	3 %	4 %	5 %	6 %	7 %	all %	%	%	%	no.
HIGH FLATS													
Cruddas Park*	–	56	31	2	–	13	–	4	96	4	–	100	52
Cruddas Park**	3	62	22	6	3	12	–	–	97	–	–	100	32
Gateshead	7	61	18	–	7	14	9	5	93	–	–	100	44
Wallsend	–	(16)	(2)	–	(1)	–	–	–	(19)	(1)	–	100	20
LOWER FLATS													
Longbenton	–	(7)	–	(4)	(8)	(3)	–	(4)	(19)	–	–		19
Wallsend	2	46	12	15	27	2	–	2	98	–	–	100	52
MAISONETTES													
Cruddas Park	(2)	(8)	(2)	(1)	(4)	(1)	–	(2)	(15)	–	–		17
Wallsend	4	22	26	–	35	4	–	9	96	–	–	100	23
HOUSES													
Cruddas Park	36	–	–	53	–	–	–	–	53	–	11	100	36
Longbenton	(12)	–	–	–	–	–	–	–	–	–	(1)		13
Wallsend	75	–	–	3	8	–	–	3	14	–	11	100	36

TABLE 34a. Preference for house or bungalow (respondents in multi-storey dwellings only)

Type of dwelling	Reasons for preference***								Other respondents	All	
	1	2	3	4	5	6	7	all			
	%	%	%	%	%	%	%	%	%	%	no.
High flats	62	22	2	3	11	3	3	95	5	100	148
Lower flats and maisonettes	40	13	12	31	5	–	8	96	4	100	111

* 6th floor or above
** below 6th floor
***reasons for preference:
1 to have a garden
2 better for children
3 more space
4 more privacy
5 more independence, 'own front door'
6 easier to clean
7 other or none given

found that this applied to 70 per cent of his sample, while most of the rest preferred their flat, mainly because of the high standard of amenities (disregarding the facilities for play) that they had come to appreciate. (41)   The Ministry of Housing investigation reported a very similar result in all block dwellings, regardless of their elevation. (42)

The volume of the response on Tyneside may have been induced by the phrasing of the question, with its emphasis on respondents' freedom to move elsewhere.   Moreover, the question came at the end of the interview, after mothers had aired their views on many problematic aspects of their home and environment, and it was not surprising that almost all of them opted for a change.   They were not asked whether they had applied for a transfer to a local authority house, or whether they had ambitions, or prospects, of becoming owner-occupiers, so one cannot assess the degree of fantasy in the replies here.

The Melbourne study found that all but one in the lower, walk-up flats (including most of the younger families in the sample), said that they would prefer to move to a house. (43)   All but three would have liked to be owner-occupiers, but, for the majority, there was little prospect of their ever doing so.   Still, about half the sample were satisfied with the flats.   They had only vague reasons for their desire to own a house.   On the other hand, those who were less satisfied or overtly critical of the flats explained their preference for a house in much the same terms as did the respondents on Tyneside - the strains of communal living and the effects on their children.

For the present survey, the reasons for preferring a house may similarly be set against the earlier questions on mothers' attitudes to their home.   As shown in Chapter 5, current opinions were most divided in all the multi-storey dwellings, apart from those in Longbenton, where satisfaction was more general. (44)   In Cruddas Park and Gateshead, mothers' attitudes to their home, at the time of the survey, did not appear to be related in any systematic way to their reactions when they first moved in. In Wallsend, however, there were signs of persistent and growing dissatisfaction.   Nevertheless, the majority in all areas recognised that their living conditions were a great improvement on the decaying, overcrowded housing from which most of them had moved.

As seen above, virtually all the mothers in multi-storey dwellings, whether or not they were satisfied with their home, gave a house as their ideal choice.   The reasons given by these two groups were however somewhat different.

In all the high flats, more of those who had reservations about their home, or who were definitely unhappy
with it, said that they would prefer a house in order to
be more private or independent or to have their own front
door; (one in six of them answered in this way, compared
with one in twelve of .those currently satisfied). In the
lower flats and maisonettes at Wallsend, mothers who were
most dissatisfied with living there tended more often
than the rest to prefer a house because of their own
desire for privacy. The more satisfied tenants in all
areas wished mainly for a garden. Correspondingly fewer
of them gave other specific reasons for their choice.

In the Melbourne report, the authors explain that, in the
Australian setting, there is an overwhelming emphasis on
the suburban villa as a symbol of status and success, and
that ideals of child-rearing are therefore very much associated with the suburban way of life. (45) In intro-
ducing their theory to housing classes, for this country,
Rex and Moore maintain, from their experience in Spark-
brook, that the suburban house is a scarce resource that
is generally desired. (46)
    From the relatively simple questions included in the
present survey, it is clear that people's views of their
'housing situation' are complex and not always consistent.
Feelings of satisfaction or displeasure derive from many
sources and are relative, not absolute. The analysis of
the Tyneside data must be set against the background of
all the topics covered in the survey, and, even here, it
has been seen more than once that people in ostensibly
similar circumstances may assess their position very
differently. (47)
    Any attempt to assess 'housing satisfaction' must take
account of a range of variables, including past experience, or 'housing history', present aspects of life beyond
the confines of the home itself, and future aspirations,
and perhaps try to relate them more analytically than has
been done here. This exercise is not solely of academic
interest, in the study of one aspect of social stratifica-
tion. It will be a necessary part of any endeavour to involve individual citizens in planning schemes affecting
how and where they shall live.
    Here, even the notion that the suburban house is the
accepted ideal was not fully supported. True, almost
everyone would have preferred to have a house, but, when
asked about the locality that they would choose, a considerable number wished to return to the area from which
they had moved, where houses, and especially those with

TABLE 35 Preference for other locality

Locality and type of dwelling	No change	Preference if free to choose*									No reply	All	
		anywhere but here	*1	2	3	4	5	6	7				
			\[other area because\]											
	%	%	%	%	%	%	%	%	%	%	%	no.
CRUDDAS PARK													
high flats	32	5	21	2	14	4	4	6	7	5	100	84
maisonettes	(4)	(1)	(2)	–	(2)	–	(5)	–	(2)	(1)		17
houses	44	–	19	–	8	–	11	–	6	11	100	36
GATESHEAD	34	9	5	16	27	16	2	5	5	–	100	44
LONGBENTON	62	–	16	9	3	6	–	–	–	3	100	32
WALLSEND													
high flats	(6)	(3)	(1)	(1)	(1)	(1)	–	–	(5)	(2)	100	20
lower flats	33	19	12	12	6	–	4	–	12	4	100	52
maisonettes	17	26	22	4	22	4	–	–	4	–	100	23
houses	75	–	14	–	6	3	–	–	3	–	100	36

*reasons for preference:
1 nearer relatives or friends
2 nearer to shops or husband's work
3 situation – outlying, healthier, etc.
4 people – 'better-class', quieter, etc.
5 better houses
6 better for children's recreation and/or schooling
7 other or none given

gardens, were likely to be in short supply (Table 35).

In the choice of area, it seemed that the most general factors were the pull of the family and of the old circle of friends, or the convenience of proximity to shops and to the husband's place of work. Though there were those, too, who said that they would rather live in a more out-lying or 'better class' area, they were not so numerous as to validate the model put forward by Rex and Moore.

Table 35 does illustrate the point made in the previous section about the loneliness experienced by mothers in the multi-storey dwellings. (48) This seemed to be a combina-tion of nostalgia for their old surroundings with the social isolation to which flat-dwellers are particularly susceptible (and which incidentally might be relieved to some extent if mothers could be persuaded to share in some communal venture to provide for their children's play).

COMMENT ON LOCAL AUTHORITY POLICY (49)

The last questions were intended only for those interview-ed in the high blocks, in order to see whether they knew of the policy of their own local authority regarding the placement of young families in such accommodation, and to invite their comments.

The position, in this matter, of the various local authorities on Tyneside, at the time when the survey was planned, has been outlined in Chapters 1 and 3. (50) Some, as Gateshead, had definite rules; others tried, though less explicitly, to avoid housing young families in this way.

Only a handful of respondents in Gateshead were vague or uncommunicative about the official position. Of the rest, in that area, just two stated that, as far as they were concerned, there was no problem. One of these said that flats could be all right for young children, given an effective janitor. The other said that she herself had had no trouble over living there, and that it was up to individual parents to decide for or against flat life.

Five of the mothers in Gateshead reckoned that they had good and fairly immediate prospects of being moved out, but three spoke of injustice and discrimination, alleging that only the largest families were being transferred, or that those who were 'favourites with the housing depart-ment' were given priority.

The great majority in Gateshead, as one would expect, were agreed that the official policy was sound and that their flats, while satisfactory for households without children, or maybe for families with children old enough

to take care of themselves, were not good for the very
young - mainly because of the restrictions on their play,
or of the dangers and other inconveniences of living high.

Of the 104 mothers in the high blocks in Cruddas Park
and Wallsend, only seven said, in reply to this question,
that they had met no problems at all in living there. In
all these cases, either there were no children beyond the
toddling stage, or the mother was working and had made
satisfactory arrangements for the family, or the conditions were recognised as so much better than where they
lived before that they felt that they had no cause to
complain.

The majority replied, as in Gateshead, and for a variety of reasons elaborated in the text, that high flats
were unsuitable for the under-fives.

The response to this set of questions was uneven and
not particularly informative, except in showing that the
Gateshead people were generally aware of the official
line. There was little evidence of ignorance, though, not
unnaturally, there were signs of impatience and
disgruntlement.

However, despite such reactions, Gateshead was already
vigorously implementing this aspect of its housing policy
when the survey began. Shortly afterwards, in Newcastle
and in Wallsend, the desirability of offering transfers to
young families in high blocks was incorporated into housing management practice. (51) And similar definite
measures have been taken by many local authorities
throughout the country, in recognition of the social disadvantages of 'living high'. But young couples in high
blocks will still have children. In some areas, too, the
high-rise solution to the housing of young families cannot
be abandoned altogether, that is not in the short-term.
It is hoped that the insights derived from this survey may
further underline the problems that may be faced by young
families in these circumstances, and by the larger group
in the lower blocks, who experience at least some of the
same restrictions and privations.

The high-rise, low-rise debate and the needs of the
pre-school child have been presented as important issues
in the intervening years, by those responsible for policy
at local and at national level, and have been frequently
discussed in the press. In Parts two and three these two
themes will be developed.

Appendix A

THE QUESTIONNAIRE

UNIVERSITY OF NEWCASTLE DEPARTMENT OF SOCIAL STUDIES &
NORTHUMBERLAND AND TYNESIDE COUNCIL OF SOCIAL SERVICE

'Children's Play' Survey

Serial no. ...

Type of dwelling ...

Address ...

Interviewer ...

Date of interview ...

Time ...

Respondent ...

Others present ...

1 to 10 for members of the family living at home:

1 Name

2 Relation to housewife

3 Marital status

4 Date of birth

5   Employment:
    Occupied
    Unemployed
    Retired
    At school
    Unoccupied

    If occupied:
    (For those unemployed, items 6-10 should be recorded
    for their last employment.)

6   Full-time
    Part-time

7   Regular
    Shifts

8   Days only
    Some nights

9   Occupation

10 Firm (or school)

11 Is there anyone else belonging to the family but away
    from home (e.g. at sea, at school, in hospital)? If
    so record above (questions 1-4).

12 (a) For how long have you lived at this address?
    (b) Where did you live before you came here?
    (c) Was that property 'local authority' or 'private'?
    (d) Was it a house/maisonette/multi-storey flat/other
        flat/other type (specify)...................?
    (e) Why did you move?
    (f) Did you have any choice about where you could go?
        Yes/no
        about the type of accommodation? Yes/no
    (g) Did you get what you wanted at the time?

13 (a)   (i) What do you yourself think of your present
               (house, etc.)?
         (ii) What does your husband think of it?
        (iii) How does it compare with the (house, etc.)
               that you had before?

    (b)   (i) What do you yourself think about living in
               this area?
         (ii) What does your husband think of it?
        (iii) How does it compare with living where you
               were before?

14 (a) How many rooms have you?   kitchen & living room(s)
    ....
    bedrooms...............
    (b) Which rooms do you use for:
    meals?.......................................
    sitting, reading, TV, radio, etc.?................
    children's recreation?.......................
    (if approp.) children's homework?................
    (c) In which room(s) do your young(er) children play?
    (i.e. those not yet at school)
    (d) (if approp.) Do you use the balcony?

15 (a) Have you had any difficulties in bringing up your
    children in this (house, etc.)?
    (b) (If so) what would you say were the main problems?

16 (a) What do you think of the facilities for play?
    (i) for your children generally?
    (ii) for your young(er) children?

17 (a) Do you have any help with your young(er) children
    from your parents?
    other relatives?
    neighbours?
    other friends?
    (b) Who would look after them if you were ill?
    (c) Did you have any help of this kind where you lived
    before?
    If so, from whom?

18 (a) Are there any organisations around here for look-
    ing after young children?
    (b) Do you ever make use of them?
    (c) Have you any comments or suggestions to make about
    this?

    Thinking now particularly of the play of your children
    under 5:
19 Whereabouts do they play?
    Outside (the building)?
    Inside (the flat, etc.)?
    Elsewhere indoors?
Interviewer (You will probably find it more convenient to
name the children in whom you are interested.)

20 (a) Do your neighbours have children of ......'s age?
    (b) Do they live:
    (house or mais.) next door/elsewhere (specify)?
    (flat) same floor/floor above/floor below/else-
    where (specify)?

21   (a) With whom do(es) .... usually play?
    (b) What sort of things does (he) play with?

22   Is .... restricted at all
    (a) because of noise?
or (b) because of neighbours?

23   (a) Do young children run any special risk of acci-
       dents here?
       Outside the building?
       Inside (the flat)?
       (as approp.) Elsewhere indoors?
    (b) Has this situation restricted ....'s play at
       all?
       In what way?
       What, if anything, do you think could be done
       about it?

24
        (a)   (b)
Do you have any of the   How often do you (or some-
following near here?   one else) take.......there?
(cf Qn. 18)   (daily/several times a
                      week/occasionally/never)
                      (a)   (b)

      (i) park
     (ii) play area
    (iii) playground
     (iv) play centre
      (v) nursery
     (vi) nursery school
    (vii) community centre
  (viii) clinic
     (ix) shops
    (c) Do you take........to visit relatives and/or
       friends?
       If so, where do you go?
       How often? (as 24b)
    (d) Do you take any of your children to school or
       bring them home?
       Do you take .... with you?

25   (a) To fill in the picture, could you tell me how
       (eldest 2-4 yr-old) spent yesterday? (may need to
       prompt here)
       Morning

       Afternoon

       Evening

(b) Was there anything special about yesterday?
or (c) Would you say that it was a normal sort of day for (him)?

26 (a) Do you have a pram for (the baby)?
   (b) Do you put .... outside at all?
      If so, where?
   (c) Is any storage space provided for the pram?
   (d) Where do you keep it usually?

27 (a) How do the facilities here for ....'s play
      compare with those where you lived before?
      better/worse/same/no children under 5 where lived
      before
   (b) In what ways do they differ?

28 (a) Where is your doctor's surgery?
   (b) How often do you take .... there?
   (c) When did you last take (him)?

29 (a) What is your own assessment of ....'s health?
   (b) What was it like where you lived before?
   (c) Would you say that now, on the whole, it is
     (i) better/worse/about the same/don't know/not
        applicable?
     (ii) if different, any reasons for this?

30 Has living in this (.....) had any effect:
on you yourself?
on ....?
on your other children?

31 If you could choose somewhere else to live, what would
be your preference
   (i) for type of accommodation?
      why?
  (ii) for locality?
      why?

32 For families in multi-storey blocks:
   (a) Are you aware of the policy of the local Housing
      Dept in regard to placing families with young
      children in multi-storey blocks?
   (b) Have you any comments to make on this?
      (i) from your own experience?
&/or (ii) in general?

33 Thank you for answering our questions. Is there anything else, apart from what you have told me already,
that you would like to say?

Part two

Flats in local authority housing: the record of the 1960s

8   Flats in local authority housing

The children in the Tyneside survey will now be in primary
school. Wherever they are living, they will be removed,
for most of their waking hours, from the restrictions and
dangers which many respondents in the survey associated
with the high blocks, the maisonettes and the busy estate
roads. They will all have children of their own age to
talk to and somewhere to play in safety with them. But
will any of them have had an 'unfair start'? Will they be
shy, withdrawn, find it hard to make friends? More particularly, will their ability to learn and to enjoy learning
be impaired?

To suggest that these consequences are inevitable,
would be to indulge in a degree of environmental determin-
ism that is neither theoretically acceptable nor logically
justified by the findings of the survey. For, in each
type of dwelling, and in each area, mothers were by no
means unanimous about the difficulty of bringing up their
children in the kind of atmosphere that they would wish
for them. (1) Nevertheless, the conclusions of the
Plowden report, (2) the rationale underlying the EPA projects, (3) and much contemporary thinking in educational
and child psychology, (4) would maintain that some of
these children have been at risk of missing certain essential elements of their most formative years.

During the last five or six years, in the context of
public housing, the circumstances of young children in
high-rise flats have been the focus of attention. For the
young families studied here, some of the problems seemed
to be associated with the fact that they were housed off
the ground, regardless of the height of the building. (5)
Nor can the worries of some of the relatively more fortunate occupants of the houses be altogether discounted as

those of a convenient 'control' group. (6)

It would be correct to say that the wave of high-rise construction by local authorities has now receded. But certain implications of the whole pattern of local authority building in the last decade are now viewed with concern and all the more so, given the slump in new construction of all kinds in the last few years.

Pearl Jephcott has drawn attention to the situation in Scotland. (7) This chapter will be restricted to England and Wales. It will document some of the factors underlying the provision of flats as a form of public housing in the last decade, and will sketch out their present distribution at regional and local level.

It may be objected that 'to amass statistics is not to confront reality.' (8) And this is true unless one looks behind the numbers into the several dimensions whose kaleidoscopic patterns may be concealed in the printed table. With regard to the provision of public housing during the last decade or so, there are many such dimensions to consider. They include trends in architectural style, the economics of building and construction, the financial policies of central and local government in relation to housing, the varying demographic structure and hence differing housing needs of local populations, the articulated preferences of those to be housed, more euphemistically termed 'housing demand', and the whole decision-making process whereby these 'dimensions', and possibly others, are brought together and argued over, time and again, in Whitehall and in council chambers from Carlisle to Dover and from Berwick to Penzance. Nor, in the matter of building high, can one ignore the tenor of opinion among the general public and among professionals - social workers, doctors, educationalists - who are very much concerned with the housing situation of their clients.

Some simple questions will help to set the scene. For instance, how much of the current stock of dwellings is in the public sector - including properties both of local authorities and of New Towns? How much is privately rented and how much owner-occupied? How do these proportions vary among the regions and how do the four authorities studied here compare with regional and national aggregates?

Table 36 shows that while, in December 1971, some 28 per cent of all occupied dwellings in England and Wales as a whole were rented from local authorities or New Town corporations, there were marked regional differences, the Northern region having the largest overall percentage of dwellings in this category and the smallest percentage in owner-occupation.

TABLE 36   Tenure of dwellings, December 1971

Region	Owner-occupied	Rented from LA or New Town Corp.	Rented from private owner	Other ten-ures	All
	%	%	%	%	%
Northern	42	38	14	6	100
Yorks. and Humberside	49	31	15	5	100
North-West	55	27	15	3	100
E. Midlands	52	27	15	6	100
W. Midlands	51	35	10	4	100
East Anglia	52	26	13	9	100
South-East:	53	26	17	4	100
Gtr London	46	28	23	3	100
Outer Metrop. Area	57	28	10	5	100
Outer South-East	58	21	14	7	100
South-West	58	24	11	7	100
England	52	28	15	5	100
Wales	54	29	12	5	100

Source: 'Social Trends' no.3, 1972 (HMSO, London), Table 102, p.137.

There is, of course, still more variation among local authorities within the regions than between the regional averages. In each of the areas studied here, over 40 per cent of household heads were local authority tenants, and, except in Longbenton, and, most recently, in Newcastle, tenants of private landlords were more numerous than owner-occupiers (Table 37). In each area, too, the class of local authority tenants has increased, both absolutely and relative to all households, between 1961, 1966 and 1971. Against this, the number of households renting from private landlords has fallen consistently, and the proportion of owner-occupiers has changed very little, though their absolute numbers have declined. (9)

Census returns for 1961, 1966 and 1971 show that, between each date, Newcastle, Gateshead and Wallsend lost population on balance, by migration. Net gains are recorded for Longbenton, for the rest of the Tyneside

TABLE 37 Household tenure: local variations

LA	Owner-occupiers %	Tenants of LA or New Town Corp. %	Tenants of private landlords unfurn. %	furn. %	Others %	All households %	000s
1961							
Newcastle	27	28	38	4	2	100	86·8
Gateshead	25	21	50	2	2	100	33·0
Wallsend	18	38	40	2	3	100	15·3
Longbenton	30	54	10	1	6	100	14·0
1966							
Newcastle	28	34	32	4	2	100	82·6
Gateshead	26	30	41	1	2	100	32·2
Wallsend	20	40	37	1	2	100	15·2
Longbenton	30	55	10	1	4	100	14·6
1971							
Newcastle	28	41	25	5	1	100	78·7
Gateshead	27	42	30	1	–	100	32·5
Wallsend	22	43	34	1	–	100	15·7
Longbenton	31	60	9	1	–	100	16·4

Source: census 1961, 1966, 1971; see note 9.

conurbation, and for the remainder of the Northern region, taken as a whole. (10) An analysis of population change in local authority areas throughout the region, along with the proportion, in each area, of house completions that were in the private sector, over the whole period 1945-69, shows a fair degree of correlation between these two measures. (11) The statistical association would be stronger, were it not for the inclusion in the reckoning of authorities such as Longbenton, whose population growth has been largely due to overspill.

There is some evidence, then, in this analysis, of a selective migratory process within the region, with households moving out from the inner boroughs into home-ownership within the rural or semi-rural areas along the Tyne, and to the south, in Durham County, including Washington New Town. Nevertheless, from such evidence as is available in the 1966 census, the dominance of household movement into or within the public housing sector remains, whether one considers moves within the Tyneside conurbation, or within the rest of the Northern region. On the other hand, most of the relatively small group of households who moved into the region from other parts of Britain owned the homes to which they came. (12)

More recent figures are not yet available, but it is unlikely that the role of the local authorities in the provision of housing will have diminished, and certainly not in our study areas. For, during the 1960s, extensive programmes of clearance and redevelopment of the inner areas have been under way. In Newcastle, the comments of respondents in Cruddas Park would suggest that, among families displaced by such schemes, there is a strong preference for remaining within or within easy reach of the central areas - an attachment which has often been observed elsewhere, but which, on Tyneside, is reputed to be particularly strong. (13)

Stone has claimed that the nature of the housing stock in terms, for example, of the distribution of dwelling units of varying size, type and elevation, is changed very slowly by injections of new building. (14) This may be so at national, or even regional level, but within a relatively small area, the situation is much less static. The flexibility with which a local authority may assist families to move into accommodation that seems, on all counts, to offer an 'enhancement, not a deterioration in the quality of life', (15) will be greater or less, numbers apart, according to the range of dwelling-types that is available for letting, and how far these match the needs of potential tenants. Throughout much of the 1960s, the provision of more large dwellings has been given priority

in Newcastle's building programme. But the increasing
number of small households to be accommodated and the
growing shortage of small units available for letting have
led to a reversal of this policy and, since 1970, the need
to increase the number of dwellings with one or two bedrooms has been recognised. (16) This may require more
flats, more maisonettes, and since land is in short
supply, and possibly too, given an already declining population, to avoid further losses of revenue to the rate
fund - less overspill, fewer peripheral estates, more
high-density, inner-city redevelopment.

The housing managers of Newcastle and Gateshead claim
that their position is relatively favourable - more so,
that is, than when the survey was mounted. They do have
dwellings to offer to those who are seeking transfer. No
family with young children that does not wish to do so
need live in a high-rise flat. Nor is there occasion for
tenants to be deterred from moving from such accommodation
by the prospect of increased rent. To achieve maximum
benefit from such a situation to the clients of housing
departments, requires measures for promoting the articula-
tion of the former's needs, as they perceive them. These
may not square with the conventional wisdom, and one can
appreciate the possible impatience of housing managers
with tenants who are nostalgic for the cramped little
yards and dingy back lanes where their children used to
play. (17) But public participation is a pretence unless
such objections can be given a hearing. For out of the
high-rise into the maisonette or two-storey flat may not
be universally regarded as a favourable exchange. The intention is not to trivialise this aspect of housing provision and management. Nor is it to suggest that such
limited options are likely to prevail on Tyneside. But
there are other parts of the country where such prospects
are not unrealistic and where the room for manoeuvre in
housing allocation is likely to be more limited than in
the north-east. In support of this contention the general
pattern of local authority building in recent years will
now be reviewed, for the country as a whole and for some
major urban areas.

HIGH-RISE, THE STYLE OF THE 1960S

Each generation of house-builders bequeaths a legacy for
succeeding generations to enjoy or to tolerate, to prize
or to decry. Victorian mansions, Edwardian villas, grim
urban tenements, dense acres of terraced houses, the
sprawl of inter-war council estates, with their equally

sprawling middle-class counterparts, 'semis', maisonettes,
luxury flats - we have them all; some preserved, con-
served, revitalised, some stout and seemingly indestruc-
tible, some ripe for demolition, some blighted already by
its more distant prospect, some converted into erstwhile
unimagined uses, some enduring testimonies to their occupiers' pride in them, some noble reminders of man's skill
and craftsmanship, some grim memorials to his mistakes,
some a delight to live.in, some just a space to occupy.

The 1960s, for all their proliferation of buildings,
will be remembered by many as the era of the high-rise,
which seems to have generated more professional and public
controversy than any previous building form.

Table 38 gives an indication of the pattern of building
within the public sector, though in terms of tenders, not
completions, since detail for storey height is only published on this basis. In the spirit of the remarks above,
it is relevant to consider some of the factors underlying
these general trends.

HIGH-RISE AND ARCHITECTURE

Notions of aesthetic appeal and the constituents of good
architectural design have contributed to arguments for and
against high-rise schemes. In 1966 Jensen, an architect
enthusiastically committed to high-rise, concluded, from a
review of housing schemes throughout the world: (18)

There is now a considerable prospect of an increasing
volume of high-density housing in flats and apartments
getting under way in many countries. Higher densities
do not necessarily imply slums ... rather, in fact,
where coupled with good planning and good design (they
may) have the reverse effect.

More sweepingly he claimed: (19)

If the architect sees in the pattern of high-density
urban areas an important future plan for the millions,
the pattern of whose work and daily normal activity
necessarily keeps them in close proximity with the
metropolis for a considerable part of their lives, it
is only because the architect has, of all those concerned with town planning, shown himself to be signifi-
cantly able and anxious to meet the sociological needs
of the age.

He foresaw the future city residential area as 'a combina-
tion of tower blocks, of at least 15 storeys, interspersed
with 2- and 4-storey garden maisonettes, some with their
own patios'. (20) Though Jensen was unequivocal in his
advocacy of blocks that are really high by the standards

TABLE 38   Tenders approved* (gross) for local authorities and New Towns in England and Wales

| Year of approval of tender | Type of dwelling | | | | | | All dwgs 100% |
| | Houses and bunga- lows % | Flats** in bldgs of storey ht*** | | | | | |
		2-4 %	5-9 %	10-14 %	15+ %	5+ %	000s
1960	52·8	33·0	4·6	6·5	3·1	14·2	110
1961	51·3	32·2	5·6	7·1	3·8	16·5	104
1962	50·1	32·6	4·6	7·7	5·0	17·3	109
1963	46·9	31·2	4·3	8·6	9·0	21·9	125
1964	44·8	31·0	5·4	6·8	12·0	24·2	147
1965	48·3	30·2	4·6	6·3	10·6	21·5	162
1966	47·5	26·8	9·0	6·2	10·4	25·7	173
1967	50·0	27·0	9·4	3·9	9·7	23·0	170
1968	49·3	30·8	10·5	3·5	5·9	19·9	154
1969	50·6	35·9	8·0	1·8	3·8	13·5	112
1970	51·5	38·6	7·0	1·2	1·7	9·9	98
1971	50·0	41·4	5·2	1·5	1·9	8·6	97
1972	48·3	44·5	5·2	0·7	1·3	7·2	73

Sources: 'Housing Statistics, Great Britain', 1968, 1970, 1971 (HMSO, London) and 'Housing and Construction Statistics', no.5, 1st Qtr 1973 (HMSO, London).
*   gross tenders relate to all those approved in the given year, dated as follows:
    Date of approval
    LAs to 30 June 1967:   date of approval by Minister
          from 1 July 1967:   date of acceptance by LA of
                                    tender or direct labour estimate
                                    (and previously for GLC or LCC)
    New Towns: date when Minister notified of acceptance
** including maisonettes
***data are not available for storey height of dwellings

of this country, he usually preferred them in conjunction with other building forms. Moreover, while citing man's gregarious instincts as providing a unique stimulus for such high-density schemes, he conceded that there was more to learn about human needs and reactions under conditions of extensive occupation. (21) While the use of such building style, in this country, considerably pre-dated Jensen, his advocacy of high-rise development was not un-influential, especially in the early part of the decade that is of interest here.

In similar vein, prior to the development of the well-known Parkhill scheme in Sheffield, the city architect concluded, from a tour of multi-storey housing projects in Europe, that 'high flats could provide living standards in every way adequate as an alternative to 2-storey housing' and hoped that, within a comprehensive development, they might appeal to the younger group of parents. In 1960, Parkhill was described as a spectacular success, one of the most heartening architectural prospects in England, and of international quality. (22)

Cullingworth, in 1964, was doubtful, however, of the prospect of producing fine architecture when the dominant feature of the architect's brief was so often to achieve the largest area of lettable floor space that would be consonant with planning permission, on small restricted sites. For, as he pointed out, whatever the architectural merit of individual buildings, the problem of their siting remains. (23) This problem has been recognised for example, by the GLC, in its Development Plan, which includes a classification of sites, according to their suitability or otherwise, on the basis of aesthetics and amenities, for the erection of high buildings. (24)

Eversley has recently voiced increasing scepticism about the resort to high-rise: (25)

To 'solve' the housing problem by, for example, creating residential units with minimal amenities in an otherwise unpromising environment is to solve only part of it. Where, as in parts of East London, high tower blocks have been built right in among the docks, the semi-derelict wharves and former industrial plants, it is very hard to see what has been gained. It is said that such schemes are now out of favour, but they are still being built (new forty-storey block schemes were announced in 1972), and one cannot help wondering what kind of people will want to inhabit them.

His last comment is apposite and ties in with Jensen's agnosticism, for however architects and planners evaluate them, however attractively it may be possible to site them, antipathy towards high flats, within the realm of public housing, has arisen from doubts as to their suitability for certain kinds of families, especially those with young children. Van der Eyken described them as 'hollow towers - an environment that is anti-child', (26) and Pearl Jephcott, with such antipathy in mind, warned that they might be found 'among the most ponderous ruins of the age'. (27)

HIGH-RISE AND INDUSTRIALISED BUILDING

Another factor that has been commonly associated with the
frequency of resort to high-rise building derives from innovations in the construction industry. Once procedures
for fire-fighting had been improved and the embargo on
buildings over 10 storeys high had been lifted, it seemed
likely that these new methods of construction and the new
forms of organisation within the building industry that
they entailed, would make the choice of high-rise an at-
tractive proposition.

Stone has made a most comprehensive analysis of the
economics of the production of dwellings, including cost
comparisons between schemes using industrialised building
and those employing traditional methods. But he considered that comparative data of this kind, as applied to high-
rise construction, were too sparse at the time for firm
conclusions to be drawn. (28)

More recent official tables note the absence of a hard
and fast line between their definitions of industrialised
and traditional building. For the former includes many
elements: the use of new materials, large factory-made
components, new methods for delivering materials to the
building site and the mechanisation and reorganisation of
on-site processes. Classification of schemes under one
heading or the other follows the rubric of an official
circular. (29)

Table 39 part (a) illustrates the rise and fall in the
local authorities' use of industrialised building, as defined, between 1964 and 1972. (30) Regional analyses are
available for completions only, and on a comparable basis
only from 1966, in terms of the current economic planning
regions. (31) One may expect to find a connection between
these data and the predominant building form within each
region. And it appears, from Table 39 part (b), that tenders for industrialised dwellings have been most numerous,
in relation to all tenders, in parts of the South-East, in
the North-West and in the East and West Midlands, where
the emphasis on flats, both high- and low-rise, has been
marked. (32)

The reality is more complex, however. For when the
series for approved tenders is partitioned by type of
dwelling, as in Table 40, the simple assumption that the
increase in the percentage of high-rise dwellings was a
response to developments in industrialised building cannot
be supported, at least at national level and excluding
tenders for the GLC or LCC. (33) For the use of these
methods of construction, while consistently greatest for
high-rise, has increased most markedly from 1964 to the
peak year of 1967 for houses and for low-rise.

TABLE 39 Industrialised building for local authorities
(a) England and Wales

| Year | Industrialised dwellings % of all dwellings: | | |
	completed %	started %	in approved tenders* %
1964	14	20	19
1965	19	27	25
1966	26	33	37
1967	31	39	44 P
1968	34	41 P	42 P
1969	38 P	40 P	27
1970	41 P	25	19
1971	32	24	16
1972	26	17	not available

(b) regional analysis for completions

| Region | Industrialised dwellings % of all completions in | | | |
	1966 %	1968 %	1970 %	1972 %
Northern	18	27	32	13
Yorks and Humberside	36 A	39 A	38	19
North-West	32 A	40 A	50 A	36 A
E Midlands	27 A	33	48 A	33 A
W Midlands	40 A	40 A	52 A	33 A
E Anglia	12	16	3	2
S-E: Beds, Ess, Herts	26 A	36 A	35	34 A
Gtr London	18	33	50 A	34 A
S-E counties	20	33	29	17
S counties	17	39 A	42 A	16
South-West	18	24	10	9
Wales	30 A	28	29	24
England and Wales	26	34	41	26

For sources and notes see note 30
*excluding tenders for GLC (or LCC) as in Table 40, and
 see Table 38, note *
P denotes peak years
A denotes above the average for England and Wales

TABLE 40 Industrialised and traditional building for local authorities in England and Wales, excluding GLC or LCC

(a) tenders approved (thousands) for each type of dwelling

Year	Industrialised houses and bungalows	Industrialised flats** low-rise	Industrialised flats** high-rise	Industrialised flats** all	Traditional houses and bungalows	Traditional flats** low-rise	Traditional flats** high-rise	Traditional all
1964	10.1	3.8	10.1	23.9	49.3	33.1	19.3	101.8
1965	17.8	6.0	12.1	35.9	53.5	35.0	17.6	106.1
1966	27.0	8.2	18.6	53.8	46.4	30.4	15.8	92.6
1967	32.6	11.3	20.5	64.4	43.9	27.1	13.3	84.3
1968	30.2	10.0	14.1	54.3	41.6	24.3	9.4	75.4
1969*	12.8	6.3	5.5	24.6	35.5	25.6	4.3	65.4
1970	8.2	4.6	1.5	14.3	33.6	23.3	4.2	61.2
1971	7.0	4.2	0.8	11.9	33.7	24.2	3.4	61.3

Percentage of all dwellings

Year	Industrialised houses and bungalows %	Industrialised flats** low-rise %	Industrialised flats** high-rise %	Industrialised flats** all %	Traditional houses and bungalows %	Traditional flats** low-rise %	Traditional flats** high-rise %	Traditional all %
1964	42	16	42	100	48	32	19	100
1965	50	17	34	100	50	33	17	100
1966	50	15	35	100	50	33	17	100
1967	51	18	30	100	52	32	16	100
1968	56	19	26	100	55	32	12	100
1969*	52	26	22	100	54	39	7	100
1970	58	32	10	100	55	38	7	100
1971	58	35	6	100	55	39	6	100

(b) industrialised dwellings per cent of all approved dwellings

Year	1964	1965	1966	1967	1968	1969*	1970	1971
Houses, etc.	17	25	37	43	42	27	20	17
Flats, low-rise**	10	15	21	29	29	20	16	15
Flats, high-rise**	34	41	54	60	60	56	26	18
All (as Table 39a)	19	25	37	44	42	27	19	16

For sources and notes see note 33
* New Towns also excluded from 1969
**here low-rise = buildings of 2–4 storeys
       high-rise = buildings of 5 or more storeys

Comparing the industrialised and traditional groups for all tenders, and for each type of dwelling, increases in approvals to 1966 or 1967 are accounted for by growth within the first group only. The number of tenders for dwellings to be built by traditional methods shows a consistent decrease, from 1965, for each type of dwelling. More particularly, tenders for industrialised construction, per cent of all tenders for houses, low-rise and high-rise respectively, increased from 17, 10 and 34 in 1964 to 42, 29 and 60 in 1967 (Table 40 part (b)), a greater proportionate increase for houses and low-rise than for high-rise flats, despite the more advantageous costing of industrialised over traditional methods for high-rise, as compared with the other dwelling types. (34) Between 1964 and 1968 the percentage of tenders that were for high flats fell in industrialised as well as in the traditional group, and in a similar ratio (Table 40 part (a)). By contrast, the percentage of houses among all dwellings for which tenders were approved, increased more sharply for industrialised than for traditional construction. The statistics alone would suggest that industrialised methods were developed partly in response to the urgent need for more homes. The economy of these methods in time and cost has led to an increase in high-rise construction, but not disproportionately so.

This analysis, however, is the total effect of a number of factors, including aspects of the organisation and economy of the construction industry, whose influence may vary from one part of the country to another. The supply of operatives, and policies for their employment, the availability of materials and of transport, the volume of work for private developers and for non-residential building, are obvious examples, too complex to consider here. (35) But one event whose effects may be more confidently inferred was the partial collapse of the systems-built flats at Ronan Point on 16 May 1968. The disaster had repercussions in many parts of the country and no doubt contributed to the relatively sharp decline from 1969 onwards in tenders for high-rise construction, especially by industrialised methods.

Immediately after the collapse, a tribunal was commissioned to inquire into its cause. Acting on the advice of the tribunal's preliminary report, the Minister urged all local authorities with tall 'systems' buildings to carry out an inspection of their properties. (36) Some seventy-three local authorities were involved in this review, although it was found that some of them were not affected, since their high-rise was not of the Ronan Point type of structure. (37) In the North-East, for example, direct

measures were called for in Felling and Sunderland only.
(38) Nevertheless, the effect of the disaster was not
only to involve certain authorities in the expense of a
review, and to inflate the likely cost of future schemes
by government prescriptions for the inclusion of new pre-
cautionary features in building design. (39) 'The Times'
predicted that it would send its tremors through every
such block in the country. (40) Whether the outcome was
quite so dramatic one cannot say. But to judge from the
coverage given to the incident in the national and local
press, it gave expression to misgivings about high-rise
building, at least as a form of public housing. Newcastle's housing architect, for instance, affirmed that
the council would not resort to high blocks unless forced
to do so by shortage of land or 'other circumstances' - a
policy which, he said, had pre-dated the Ronan Point incident and which reflected the council's intention to give
their tenants, especially those with young children, the
option of keeping their feet on (or close to) the ground.
(41)

Variations in this aspect of housing provision among
the regions and between some of the larger local authorities, will be discussed presently. (42) Meanwhile, Table
38 above gives some indication, at the national level, of
a move away already between 1964 and 1968, from the use of
really high-rise buildings towards those of 5-9 storeys.
The table includes tenders for the GLC (or LCC), and presents a finer breakdown of storey height than was available for the analysis of industrialised building. From
1968 onwards, tenders for low-rise, at between 2 and 4
storeys, have consistently increased. Within the highest
group however, approved dwellings in blocks of 20 storeys
or more, which first appeared in 1959 (under 400 dwellings), reached nearly 8,000 by 1967, and decreased thereafter. Tenders for flats in blocks of 15-19 storeys -
always more numerous - had reached a peak already by 1964,
when, at over 12,000, they represented nearly 9 per cent
of all tenders. As the table shows, 1963 was the peak
year for approvals in 10-14 storey buildings, with 1966
running close to it, in terms of numbers. The 5-9 storey
group continued to rise, in absolute and in percentage
terms, until the aftermath of Ronan Point and other considerations led to an increasing preference for low-rise
construction.

HIGH-RISE AND DENSITY

Underlying these trends are the various densities to be
achieved by individual schemes, for, in each case, it is
on the basis of the required density that the appropriate
mix of dwellings is determined, having regard also to the
physical features of the site and substructure, the kind
of environment that is desired and the acceptable cost.
Density distributions, excluding schemes for the GLC (or
LCC), may be compared with those by type of structure, the
latter being a combination of the data in Table 40 part
(a), above, for industrialised and traditional building
methods.

There is some evidence, in Table 41, of an increase
from 1966 in the percentage of approvals for dwellings in
the lower-density schemes, with a corresponding decrease,
especially, for developments at 140 or more persons, or
bed spaces, per acre. (43)

Stone's analysis of the densities of various forms of
public authority housing, in the early 1960s, may be set
against these figures. According to Stone, the majority
(86 per cent), of new houses for public authorities were
planned at net residential densities of up to 80 persons,
or bed spaces, per acre. (44) Low-rise development, in
blocks of 2-4 storeys, came in these units within the 70-
120 range, while high-rise densities extended from 140
persons per acre, at 5 storeys, to around 200 when blocks
of 20 storeys were employed. (45)

If these criteria are applied to the distribution by
type of dwelling, as in Table 41, it appears, as one would
expect, that in each year a considerable proportion of
low-rise construction has been included, along with
houses, in the lower-density schemes. Moreover, the distinction between tenders at densities of under 140 and
those at or exceeding 140 persons per acre is almost equivalent, at each date, to the distinction between dwellings, whether houses or flats, in buildings of up to 4
storeys and those in structures of 5 storeys or more.

One small, but interesting, deviation illustrates a
change in practice since 1968. For it is only since that
date that approvals in the highest density band have exceeded those for high-rise development. As mentioned already, the data exclude tenders for the GLC (or LCC), who
may have found it especially difficult to avoid planning
at the highest densities and with an emphasis on high-
rise. Moreover, the overall picture masks both the forms
of high density development that are employed in the major
provincial cities, and the effects of differences in the
size of individual schemes. (46) But, within its limits,

TABLE 41 Dwellings by net residential density of scheme:
tenders approved for local authorities in England and
Wales, excluding GLC or LCC

(a) dwellings per cent of all approvals

Density: persons or bed spaces per acre	Year of approval							
	1964	1965	1966	1967	1968	1969	1970	1971
	%	%	%	%	%	%	%	%
under 60	37	34	33	34	26	37	35	38
60–79	24	29	28	31	37	30	34	30
80–99	10	11	8	8	13	10	11	15
100–139	9	9	11	8	10	10	12	9
140+	20	16	20	19	15	14	8	8
All approved dwellings	100	100	100	100	100	100	100	100

(b) dwellings per cent of all approvals (cf. Table 40
part a)

Type of building	Year of approval							
	1964	1965	1966	1967	1968	1969	1970	1971
	%	%	%	%	%	%	%	%
Houses and bungalows	47	50	50	52	55	54	55	56
Flats, etc. in buildings of 2–4 storeys	30	29	27	25	27	35	37	38
5+ storeys	23	21	23	23	18	11	8	6
All approved dwellings	100	100	100	100	100	100	100	100

For source see note 43

the statistical evidence provides a backcloth to the discussion of other modifications in attitudes to the use of
high buildings, even when density targets have remained
high, and the absorption of certain elements of this
thinking into public housing policy.

HIGH-RISE AND COSTS

Financial aspects of alternative forms of high-density development have been consistently to the fore. The evidence is difficult to summarise accurately, since the
bases of the various estimates are not strictly comparable. But the general impression, from the sources quoted
here, is of a pattern of differences between the costs of
high-rise, low-rise and 2-storey schemes that has changed
relatively little in almost twenty years.

     In the mid-1950s, Peter Self described the expensive-
ness of flat construction as one of the mysteries of the
British building trade. (47) On his reckoning, the cost
of the average 2-bedroom, or 4-person flat, in a block of
6 or more storeys, was more than twice that of the
'ordinary' council house. The cost per square foot ranged
from £2·75 to £4 for flats, against a mean of £1·60 for
houses.

     The Parker-Morris Committee, basing their calculations
on provisional prices for local authority dwellings in
mid-1961, gave £2,500 as the notional cost of a flat designed for 4 persons, in a block of 11 storeys, compared
with £1,800 for a 4-person, 2-storey house. (48) Their
figures are complicated by the fact that site development
was excluded from the first estimate, but included in the
second. Moreover, it was noted that the constructional
costs for flats were subject to wide variations.

     In 1963, the Housing Yardstick Manual quoted building
costs, excluding outlay on roads, sewers and external
works, for 4-storey flats, and for those in higher blocks,
as between 125 and 135 and as over 175 per cent respectively of the cost of providing similar accommodation in
houses. (49)

     A year later, Stone maintained that in London, the con-
struction cost of dwellings built to Parker-Morris standards of space per unit was 44 per cent greater for those
in 15-storey blocks than for houses of the same size and
that, for low-rise, the increment was around 20 per cent.
(50) In the provinces, the differentials were wider, and
of the order of 70 and 40 per cent respectively. The regional disparity was due to the fact that while houses
could be erected more cheaply outside the London area, the

building costs for flats, and especially for those in systems-built, multi-storey blocks, were relatively more uniform throughout the country.

Official data on costs are published for dwellings in approved tenders, again excluding those for the GLC (or LCC). (51) The basis of the figures differs slightly according to the type of contract negotiated for each scheme. In the majority of cases, the data relate to the average cost per square foot (i.e. average cost/average area, per dwelling), as calculated from the contractors' agreed price for the structure, superstructure and external works (Table 42).

It appears, from the table, that the cost differential between low-rise flats and houses has remained of the order of 30 per cent, and rather higher from 1969 than previously. That between high-rise and houses has been more variable, but was still, in 1971, near 60 per cent for industrialised schemes and 70 per cent for the rest.

(In advance of the discussion on high-rise and legislation below, it should be noted that new legislation was introduced, in 1967, setting out minimum standards and maximum costs for dwellings that might qualify for loan sanction. Tenders from 1967 or 1968 onwards will be affected by these changes.)

From 1956 to 1967, the costliness of medium and high-rise construction has been mitigated by subsidies provided by the central government. (52) Under the Housing Subsidies Act of 1956, the basic subsidy for dwellings in slum-clearance and redevelopment schemes was £22 1s. for those up to and including 3-storeys, £32 for 4-storeys, £38 for 5, £50 for 6 storeys and over, plus an additional subsidy of £1 15s. per dwelling for each storey height above the sixth, i.e. £57 for 10 storeys and near £66 for 15. The storey-height in each case referred of course to the whole building, not to the elevation of the dwelling itself. The Housing Act of 1961 changed the rate for dwellings in the first category to either £24 or £8 according to the level of the local authorities' expenditure on housing, but the incremental scale, where buildings exceeded 3 storeys, remained the same.

Self noted that the rise in the scale was greatest for buildings of from 4 to 6 storeys (an increase of £18). He saw this as an inducement to housing authorities to concentrate on standardised blocks of medium elevation, rather than a mixture of ordinary housing and really high-rise. (53) In the early 1960s, however, the additional payments for each storey above the sixth were more often regarded as encouraging the use of tall buildings, especially as construction costs per dwelling were reckoned to

TABLE 42 Cost of construction* by type of dwelling and building method: for dwellings in tenders approved for local authorities in England and Wales**

Year of approval	Industrialised			Traditional			All		
	houses and bungalows	flats*** low	high	houses and bungalows	flats*** low	high	houses and bungalows	flats*** low	high
	Average cost (£) per square foot****								
1964	2.77	3.57	4.71	2.60	3.46	4.94	2.63	3.47	4.80
1966	3.08	4.17	5.30	3.01	3.99	5.50	3.04	4.03	5.39
1968	3.25	4.26	4.99	3.27	4.16	5.75	3.27	4.19	5.28
1969	3.35	4.61	5.53	3.47	4.68	5.91	3.44	4.67	5.69
1970	3.58	4.75	6.35	3.72	5.05	5.85	3.69	5.00	5.99
1971	3.98	5.18	6.33	4.32	5.86	7.45	4.25	5.75	7.24
	Average cost of houses = 100****								
1964	100	127	170	100	133	190	100	130	182
1966	100	135	172	100	132	183	100	132	176
1968	100	130	152	100	127	176	100	128	161
1969	100	138	165	100	135	170	100	136	165
1970	100	133	177	100	136	158	100	136	162
1971	100	130	159	100	136	172	100	135	170

* costs include superstructure, substructure and external works (for source see note 30 and see also 51)

** excluding tenders for GLC or LCC, and also for New Towns from 1969

*** here low-rise = buildings of 2-4 storeys
    high-rise = buildings of 5 or more storeys

****no. of dwellings in each group as in Table 40

increase more slowly as storey-height increased. (54)
Moreover, the availability of subsidies for expensive
sites added to the financial attractiveness of high-rise
solutions to high-density inner city development. (55)

These aspects of the finance of high-rise building may
be illustrated by reference to the record, in the Newcastle City Council minutes, of the costing of developments within the Cruddas Park estate. (56)

The analysis covers all of the 2-storey and 4-storey
dwellings and two of the eight 15-storey blocks included
in the interview study in Cruddas Park. Data for the remaining high blocks have been omitted, since revision of
the original tender for these, and for schemes in other
parts of the city negotiated at the same time, have made
it difficult to disentangle the relevant items. (57) It
is interesting to note the considerations that prompted
the revision. They are of two kinds. In the first case,
as a result of trial borings, it was recommended that, because of the nature of the site, the substructure of the
flats be changed from one using bored piles to a more
costly cellular raft construction with pre-cast concrete
piles. In an area with extensive mine workings, similar
problems regarding the foundations have contributed, in a
more recent scheme, to the decision not to incorporate
high-rise. In the second instance, the additions to the
tender were recommended so as to achieve a higher standard
of finish within the superstructure. The largest item included estimates for the increased width of public staircases, improvements in fittings and in lighting within the
flats and in measures for protection against fire. Also
on the list was the design and provision of specialised
play equipment. The debate on this issue illustrates the
difficulties faced by the City Council in providing flats
with a high standard of amenity on sites that present certain technical problems - factors which go some way to ex-
plaining the local balance of dislike of high-rise construction and the relatively low degree of resort to it.
(58)

The comparison of costs for each building type in
Cruddas Park must allow for variation in the size of
dwellings. The average number of bedrooms per dwelling
here was 1·65 for the 180 dwellings in the high blocks,
2·50 for the 64 maisonettes and 2·41 for the 179 2-storey
dwellings (which included 38 2-storey flats). The number
of rooms, rather than the number of persons (or designated
bed spaces) has been used to adjust the figures for comparative purposes, since complete information was provided
on the former basis only. Differences in the standards of
equipment within the dwellings also confuse the comparison

TABLE 43   Construction and associated costs for dwellings within Cruddas Park, Newcastle

	A 2-storey houses flats	B 4-storey maisonettes	C 15-storey flats	A	B	C Type A = 100
No. of dwellings	141 38	64	180	100	104	69
No. of bedrooms/dwg	2·41	2·50	1·65	100	104	69
Costs per dwg (excl garages)	£	£	£			
superstructure	1832	2389	2233	100	130	122
substructure, external works	345	506	620	100	147	180
(1) Total including fees	2292	3032	2989	100	132	130
roads, sewers, cost of land	1370 (16·8 acres)	874 (4 acres)	232 (2 acres)	100	64	17
(2) Total costs	3662	3906	3221	100	121	88

	Type of dwelling			Type A = 100		
	A 2-storey houses flats	B 4-storey maisonettes	C 15-storey flats	A	B	C
	£	£	£			
Housing Revenue Account						
Annual expenditure/dwg						
loan charges (60 years)	257	295	223			
repairs, management, etc.	17	17	24			
(3) Total expenditure	274	312	247	100	114	90
Annual income/dwg						
exchequer subsidies						
dwelling	24	32	66			
expensive site	22	32	15			
rate fund	8	8	8			
total income	54	72	89	100	133	165
Balance of expnr charged to HRA	220	240	158	100	109	72
(4) excl garages	211	221	158	100	105	75

For source and notes see note 56

of building costs, at least for dwellings completed before
1969, when certain Parker-Morris standards became mandatory. Within one estate, as here, it may be assumed that
standards are unlikely to vary substantially by type of
dwelling.

The analysis is set out in Table 43. Remembering that
these figures relate to the approved tenders, and thus
presumably to the most economical costings in each case,
several points may be made from the comparisons in the
table.

Though the high-rise flats are smaller than the houses
their construction costs are very much greater. Costs for
the substructure and external works are particularly high.
Close to the time when this tender was approved, a similar
figure of £600 per flat was quoted for the substructure of
a similar scheme in another part of the city. The costliness of this foundation work was viewed with some concern
by members of the City Council. (59) Nevertheless it was
conceded that the overall construction costs were not ex-
orbitant. Rather it was claimed that Newcastle was erect-
ing flats of high quality for an outlay that was low in
comparison with the national average. (60) In the case of
Cruddas Park, the external works component included an
allocation of £180 per dwelling for play areas and under-
ground parking.

Savings in the expenditure on roads, sewers and the
purchase of land, achieved by building high, appear dramatic in the table. But the three building schemes cannot
fairly be costed separately under this heading since they
are all part of the one estate. The density, in terms of
dwellings per acre, for the whole estate, assuming a land-
allocation for the remaining six high blocks similar to
that for the two blocks included here, works out at 33
dwellings or, using an estimate of the intended number of
occupants, in the range of 100-120 persons per acre. (61)
This may be an over-estimate, since the more high blocks
are included in any scheme, the greater the ancillary
space that is required, and the plans for Cruddas Park
were praised by the Chairman of the Housing Committee for
the use of open space within the estate as a whole. (62)

The need for extra space around high-rise development
is one factor that has been said to limit the economic
viability of high-rise construction to areas where the
purchase of land is open to a high level of Exchequer subsidy. (63) Even so, the need to accommodate as many
dwelling units as possible on such expensive sites has no
doubt resulted, in developments such as the Gateshead
scheme, in a parsimonious allotment of communal space, as,
for example, the shortage of play areas outside the

buildings, which many respondents in the survey deplored. (64)

In Table 43 total expenditure from the Housing Revenue Account is proportional to the total costs. Within this item, the outlay per dwelling for repairs and management is greatest for the high flats. This illustrates another argument that has been made against their use, and for which more detailed evidence is provided, for individual authorities, in the returns of the Institute of Municipal Treasurers and Accountants. (65)

Income to the Housing Revenue Account is heavily weighted, in the case of the high flats, by the Exchequer subsidy for dwellings of this elevation, assuming that the basic subsidy of £24 is appropriate here. (66) As a result, the balance to be charged to the Account, and thus at least the notional rent, for each dwelling type, is not disproportionate to the size of the accommodation. (67) Without the differential by storey height, the charges would be £211, £229 and £200 respectively, making the high flats potentially the most expensive to rent, given their size.

In order to relate the main elements in Table 43 more directly to the dwelling size within each group, items marked 1 to 4 in Table 43 have been divided by the average number of rooms. The results are as in Table A:

TABLE A

Item, as in Table 43		Type of dwelling		
		A 2-storey houses and flats	B 4-storey maisonettes	C 15-storey flats
		£ per room		
1 (a)	per bedroom	951	1213	1805
(b)	per bedroom and living-room*	672	866	1124
(c)	per bedroom and living-room and kitchen*	520	674	817
2 (a)		1519	1562	1945
(b)	as above	1074	1116	1211
(c)		830	868	880
3 (a)		114	125	149
(b)	as above	80	89	93
(c)		62	69	67
4 (a)		88	88	95
(b)	as above	62	63	59
(c)		48	49	43

*see p.145 above, and Hole (68) for discussion re dwg size

The effect of increasing the denominator is to narrow
the differential and, in the case of item 4, the final
charge per dwelling, to make the high flats the cheapest.
Two points may be made from these crude calculations, in
support of the preceding general discussion. First, however 'size' is evaluated, the construction costs for the
high-rise dwellings (item 1) range from 57 to 88 per cent
more than for those of 2 storeys. The estimate for the
remaining high blocks within Cruddas Park seemed to be
lower than for the two included here. (69) However, their
cost would still exceed that of the 2-storey dwellings by
some 20 to 50 per cent, despite the fact that tenders for
these other high blocks were made two years earlier.
Second, without the extra subsidy for buildings of more
than 6 storeys, the net charge per room to the Housing
Revenue Account would become (item 4), for the high-rise,
£105, £65 and £47 respectively. Thus, taking size into
the reckoning, the high flats would become more costly, or
only marginally cheaper to occupy than the houses.

HIGH-RISE AND LEGISLATION

To return to the wider scene - although, as shown already,
the high cost of tall buildings had been mentioned in the
official literature from the beginning of the 1960s, it
was not until the Housing Subsidies Act of 1967 that measures were taken actively to discourage local authorities
from building high. (70) The Civil Appropriation Account
of 1966-7 (published in 1968), drew attention yet again to
the fact that high-rise was 30 per cent more costly than
low-rise (cf. Table 42). (71) Under the Housing Subsidies
Act of 1967, a completely new form of basic subsidy was
introduced. This was related, in a given year, to the interest charges incurred by each local authority on borrow-
ing in respect of all approved dwellings completed in that
year. In addition, an extra provision was made per dwelling for those in blocks of 4 storeys and over, namely £8
for 4 storeys, £14 for 5 and £26 for 6 storeys or more
(72) - all payments, as before, to cover a period of 60
years. The extra subsidy for buildings exceeding 6
storeys, so frequently regarded as an inducement to local
authorities to build high, was withdrawn under this new
legislation. At the same time, other measures were introduced which, together with the abolition of the high-block
subsidy, could be interpreted as a disincentive to local
authorities to settle for a large complement of tall
buildings in their housing programmes, save in exceptional
circumstances. A circular issued by the Ministry of

Housing and Local Government in 1967 announced that housing schemes submitted for loan sanction and/or subsidy
from January 1969 would be required to conform to Parker-
Morris standards. (73) Furthermore, a cost yardstick
system was to become operative from July 1967, represent-
ing a level of expenditure beyond which, or beyond 110 per
cent of which, full loan sanction would be refused, save
in certain special circumstances, and subject to negotiation wherever these were considered to apply. The force
of these measures lay in the fact that they were imposed
simultaneously - or almost so.

The Parker-Morris report in 1961 set out minimum standards of space, heating and other aspects of design and
equipment which would provide 'good homes, fully reflect-
ing the needs of the people who (were) to live in them'.
(74) For homes in flats or maisonettes special attention
was given to lifts, balconies, sound insulation, refuse
disposal, safety and to the design and management of play
space, on the general principle that such accommodation
should provide, for their occupants, an environment 'as
workable and as satisfactory as for people who lived in
houses'. (75) It was estimated that the extra cost of in-
corporating the Committee's recommended minimum standards
in relation to floor space (including room for storage),
bedroom cupboards, kitchen fittings and electric sockets,
within 4-person flats in 11-storey blocks, might amount to
near 10 per cent of the average cost, in 1961, of a dwelling of that type, with the possibility of a further allowance for improved heating. To build a 4-person house at
these standards, and with adequate heating arrangements,
would involve a slightly smaller outlay, on average, over
the current price. (76) These estimates take into account
all six 'improved standards' by which dwellings are
classified in the housing returns. They do not allow for
the cost-implications of those other items, mentioned
above, that were considered to merit special attention in
flats and maisonettes.

Of the six internal standards, all except those relat-
ing to kitchen fittings and electric sockets became mandatory, under the Ministry's Circular 36/67, for schemes
submitted for loan sanction and/or subsidy as from the beginning of 1969. Local authorities were therefore advised
to incorporate them in designs prepared from 1967 onwards.
(77) What the recognised desirability, and finally the
necessity of conforming to these standards, meant in terms
of building costs it is impossible to say for all types of
dwelling. (78)

From data provided from 1964 it appears that more 1-
and 2-bedroomed flats than houses of similar size, were

already at or above the minimum level on all six counts.
The percentage of such dwellings in approved tenders in
each year was as in Table B: (79)

TABLE B

	Flats		Houses		All
	1 bedroom %	2 bedroom %	1 bedroom %	2 bedroom %	dwgs
1964	16	15	9	11	14
1965	19	22	15	19	21
1966	38	48	26	33	40
1967	49	60	42	55	54

(excluding tenders for GLC or LCC)

Although, in the early 1960s, few new dwellings in
the public sector, whether flats or houses, met all six of
their main recommendations, the Parker-Morris Committee
recognised that some local authority flats, built since
the war, were of a quality that was 'previously scarcely
dreamt of for anything but the luxury market'. (80)   In
Sunderland, which heads the list of the largest provincial
boroughs for the rate of new council building in that
period, per head of population, Norman Dennis has drawn
attention to the high level of design and amenity achieved
in many of its schemes, and especially in those incor-
porating high flats. (81)   Estimates for the part of the
Cruddas Park estate, based on the analysis in Table 43,
would place the whole plan above the yardstick costing.
(82)   Nevertheless, from the evidence presented above, it
appears that in 1967 around 50 per cent of 1- and 2-
bedroomed flats, those in Greater London Council tenders
excluded, were below the minimum standards in one aspect
at least.

The published data on standards do not distinguish between flats in high and low rise.   But, given the roughly
even balance between dwellings of these types in tenders
approved by local authorities, other than GLC, in 1967,
(83) it cannot be concluded that the necessity to meet
Parker-Morris requirements would have had no repercussions
for the cost of high-rise schemes.   Indeed, Circular 36/67
included a request to local authorities 'to reappraise
their policies for housing densities and layouts where
these appeared to demand a high percentage of high-rise
dwellings'. (84)   The added complication of meeting or

negotiating the cost yardstick, and the abolition of the
extra subsidy, coupled with rising doubts as to the suitability of high flats, however well appointed, as family
homes - the non-quantifiable 'social costs' - all ensured
a wide response to the Ministry's directive.

The cost yardstick system was introduced by the Minister of Housing and Local Government within the Conservative government of the early 1960s. It represented a
scale of costs which were considered reasonable for housing people at medium and high densities, that is at or
above a net density of 80 persons per acre. Tables were
produced giving estimates for expenditure on superstructure, substructure and external works (as defined in the
discussion of Table 43), in relation to the average number
of persons per dwelling and the overall density to be
achieved within a particular scheme. These were intended
to be a guide to local authorities and an encouragement to
'architects and all concerned with a housing scheme to explore the use of different combinations of layout and
height and type of building before a final decision (was)
made'. (85)

Purely as a guide, the degree to which the yardstick
affected such decisions or the prospects of schemes gain-
ing ministerial approval is a matter for conjecture, or
for study at the local level. Norman Dennis tells, for
instance, of a development in Sunderland, in the early
1960s, whose cost was so much in excess of the yardstick
that the Ministry 'intimated that no more blocks of that
design should be planned'. (86) In any event, the innovation could scarcely fail to underline the cost factor
among the variables to be considered in choosing between
alternative ways of achieving a given density, and to draw
attention, yet again, to the expensiveness of building
high.

When the next Labour government formally imposed the
yardstick in 1967, it began to be associated with the relative decline in high-rise construction. (87) Indeed,
the pressures to keep within or close to the yardstick
costing has been said to have contributed to the general
fall in local authorities' output of new dwellings. (88)

Under the 1967 Act, plans were open to close scrutiny
at both local and ministerial levels. Designs for schemes
which were not to be supervised by a registered architect,
responsible to the local authority, were to be submitted
to the Ministry for approval at all stages. (89) Moreover, the added obligation to conform to Parker-Morris
standards meant that local authorities would either have
to settle for the most economical solution that would be
in keeping with these standards or attempt to justify, to

the central government, their choice of a more expensive
scheme. (90)

The yardstick costings have been criticised as un-
generous, and thus tending, in some cases, to transform
the Parker-Morris standards, which had been suggested some
years previously as minima, into maxima also.   Further,
they have been regarded as insufficiently sensitive to in-
flation and its effects on the cost of construction, despite the recent 'market forces allowance' which permits a
discretionary adjustment of the yardstick figure. (91)
Such criticisms apart, the procedure embodied in the 1967
Act complicated the task of local housing authorities, by
requiring them to consider, for example, the relationship
between storey height and overall density, and to weigh up
the relative costs and benefits inherent in alternative
designs, or to face the prospect of delays in the building
programme where the approval of exceptional schemes was a
matter for negotiation with the Ministry. (92)   It is
significant, therefore, that it was during the period when
these changes in housing legislation were introduced that
the growing preference among architects for medium- or
low-rise solutions to high-density provision became publicised in the professional journals and in the national
press.

A CHANGE IN EMPHASIS

The measure of density that is of interest here is of
course the net residential density, that it to say the
number of persons, or bed spaces, per acre within the area
allotted to a housing scheme, including half the width of
surrounding roads.   For simplicity, too, densities will be
regarded as high when they exceed the level beyond which
the inclusion of some form of multi-storey building,
though not necessarily high-rise, may be required - that
is, in these units, beyond the 70 to 80 range. (93)   Vere
Hole has pointed out that the density levels within new
building schemes are contingent upon current building
regulations and cannot be compared with the often higher
occupancy rates found for example in areas of nineteenth-
century terraced housing. (94)

A decade ago, Cullingworth described high densities in
new public housing as synonymous with flat development,
but noted the possibility of achieving levels exceeding 70
persons per acre with a high percentage of houses. (95)
In the same period, Stone maintained that any future increase in density was likely to be obtained by building
flats, especially high flats, though he modified the

prediction by recognising that an increasing percentage of households might require accommodation closer to ground level. (96) It was commonly supposed, however, that when densities exceeded 140 persons per acre, dwellings in high blocks would be predominant (cf Table 41 above).

In 1967, when, as has been shown above and in Tables 38 and 41, the resort to high blocks of 20 or more storeys had reached its peak, when among other high buildings, only those of 5 to 9 storeys continued to rise, when the percentage of approvals for dwellings in the most densely occupied schemes had already begun to fall, and at the time of the official directive to local authorities to re- consider their plans for building at this level, an issue of the 'Architectural Review' was devoted to a critique of the recent pattern of new housing development. (97) A number of the schemes that were examined in detail were described as 'brutal' in style - a profusion of 'off-the- peg' tower-blocks, destined to be the slums of the future. A slum was defined, more widely than usual, as a dwelling that, for all its Parker-Morris internal equipment, denied to its occupants the freedom to express and to fulfil themselves - in short, the ability to make it 'home'. (98) The economic attractions of the subsidy system (about to disappear) and the practical advantages of engaging con- tractors specialising in heavy concrete building systems, were mentioned as having contributed to the tendency to build high. Against this, progressive architectural opinion was said to have moved decisively on again, recog- nising that towers were unsuitable for children, and to have given up the attempt to cram families into them. (99) Various schemes were evaluated in terms of the distribu- tion between private and public space and of the link be- tween the two - the threshold, which was too often a dreary lift-hall or wind-swept access balcony, and one of the places where, in spite of regulations, young children would often choose to play. (100) On the positive side, reference was made to experiments at reaching high densi- ties with as many families as possible housed at ground level, as for example a development for the GLC, in South- wark, which would provide gardens and garages at a density of 140 to 160 persons per acre. (101)

Since the 1967 'watershed', and for a variety of reasons that have been intimated already, medium- or low- rise has become increasingly associated with high-density schemes. Other schemes, similar to that in Southwark, have been publicised in the national press. Among these are the estate at Lillington Gardens, Pimlico, where at 200 bed spaces (or persons) per acre, 40 per cent of fami- lies (and all of those with young children) were provided

for at ground level, each with their own garden or patio,
and the (then) projected Marquess estate in Islington
where, at even higher densities, some two families in
three were to have their own private space outdoors. (102)
'Low-rise high-density' has been reported as the new enthusiasm in housing development, though with some apprehension about the problems that this too might engender
and with a definite rejoinder from the Chairman of the
Housing Committee of the GLC that, in parts of London,
high density planning would necessitate high flats,·and
that some families with young children would inevitably be
found in them. (103)

By 1972 the annual output of new dwellings for local
authorities, in terms of those in approved tenders, had
fallen by some 60 per cent from the peak year of 1966.
The change in pattern and some of the factors behind it
are illustrated by Table 38 and have been elaborated in
the preceding discussion, for the country as a whole. But
housing is ultimately a matter for local decisions, and
the influence at the local level of the various matters
that have been discussed here would demand a series of
micro-studies. (104) Moreover, the policy of individual
local authorities, in respect of new building, could not
realistically be considered in isolation from other aspects of the local housing situation, not least the com-
plementary emphasis, within the public sector, on the improvement of existing dwellings. (105)

The overall picture that has been presented here has
been largely confined to the 1960s, and this was not just
for statistical convenience, but because it was during
this time that the high-rise problem became a matter of
national concern. The period ends, in 1972, on the threshold of the changes implicit in the Conservatives' Housing
Finance Act of that year and in the subsequent measures to
be taken by the present government. (106) At the local
level, the reorganisation of local government will clearly
also affect the provision of public housing.

Meanwhile, however, the consequences of the pattern of
new building for the housing of young families remains the
focus of this study. As such, it comes within the general
expectation that local authorities should take a wider
view of their function in meeting all physical and social
aspects of housing needs within their area. (107) The
needs of young children in multi-rise housing cannot be
assessed from national trends alone. They will clearly be
more urgent in some areas than others. In order to illustrate this very obvious statement, trends in the provision
of new dwellings within the regions, and for some individual authorities, will now be considered.

SOME REGIONAL PATTERNS

To focus first of all on regional differences in the housing stock, especially in the proportion of flats and maisonettes within the public sector: according to the population census, and in terms of census definitions, the
proportion of private households in England and Wales that
were housed in buildings containing more than one structurally separate dwelling, increased between 1961 and 1966
from 9 to 11 per cent.   The General Household Survey gives
an indication of more recent and greater changes by
putting the 1971 figure at 17 per cent. (108)   The picture
for and within the Northern region is given by Table 44,
together with a breakdown by type of tenure for 1966
(available for that date only). (109)

Local comparisons must be treated with caution.   It
appears, for instance, that, in the Northern region and
primarily on Tyneside, the proportion of households accommodated in this way more than doubled in the first half of
the 1960s.   The net increase is shown as some 60,000
households, including 30,000 in Newcastle and Gateshead
combined.   But, in the absence of corresponding data, by
tenure groups, for 1961, it is impossible to judge from
this source how much of the increase reflects the activity
of local authorities in their demolition and rebuilding or
new housing programmes. (110)   In the Tyneside conurbation, for example, the increase of over 50,000 households,
in all tenure groups combined, by far exceeds the number
of households, renting from the local authorities, who
were living in multi-dwelling buildings in 1966, and some
of these would have been there already in 1961.   Neither
is it possible to discern the nature of the changes in the
privately-rented sector, by far the largest remaining
tenure group, within which most of the balance must be
found.

Admittedly the 1966 data were based on a 10 per cent
sample of households.   But assuming an unbiased selection,
one would not expect the degree of sampling error substantially to affect the regional or conurbation aggregates.
A further problem lies in the definition of a separate
dwelling, and possible inconsistencies in the application
of the official criteria cannot be discounted.   In any
event, although their numbers at these dates cannot be
assessed, the 'Tyneside flats', usually in 2-storey terraced buildings, have remained a distinctive feature of
the privately-rented sector within the Northern region.

There are no data in this form, from the census of
1971, but other evidence of changes, during the decade,
within the stock of local authority dwellings in Newcastle
and Gateshead is given in Table C.

TABLE 44 Households in multi-dwelling buildings 1961 and 1966, Northern region

(a) number of households* (thousands)

| Area | 1961 | | | 1966 | | | | |
	in multi-dwelling buildings no.	%	all h'hds no.	in multi-dwelling buildings** pb no.	c no.	all no.	%	all h'hds no.
England and Wales	1,354	9	14,890	1,225	427	1,652	11	15,694
Northern region	64.5	6	1022.9	113.0	11.5	124.5	12	1061.9
Tyneside	39.2	14	276.7	89.2	3.0	92.2	33	277.7
rest	25.3	3	746.2	23.8	8.6	32.4	4	784.2
Newcastle	13.1	15	88.4	32.3	1.2	33.5	39	83.8
Gateshead	2.5	8	33.5	16.0	0.3	16.3	49	33.4
Rest of Tyneside	23.6	15	154.8	40.9	1.5	42.4	26	160.5

(b) 1966 analysis by household tenure*** (no. of households in thousands)

Type of tenure	England and Wales			Tyneside			Northern region remainder			all		
	pb	c	all h'hds	pb	c	all h'hds	pb	c	all h'hds	pb	c	all h'hds
Owner-occupiers	104	72	7,170	11	–	83	2	2	306	13	2	389
Tenants of:												
LA or New Town corp.	758	21	3,942	24	–	102	16	–	266	40	1	368
private landlord												
unfurnished	280	198	2,935	50	2	77	5	4	120	55	6	197
furnished	16	95	526	1	–	5	–	1	9	1	2	14
Others	31	20	787	1	–	6	1	1	65	2	1	72
All households	1,189	407	15,360	87	2	273	23	8	767	110	11	1,040

For source and notes see note 109
* all households, including those absent on census date
** pb: purpose built; c: converted
***excluding absent households

TABLE C

	Percentage of local authority dwellings (111) in buildings of			
	5-9 dwgs	10+ dwgs	3+ storeys	
	1961		1966	1971
	%	%	%	%
Newcastle	4	10	32	35
Gateshead	2	8	21	22

The sources and categories differ between 1961 and the later years. But the estimates confirm the expectation, from the general discussion of local authority building in the 1960s, that in certain areas such as these, the amount of multi-rise building would have contributed to a marked change in the composition of the stock of public housing by the end of the decade. (112) Whereas in Newcastle and Gateshead construction of buildings of this elevation was greatest in the first half of the decade, the reverse was the case in many county boroughs. For this reason, and since appropriate data are available from 1966, the analysis by region and by local authority will start from that date.

Table 45 shows the distribution of flats and maisonettes, as defined in the census, for each of the present economic planning regions, and separately for the public and private sectors. (113) The contrast between Greater London and elsewhere is striking. In the former area more than half of the local authority dwellings in 1966 were in buildings containing more than one dwelling, and, of the buildings, the great majority in this sector were purpose-built. In the rest of England and Wales, the overall proportion was one in seven. Among the regions, and still within the public sector, the proportion of such dwellings was highest in the North-West, West Midlands, South-West and in the South-East outside Greater London. Within the private sector, purpose-built flats (not shown separately in the table), were most numerous, by far, in Greater London. Other parts of the South-East and the Northern region stand out from the remaining areas. (114)

The General Household Survey suggests that in these somewhat nebulous terms 'flats' had become more prevalent, by 1971, in every region. From the statistics of completions and demolitions in the period, and on some simple assumptions, it is possible to account for a good deal of the increase for the country as a whole by the emphasis on

TABLE 45 Occupied dwellings: regional variations, 1966

Economic planning region	Rented from local authority or New Town corporation (a)			All other dwellings (b)			All dwellings (b)			1971 General Household Survey h'hlds in flats as % of all h'hlds
	flats and maisonettes (c) no. (000s)	% of total	all no. (000s)	flats and maisonettes (c) no. (000s)	% of total	all no. (000s)	flats and maisonettes (c) no. (000s)	% of total	all no. (000s)	
Northern	40	11	367	82	12	681	122	12	1,048	15
Yorks and Humberside	62	14	436	23	2	1,122	85	5	1,558	10
North-West	104	20	526	36	2	1,616	139	6	2,142	12
East Midlands	20	7	288	12	2	780	32	3	1,069	5
West Midlands	80	16	488	33	3	1,044	113	7	1,532	14
East Anglia	13	10	129	10	3	382	24	5	511	7
South-East										
Gtr London	296	54	551	361	21	1,730	657	29	2,282	45
rest of S-E	96	15	648	156	7	2,218	253	9	2,866	14
South-West	40	15	265	38	4	870	78	7	1,135	12
Wales	21	10	217	14	2	617	35	4	834	9
All England and Wales	772	20	3,917	766	7	11,060	1,538	10	14,977	17
Outside Gtr London	476	14	3,366	405	4	9,330	881	7	12,695	

For source and notes see note 113 and see note 108 for 1971
(a) dwellings where no member of any household was present on census night are excluded
(b) dwellings defined in (a) are included – the numbers are relatively small here
(c) flats and maisonettes: dwellings in buildings containing more than one dwelling

flat construction in the public sector. (115) But to
begin to explore regional and more localised variations in
this aspect of the provision of local authority housing,
it is convenient to return to the analysis of approved
tenders, and from 1966 to 1971. (116)
     The picture comes clearer when the regions are grouped
according to the relative contribution of their local
authorities to the provision of new dwellings. From the
data in Table 46, two such groups emerge, distinguishing
Greater London, with the whole of northern England through
to the West Midlands, and Wales, from the rest of the
country. (117) Without digressing on the finer differences in Table 46, and accepting the two broad groups derived from it, it can be seen, from Tables 47a and 47b and
their summary in Table 48, that within the first group,
where the local authorities' share of completions has been
greatest, their tendency to build flats, especially high
flats, has been greatest also. (118)

TABLE 46   Regional variations in new building for local
authorities and New Towns, 1966-70

Economic planning region	New dwellings completed for LAs and New Towns per cent of all completions in*					All completions for LAs and New Towns 1966-70
	1966 %	1967 %	1968 %	1969 %	1970 %	no.
Northern	50	54	56	54	55	61,053
Yorks and Humberside	48	49	44	47	43	77,975
North-West	47	44	40	48	53	105,089
East Midlands	26	35	30	30	33	38,404
West Midlands	41	52	44	52	48	93,735
East Anglia	34	34	29	29	28	24,821
South-East Gtr London	63	68	67	69	73	115,095
rest of S-E	32	33	30	32	31	126,753
South-West	30	28	24	25	23	38,810
Wales	47	52	45	46	43	42,826

For source and notes see note 117;   see also note 31 for
definition of Economic Planning Regions
*to be consistent with the analyses of tenders and with
  the general discussion, completions for Housing Associations and govt depts are not included in the numerator of
  the calculations, but contribute to the denominator in
  each case. The figures here therefore are not equivalent
  to the percentage of all completions that were in the
  public sector.

TABLE 47(a)   Regional variations in building, by storey height. Dwellings in tenders approved (gross) for local authorities and New Towns, 1966-71

per cent of all approvals in each year (all approvals, 000s)

Region*	1966 L %	1966 H %	1967 L %	1967 H %	1968 L %	1968 H %	1969 L %	1969 H %	1970 L %	1970 H %	1971 L %	1971 H %
Greater London	29	59	27	61	43	41	46	36	50	31	51	30
	(33·3)		(31·3)		(24·3)		(23·8)		(18·1)		(16·9)	
Northern	17	13	19	13	18	14	18	6	27	3	25	15
	(13·5)		(15·4)		(14·5)		(8·6)		(7·7)		(8·0)	
Yorks and Humberside	23	25	30	13	34	22	37	21	49	13	52	–
	(17·9)		(18·3)		(14·6)		(7·9)		(11·2)		(8·4)	
North-West	35	24	29	30	29	30	39	13	39	10	53	3
	(23·9)		(21·0)		(29·8)		(19·3)		(16·1)		(11·3)	
West Midlands	22	29	25	19	23	16	29	6	30	5	33	–
	(22·2)		(22·2)		(22·9)		(11·2)		(6·9)		(6·9)	
Wales	32	3	26	1	28	2	23	4	36	2	34	6
	(10·6)		(9·5)		(6·1)		(5·8)		(5·1)		(3·5)	
England and Wales as in Table 38	27	26	27	23	31	20	36	14	39	10	41	9

For source and notes see note 118
*regions with a high percentage of completions for local authorities and New Towns, as in Table 46
L: flats, etc. in buildings of 2-4 storeys
H: flats, etc. in buildings of 5 or more storeys

TABLE 47(b)   Regional variations in building, by storey height. Dwellings in tenders approved (gross) for local authorities and New Towns, 1966–71

per cent of all approvals in each year (all approvals, 000s)

Region*	1966		1967		1968		1969		1970		1971	
	L %	H %	L %	H %	L %	H %	L %	H %	L %	H %	L %	H %
South-East Beds, Ess, Herts	26	20	32	9	29	3	33	9	30	5	38	7
	(8·2)		(9·9)		(8·3)		(5·4)		(7·2)		(4·1)	
S–E counties	39	9	31	11	37	8	45	4	42	1	47	3
	(8·2)		(8·2)		(4·4)		(6·6)		(4·3)		(3·8)	
S counties	26	10	30	3	32	7	29	1	32	1	29	2
	(11·4)		(10·9)		(8·3)		(8·2)		(5·0)		(6·8)	
East Midlands	26	22	24	23	38	9	45	3	36	1	43	2
	(9·1)		(10·0)		(9·1)		(5·4)		(6·9)		(7·3)	
East Anglia	22	3	22	5	24	6	33	–	33	–	21	–
	(5·9)		(6·0)		(4·3)		(3·7)		(3·8)		(3·5)	
South-West	23	3	29	5	34	1	33	5	30	–	33	–
	(8·2)		(7·9)		(7·7)		(6·4)		(5·8)		(4·6)	
England and Wales as in Table 38	27	26	27	23	31	20	36	14	39	10	41	9

For source and notes see note 118
*regions with a low percentage of completions for local authorities and New Towns, as in Table 46
L: flats, etc. in buildings of 2–4 storeys
H: flats, etc. in buildings of 5 or more storeys

TABLE 48 (summary of Tables 47a and 47b): Regional variations in building, by storey height. Dwellings in tenders
approved (gross) for local authorities and New Towns,
1966-71

per cent of all approvals for local authorities and New
Towns; 1966-71 combined

| Region | Houses and bungalows % | Flats in bldgs of storey ht | | | | All dwgs |
		2-4 %	5-14 %	15+ %	5+ %	000s
Gtr London*	15	39	31	15	46	147·7
Northern	69	20	7	4	11	67·8
Yorks and Humberside	49	34	10	7	17	78·3
North-West	47	32	14	7	21	121·4
West Midlands	58	25	9	8	17	92·2
Wales	68	30	2	1	3	40·6
South-East**						
Beds, Ess, Herts	61	30	4	6	10	43·1
S-E counties	54	39	6	1	7	35·5
S counties	66	29	4	1	5	50·5
East Midlands	54	34	8	4	12	47·9
East Anglia	72	25	2	0·3	3	27·2
South-West	68	30	2	1	3	40·7
All England and Wales	50	32	12	7	19	
Outside Gtr London	57	30	8	5	13	

For source see Tables 47a and 47b
* see Table 47a
**see Table 47b

More precisely, several sub-groups are apparent in
these tables. The obvious dominance of Greater London in
the provision of flats of all kinds needs no comment at
this point. Elsewhere, tenders for blocks of 5 storeys or
more were most numerous in the North-West. In Yorkshire
and Humberside and the West Midlands tenders for high-rise
have also been prominent. These two regions differ, however, in that the trend has been towards more low-rise in
the former and more houses in the latter. The overall
pattern for the Northern region resembles that for Wales
(which in turn is identical to that for the South-West).
But again, over the years, the element of high-rise building has been consistently larger in the North, and that of
low-rise in Wales.

Within the second group of regions the East Midlands
and counties in the South-East closest to London are
characterised by the variety of building types, including
in each case, a smaller percentage of houses than is shown
for either Wales, the Northern region or the West Midlands. By contrast, in East Anglia, the Southern counties
and the South-West, where completions for local authorities have been relatively fewest and decreasing, the proportion of tenders for houses has been comparable and
high.

Throughout the period, and in most regions, there is
evidence of the increasing emphasis on low-rise construction and the decline in high-rise from 1967 onwards. By
weight of numbers, Greater London, the North-West and the
West Midlands contribute most to the national trends. Of
all the regions, however, it is only in the West Midlands
that the percentage of flats in local authority schemes
has decreased substantially over the years.

Considering the period as a whole, and assuming that
the majority of schemes represented here were carried
through as planned, it may be deduced that their total
effect, in most of the regions outside Greater London,
will have been to increase the number of local authority
flats, over the 1966 estimates in Table 45, by at least 50
per cent. In the East Midlands their number will have
doubled, while in the South-West, where the percentage of
flats recorded for 1966 was already fairly high, the increase will have been around 30 per cent. In Greater
London, the increment will still have been considerable
and of the order of 40 per cent.

The imprint of changes in this period and throughout
the whole era of intensified flat construction on the
housing stocks of some individual authorities will be the
final topic in this chapter. It remains to note here that
the broad regional distribution of local authority flats,

and the balance between low- and high-rise, may very
generally be explained in socio-economic terms. It reflects the degree of urbanisation, the density of population, the age and condition of existing housing stocks,
the urgency of replacement, the availability of land for
public housing, the location of New Towns, and, especially
in the Northern region and in Wales, the nature of the
terrain and the limitations imposed on high building by
the danger of subsidence - to mention some of the most
obvious factors.

But the regions are, to a certain extent, statistical
artefacts. As units of analysis, they are too large and
heterogeneous to depict the implications of the spate of
flat construction for the housing of families in those
urban areas where the choices that are open, both to the
occupiers and to the providers of public housing, may be
limited.

SOME LOCAL PATTERNS

For this purpose, a full-scale analysis for all housing
authorities was impracticable and unnecessary. Attention
is now directed, therefore, to the county and London
boroughs, relying entirely on data supplied by some or all
of them to the (then) Institute of Municipal Treasurers
and Accountants, and available in the Institute's publications. (119)

Retaining the regional framework, Table 49 shows the
distribution of the county and London boroughs according
to the percentage of flats in their public housing stocks
in early 1971. The individual authorities are listed,
with the percentage of flats in each case, in Appendix B.

One complicating factor must be mentioned here. Many
of the Inner London boroughs and some of the county
boroughs, notably Birmingham, own a number of dwellings,
other than those built under the Housing Acts, including,
for example, properties acquired prior to slum clearance.
The amount of such housing, as given in the IMTA returns,
is shown in Appendix B for Greater London, in those cases
where it comprises 10 per cent or more of the current
stock of dwellings. Elsewhere, figures of this magnitude
(at most 10 per cent) were found only in Birmingham,
Bristol and Leeds.

These 'other dwellings' affect the analysis in two
ways. Where, as in Inner London, they represent a size-
able part of all public housing, the percentage of flats,
as shown in Table 49 and Appendix B, relates to the total
stock, and would be greater if based only on dwellings

TABLE 49   Flats in local authority housing, 1 April 1971. London authorities* and county boroughs**: regional summary

Region (see Table 47 for grouping)	Flats per cent of LA dwgs								No.of auths total
	<20	20+	30+	40+	50+	60+	70+	80+	
	number of auths								
Gtr London			1	7	12	7	1	5	33
(a)									
Northern	5	1	2	1					9
Yorks and Humberside	5	5	3						13
North-West	4	3	12	1	1				21
West Midlands	2	3	5	1					11
Wales	1	3							4
All group (a)	17	15	22	3	1				58
(b)									
South-East									
Beds, Ess, Herts		1	1						2
S-E counties		1	2	1					4
S counties		3		2					5
East Midlands	2	3							5
East Anglia		1	2						3
South-West		2	4						6
All group (b)	2	11	9	3					25
All England and Wales	19	26	32	13	13	7	1	5	116
Outside Gtr London	19	26	31	6	1				83
In Table 50				6	7	4		2	19
In Table 51									
(a)		1	11	1					13
(b)			2	2					4

For source see note 119 and for individual authorities see Appendix B
* includes London boroughs (except Hillingdon), City of
   London and GLC
**all county boroughs as at 1 April 1971

provided directly by the housing authority. The reader
who prefers to think on these terms can make the appropriate adjustments for the London boroughs from the data
in Appendix B. In the second place, in a more detailed
analysis for a selection of boroughs, to be discussed
later, the results have been modified where necessary, and
as explained in the notes to Tables 50 and 51.

To return to Table 49: Among all the authorities represented here, the median percentage of flats in local
authority housing stocks was, by 1971, somewhere between
30 and 40. But only one London borough (Bexley), as
against 40 per cent of the county boroughs, come within
this range. Indeed, in 40 per cent of boroughs in Greater
London, the percentage of flats was 60 or over. Overall,
the distributions for the two regional groupings employed
in the previous analysis, are broadly similar. But there
are differences among the regions and especially within
the first group.

County boroughs in the North-West form a distinctive
pattern. The majority here have at least 30 per cent of
flatted dwellings. By contrast, in the Northern region,
Yorkshire and Humberside, Wales and the East Midlands, returns for the majority of boroughs are below the 30 per
cent level. On the other hand, Salford, Southampton,
Liverpool, Tynemouth, Brighton, Portsmouth and Coventry
report at least 40 per cent of flats among their properties - a geographical scatter that belies the superficial
regional impression. For the ten largest county boroughs,
the results are as in Table D.

TABLE D

Rank order of total population in 1971		% flats	Region
1	Birmingham	34	West Midlands
2	Liverpool	44	North-West
3	Manchester	27	North-West
4	Sheffield	32	Yorks and Humberside
5	Leeds	36	Yorks and Humberside
6	Bristol	30	South-West
7	Teesside	13	Northern
8	Coventry	40	West Midlands
9	Nottingham	21	East Midlands
10	Bradford	32	Yorks and Humberside

The median incidence of flats is higher for this group

than for the whole collection of county boroughs. And, as
will be seen, in the majority of the 'top ten', by 1971
dwellings in the high blocks exceeded 10 per cent of all
public housing (see Appendix C). But a correlation of the
percentage of flats with population size, for all the
county boroughs, shows that size, in these terms, is no
distinguishing criterion. While one could suggest other
measures that might be more discriminating, in a statistical analysis of variation in the incidence of flats, it is
doubtful whether such a procedure would be of value, since
it would tend to preclude examination of the non-
quantifiable ingredients of local policy decisions. (120)
What may be concluded from this review is that a comprehensive study of the causes and the consequences of a high
degree of flat construction should ideally be cast nation-
wide, and that problems such as have been illustrated by
the Tyneside survey may be found even within those regions
where the situation appears, on aggregate, to be most
favourable.

Finally, in the IMTA series, dwellings are also distinguished according to the storey height of the whole building. By contrast to the previous information, however,
the coverage of authorities is incomplete. (121) In
Appendix C, and using all the data available in 1971,
county boroughs are classified according to the combina-
tion of dwellings in blocks of 3 or 4 storeys, and those
in buildings of 5 storeys or more. Flats in 2-storey
buildings are not included in the returns, but some idea
of their numbers may be obtained, if required, by comparing the results in Appendix C with the percentages of all
flats in Appendix B. Data for county boroughs where 10
per cent or more of all local authority dwellings were in
blocks of 5 storeys and over, are collated in Table 51.
The equivalent information available for some of the
London boroughs is shown in Table 50.

From this table, multi-rise local authority housing is
shown to be most prevalent within the area that is defined, for the presentation of data from the population
census, as the centre of the Greater London conurbation.
(122) These central areas, in London and in the provinces, include the administrative, commercial and cultural
'hub' of each urban complex. In such areas, and in central London most of all, where sites for residential development tend to be few and costly, one would expect to
find a relatively frequent use of high-rise building, that
is by arguments that were in vogue up to the mid-1960s.

It is interesting therefore to recall the high-density
schemes, with an emphasis on low-rise construction, in
Southwark, Islington and Lillington Gardens, Westminster,

TABLE 50   Local authority flats in some London boroughs in buildings of 3 or more storeys, March/April 1971

Borough	LA dwgs built Housing Acts in bldgs of storey ht			percentage of under in all LA dwgs	All households in all LA dwgs	in LA bldgs of storey ht		Total pop'n aged 0-4
	3-4	5+	3+				5+	
	1	2	3	4	5	6 (3+)	7	8
Westminster C	17	83	99·7	63	20·0	13	11	4·1
Islington C	35	64	98·5	92	28·7	25	17	7·6
Kensington and Chelsea C	36	55	90·9	87	7·7	6	4	4·5
Southwark C	46	41	86·8	69	50·7	30	14	7·3
Lambeth	45	38	83·0	62	30·8	16	7	7·8
Lewisham	47	29	76·8	69	34·8	18	8	7·7
Newham	42	27	69·2	84	29·6	17	7	8·3
Redbridge	44	12	56·1	92	15·6	8	2	6·8
Enfield	24	24	48·0	+	20·0	10	5	7·3
Barking	30	16	46·4	+	32·2	15	5	7·0
Merton	24	22	46·0	90	19·0	8	4	6·7
Sutton	26	18	44·6	+	19·7	9	4	7·5
Ealing	27	18	44·3	+	16·4	7	3	7·7
Richmond	32	8	40·4	+	13·2	5	1	6·4
Barnet	27	13	40·3	+	17·2	7	2	6·5
Hounslow	27	11	38·3	+	24·0	9	3	7·5
Bromley	25	8	32·8	+	18·3	6	1	7·3
Harrow	29	–	29·0	+	11·0	3	–	7·3
Havering	17	10	27·3	+	23·4	6	2	7·9

Sources: cols 1 to 4 see note 121
col. 4 + approx. 100%, or close enough not to affect 6 and 7
col. 5 h'hds renting from LA % of all private h'hds.   See note 123
col. 6: $(3)\times(5)/100$ or $(3)\times(4)\times(5)/100^2$
col. 7: $(2)\times(5)/100$ or $(2)\times(4)\times(5)/100^2$
col. 8 see note 123
C = whole or part in conurbation centre

TABLE 51   Local authority flats in some county boroughs in buildings of 3 or more storeys, March/April 1971

County borough (in order by region – see Appendix B)	percentage of									Total pop'n aged 0-4
	LA dwgs built under Housing Acts as at 31 March 1971 in bldgs of storeys			completed 1966-71 in bldgs of storeys			All h'hds in all LA dwgs	LA bldgs of storeys		
	3-4	5+	3+	3-4	5+	3+		3+	5+	
	1	2	3	4	5	6	7	8	9	10
Newcastle	19	16	35	9	36	45	41	14	6	6·7
Gateshead	9	13	22	12	12	24	42	9	6	8·0
Leeds	7	19	25	no data			39	9	7	7·8
Bradford	9	12	21	23	48	71	26	5	3	8·9
Sheffield	22	12	33	41	29	70	40	13	5	7·8
Liverpool	20	19	39	20	55	75	36	14	7	7·6
Birkenhead	18	14	32	no data			30	10	4	8·5
Rochdale	9	15	24	35	36	71	34	8	5	8·8
Blackburn	8	15	24	1	45	46	25	6	4	8·8
Wigan	9	15	24	24	37	61	39	10	6	9·4
Manchester	16	10	26	21	33	54	36	9	3	8·0
Warley	12	19	31	no data			44	13	8	8·5
Wolver-hampton	7	10	17	no data			44	8	4	8·9
Southend	12	13	26	no data			12	3	2	6·3
Brighton	20	18	38	no data			20	8	3	6·3
Portsmouth	25	11	36	29	40	69	20	7	2	6·9
Bristol	10	13	22	29	70	99	31	6	4	7·2

Sources: cols 1 to 6   see notes 121 and 129
col. 7   see note 123
col. 8: $(3) \times (7)/100$ with adjustment for Leeds
col. 9: $(2) \times (7)/100$ and Bristol, where cols
1 to 3 refer to 90 per cent
of the total housing stock
col. 10   see note 123

for these boroughs are all at the centre of the conurbation. Nevertheless, in 1971, Westminster and Islington still had the highest complement of local authority properties in blocks of 5 storeys and over, that is among all the areas for which data were available for that time.

Considering potential housing 'stress', it may be more appropriate to adopt the GLC's classification, which distinguishes boroughs in inner London (group A) from those in outer London (group B). Of those boroughs where, according to Appendix B, flats comprised 55 per cent or more of local authority dwellings in 1971, all except Greenwich, Richmond, Ealing, Redbridge and Brent were in group A. And, within group A, only in the borough of Haringey was the percentage of flats smaller than this.

The distribution, given in Table 49 for Greater London, divides as in Table E for the inner and outer areas, omitting here, as before, the outer London borough of Hillingdon for which there was no information, and, by contrast to Table 49, building for the City of London and the GLC.

TABLE E

London boroughs	Number of authorities with flats per cent of LA dwellings:						All auths
	30+	40+	50+	60+	70+	80+	
Inner			4	5	1	4	14
Outer	1	7	7	2			17
All	1	7	11	7	1	4	31

Thus, by 1971, discounting Bexley in outer London and the county borough of Salford, fewer than half the authorities, even in outer London, had percentages of flats that compared with those in the top 'tail' of the distribution for the county boroughs.

Of the areas shown in Table 50, the inner London boroughs include Lewisham and Newham, besides those in the conurbation centre. And all of these have distinctly more dwellings in structures exceeding 2 storeys than the remaining authorities.

Richard Minns has studied the housing records of the London boroughs in their first term of office, 1965-8, when the majority were under Labour control, and 1968-71, during which time most councils were Conservative. (124) He found the evidence inconclusive regarding the influence

of political ideology on the provision of new homes, or on
other aspects of local housing policy. (125) But the data
which he assembled for housing starts between April 1967
and March 1970, and between April 1970 and March 1973 are
of interest here.

In Greater London as a whole, housing starts in the
public sector were fewer in the second period than in the
first. But the relative decrease was smaller for the
inner than for the outer boroughs, as in Table F.

TABLE F

Housing authorities	Number of dwellings started		Change % of (i)
	April 1967–March 1970 (i)	April 1970–March 1973 (ii)	
Inner boroughs	35,821	30,472	-15
Outer boroughs	28,020	16,093	-43
All	63,841	46,565	-27

In other words, the inner boroughs increased their
share of housing starts from 56 per cent of the total, in
the first period, to nearly 70 per cent in the second.
Moreover, Westminster, Islington, Lambeth, Newham (all in
Table 50), with Hammersmith, actually started work on more
dwellings in the second period than in the first. The increase for the five boroughs combined was of the order of
40 per cent.

Recent low-rise, high-density schemes in Westminster
and Islington have been mentioned already. Moreover, in
Hammersmith, the newly-elected Conservative council, in
1968, announced its intention to build no more tower
blocks. (126) In 1970, and again in 1971, only 600 tenders were approved, in the whole of Greater London, for
dwellings in blocks of 15 storeys and over, although the
numbers for those in buildings of 5 to 14 storeys remained
high. (127) From Table 50, high-rise or medium-rise
dwellings comprised the greater part of the stock, as in
1971, of dwellings built by or for the central boroughs of
inner London - a situation that, even with the current
preference for low-rise construction, will be slow to
change.

By using the IMTA data for 1971, together with counts,
by household tenure, from the census of that year, it is
possible to estimate the percentage of all households, in

each borough, who were occupying local authority flats or maisonettes in buildings of 3 storeys or above. Column 6 of Table 50 shows that, in 1971, by this reckoning, 25 per cent of all households in Islington and 30 per cent in Southwark were housed in this way. Moreover, one household in six in Islington, and one in seven in Southwark was living in a local authority block of at least 5 storeys. (128)

From Table 51, the position in some of the major provincial towns may be compared with that in the London boroughs. Column 8 of the table suggests that for example, by 1971, as many as 14 per cent of all households in Newcastle and in Liverpool were renting a local authority flat or maisonette, in a building of at least 3 storeys. For Sheffield and Warley the estimates were almost as high. The number of flats in blocks of 3 or 4 storeys and those in the higher buildings, relative to the total stock of local authority dwellings at that time, is given in columns 1 to 3.. As shown in Appendix C, the county boroughs to which these data refer are those where high-rise dwellings comprised 10 per cent or more of the total housing stocks in early 1971.

The considerable amount of high- or lower-rise building among all dwellings completed in the previous five years, is illustrated for some of these authorities in columns 4 to 6. (129) Of the county boroughs in Table 51, only in Newcastle, Gateshead and Liverpool did the number of high-rise dwellings, by the criterion adopted here, exceed 10 per cent or more of the stock of public housing in 1966. And among the boroughs featured here, only in Gateshead had the percentage of high-rise actually fallen by 1971.

Table 51 also illustrates the extent of multi-rise building, by 1971, among the ten largest provincial towns. Of these 'top-ten' county boroughs for which the overall percentage of flats was given in Table D, all except Birmingham, Teesside, Coventry and Nottingham appear in the table. For all but Teesside, these data were not available for 1971. In Teesside, it appears from the Appendices that local authority flats were predominantly low-rise. In Birmingham, according to a report in 'The Times', there are now 28,000 flats in blocks of from 6 to 32 storeys - more it is said, than in any other authority, outside Greater London. (130)

The data, though incomplete, suffice to illustrate the volume of multi-rise accommodation in the housing stocks of local authorities in London, and in the provinces, by the beginning of the 1970s - a situation which the Department of the Environment has announced its intention to survey. (131) The current concern is not limited to the possible problems of young families in high-rise dwellings. It questions the suitability of both high- and low-rise dwellings as homes for young children. As mentioned at the outset this question prompted the review in this chapter of some of the reasons why flats became so distinctive a part of public housing in England and Wales in the last decade, and where they now appear to be most concentrated.

How many families with young children are renting local authority flats it is impossible to estimate. The data in the last columns of Tables 50 and 51 can give no clue. For Newcastle, more telling evidence, from the 1971 census, on the distribution of families with children of pre-school age is given in the next chapter. In general where, as in many London and county boroughs, the proportion of flats, whether low- or high-rise, appears to be considerable, the possible strains on local housing management cannot be denied.

Appendix B
Housing authorities in
Table 49

GREATER LONDON (see note 119 for source)

	%		%		%
Bexley	32	*Barnet	50	*Southwark	60(31)
		*Enfield	50	Camden	62(33)
*Bromley	40	Haringey	50(26)	*Newham	62(13)
Croydon	41	Kingston-upon-Thames	53	*Redbridge	65
*Havering	41			*Westminster	65(34)
*Harrow	42	*Barking	54	Brent	66(11)
*Hounslow	43	Greenwich	55	Hammersmith	68(25)
*Sutton	43	*Lambeth	55(36)		
*Merton	49(10)	*Richmond	55	Wandsworth	74(11)
		*Lewisham	56(29)		
		*Ealing	58	Hackney	82(14)
		Waltham Forest	58(14)	Tower Hamlets	82
				*Kensington and Chelsea	84(11)
	%			*Islington	88
also GLC	56				
City of London	96				

No information for Hillingdon
% : flats per cent of local authority dwellings, 1 April 1971
( ): dwellings classed as 'other', per cent of LA dwgs. These ( ) correspond to some or all of the dwellings classed as 'acquired, purchased or other'; they are shown here when such dwellings represent 10 per cent or more of the LA's housing stock, as at 1 April 1971
*see also Table 50, for analysis, by storey height, of dwellings built under the Housing Acts

COUNTY BOROUGHS (see note 119 for source)

Northern	%	Yorks & Humberside	%	North-West	%		%
+Carlisle	11	Barnsley	7	+Warrington	11	Bury	34
+Teesside	13	+Doncaster	15	+Southport	12	+Wallasey	34
+Hartlepool	14	Rotherham	16	St Helens	15	Oldham	34
+Darlington	14	+Kingston-upon-Hull	16	Barrow	16	Stockport	36
+S.Shields	17	+Dewsbury	17	+Burnley	21	*Birkenhead	39
+Sunderland	26	+Wakefield	21	Bolton	26	*Liverpool	44
*Gateshead	34	Huddersfield	23	*Manchester	27	Salford	58
*Newcastle	36	+York	25	Preston	31		
+Tynemouth	44	Grimsby	25	*Wigan	31		
		Halifax	25	+Chester	31		
Wales	%	*Sheffield	32	*Blackburn	31		
+Merthyr Tydfil	13	*Bradford	32	*Rochdale	32		
+Swansea	20	*Leeds	36	+Bootle	33		
+Cardiff	20			+Blackpool	33		
+Newport	24						

West Midlands	%		%	E Midlands	%	E Anglia	%
+Stoke	13	*Wolverhampton	30	Derby	11	+Ipswich	21
+Solihull	19	*Warley	32	+Leicester	16	+Norwich	36
+Dudley	20	+Burton	32	Nottingham	21	+Great Yarmouth	38
Walsall	22	W.Bromwich	33	Northampton	22		
Worcester	26	Birmingham	34	Lincoln	25		
		Coventry	40				

South-East (outside Greater London)

Beds, Essex, Herts	%	S-E counties	%	S counties	%
+Luton	22	Canterbury	23	+Bournemouth	26
*Southend	35	+Eastbourne	31	Oxford	27
		+Hastings	39	+Reading	28
		*Brighton	44	*Portsmouth	41
				Southampton	49

South-West

	%
Torbay	24
+Gloucester	28
*Bristol	30
Bath	30
Exeter	30
Plymouth	35

%: flats per cent of LA dwellings, 1 April 1971
+see also Appendix C   } for analysis by
*see also Appendix C and Table 51 } storey height

Appendix C
Low-rise/high rise grouping for some county boroughs, April 1971

% OF LOCAL AUTHORITY DWELLINGS IN BUILDINGS OF:

3–4 storeys	0–5%	5 storeys and over		
		5–10%	10–15%	15% and over
0 – 5%	Carlisle Darlington Dewsbury Warrington Southport *Stoke	*Kingston-upon-Hull Wakefield Burnley *Swansea		
5 – 10%	Hartlepool S. Shields *Teesside+ Tynemouth++ Burton Solihull Cardiff Merthyr Tydfil Newport *Leicester Ipswich	*Sunderland Doncaster *Wolverhampton+ *Luton	Gateshead+ *Bradford+ Rochdale+ Wigan+ *Bristol+	*Leeds+ Blackburn+
10 – 15%	York	Chester+ *Dudley	*Southend+	*Warley+

included, with Wolverhampton in Table 51

179

3-4 storeys	5 storeys and over			
	0-5%	5-10%	10-15%	15% and over
15 - 20%	*Blackpool[+] *Bournemouth Gt Yarmouth[+] Norwich[+] Gloucester	Bootle[+] Wallasey[+] Hastings[+] *Reading	*Birkenhead[+] *Manchester	*Newcastle[+] *Liverpool[++]
20 - 25%			*Sheffield[+] *Portsmouth[++]	*Brighton[++]
25%+	*Eastbourne			

included, with Wolver-
hampton in Table 51

Source: see note 121
* among the 37 largest county boroughs, ranked by population size
[+] flats, of all elevation, 30-40% of all LA dwellings
[++] flats, of all elevation, 40% and over of all LA
  dwellings

Part three

Play and other measures for the under-fives

9   Play and other measures for the under-fives

POLICIES AND PROVISION FOR THE UNDER-FIVES

The general conclusions of the Tyneside survey and the implications, for young families, of the presence of so many flats in the current stock of local authority housing can best be appreciated against the background of recent innovations in policy for the under-fives.

The record of educational provision for this age-group, up to the time of the Plowden report and the inception of the EPA and Urban Aid programmes, has been thoroughly documented by, for example, Blackstone and van der Eyken. (1) Following the Plowden recommendations, both the report of the Seebohm Committee and the conclusions from the EPA research have reinforced the case for an extension of nursery education, and for priority to be given to the needs of children living in areas that were deemed to be in some way socially deprived. (2)

In 1972, the White Paper 'Education, A Framework for Expansion' lifted the restrictions that, for over ten years, had limited the growth of nursery education. The Minister introduced a programme of action whose aim was to ensure that 'within the next 10 years, nursery education should become available, without charge, within the limits of demand estimated by Plowden, to those children of 3 and 4 whose parents wish(ed) them to benefit from it'. (3) But the White Paper and the later circular to local education authorities represented a more complex directive than the expansion of schooling for the under-fives. Both documents recognised the distinctive role of the playgroup movement alongside a growing system of nursery education. Thus, local education authorities were encouraged to consult with their social service departments as to the most effective means of bringing the playgroups, and the energies of their voluntary organisers and helpers, within a comprehensive service. (4)

The number of playgroups, along with similar private ventures for the under-fives, had increased rapidly during
the 1960s. The Pre-School Playgroups Association was
founded at the beginning of the decade, after the government had dispelled any hope of meeting the recommendations, for this age-group, that had been part of the 1944
Education Act. (5) Circular 8/60 informed local authorities that no sanction could be given to the expansion of
nursery education, mainly because all available teachers
were needed for work with older children. A petition,
signed by 3,000 mothers of children under five, was sent
to the Minister of Education, asking that the decision be
reconsidered. (6) The protest failed, and, as parents and
other helpers organised themselves to cater for the children, the Pre-School Playgroups Association was founded as
a means of encouragement, advice and support. (7)

Although the playgroup movement derived its early mo-
mentum from the desire to compensate for the paucity of
facilities for nursery education, the two types of provision represent, according to Halsey, two contrasting
traditions of pre-schooling. (8) Moreover, there was a
class difference in their fields of application. For the
idea of playgroups took hold more rapidly, though not exclusively, among the middle classes. (A notable exception
to this was the work of the Save the Children Fund.) On
the other hand, such limited growth of nursery education
as was achieved in the early days gave priority to the
needs of children in the poorer working-class areas. (9)
From Blackstone's analysis, the differences between these
two streams of development are reminiscent of the contrasting influence, on nineteenth-century society, of
Froebel and of Robert Owen. (10)

From the inception of the Urban Aid programme in 1968
(and probably for some time to come in view of current
economic stringencies), a policy of positive discrimination has channelled resources for nursery schools and
playgroups alike into areas of special social need. For
such areas primarily, Halsey, following Plowden, has advocated the 'nursery centre', in which, with the nursery
school as main focus, all the various local services for
the under-fives would be linked together. (11) Nevertheless, from the national and local data in Tables 57 and
58, the class differential between the two streams described above is still evident. As Blackstone maintains,
it is unlikely to be removed altogether until nursery education without charge becomes available for all. (12)
Moreover, the move towards a unified system has revealed

certain conflicts between the main associations represent-
ing the two streams. (13)   A practical problem is presented by the desire to ensure that those engaged in any
formal service for the under-fives shall be professionally
qualified, and at the same time to retain the degree of
parental involvement on which the playgroup movement has
largely depended. (14)

But to describe the two lines of development in terms
of nursery schools and playgroups is to oversimplify. For
there are a number of provisions to be distinguished under
each heading. 'A tangled web of largely unrelated services, with further components supplied by private enter-
prise and charity', is van der Eyken's description of the
range of developments to 1967. (15) Those that feature
separately in the statistics will be defined presently.
(16) It remains here to bring measures for children's recreation close to home within this general framework.

Holme and Massie have discussed in detail both the
theoretical basis of interest in children's play and the
history of the provision of play facilities for children
of all age-groups, in this country, to the end of the
1960s. (17) In 1973, the Department of the Environment
published the results of a large-scale survey of children
at play. One outcome of this study was a circular to
local authorities stipulating the allowance for equipped
play space that should be made in future housing schemes.
(18) These recommendations were an improvement on those
that had been made in 1967 but they were inferior, in some
respects, to those in the Parker-Morris report. (19)

It would be quite wrong to suggest that attention to
play facilities for the under-fives will be unnecessary
when nursery groups, playgroups, or the like are available
for all. The Plowden Committee emphasised that nursery
groups should accompany, not replace, play-centres and
other amenities that cater for children all the year
round. (20) Following Seebohm, the social services departments of local authorities were to bear the responsibility for 'out of school' activities for the under-fives.
It was also recommended that supervised play for this age-
group should be considered alongside similar arrangements
for older children. (21)

A study of social planning in new communities, i.e. new
towns and other new areas besides, has drawn attention to
the 'administrative lacuna of children's play, which can
be legitimately ignored by education departments, housing
departments, planning departments and parks departments'.
(22) The new structure of local government presents an
opportunity for tackling the problems of liaison between
the various departments, and for enlisting the help of

voluntary agencies and helpers, not least the parents
themselves.

It seems likely that the principle of positive discrimination in favour of the disadvantaged will continue to give
priority, in the provision of nursery facilities, to areas
which, by various criteria, are judged to have special
claims. (23) This being so, there is a call for a further
index of need with regard to children's play, namely the
percentage of young children living in flats of all kinds,
certainly those in buildings of 3 storeys or more. Holme
and Massie included the incidence of high-rise housing in
their set of criteria for 'play priority areas'. (24)
Both the EPA report and Circular 2/73 on nursery education
recommended that the definition of social need should be
widened so as to reflect the deprivation that can exist in
new housing estates, as well as in the inner city areas.
(25) The findings in Part one of this study and the arguments in Part two lend support to the contention that
living off the ground, whether in high- or low-rise, can
be problematic for young children and those responsible
for their care.

The recent situation in Newcastle, seen against the
background of changes in the country as a whole, will put
some flesh on this skeletal framework.

Table 52 shows how households with children under 5 were
distributed among the wards of Newcastle CB at the time of
the 1971 census. (26) The wards are ranked, for the most
part, according to the percentage of such households among
all those with one member present on the census date.
Wards in the top section of the table, namely those where
the percentage of households with pre-school children are
above the city average, are all characterised by a high
incidence of households renting from private landlords, or
from the local authority, or by a predominance of both
forms of tenure. Figure 2 shows a further distinction.
For households with all their children of pre-school age
are most prevalent in those parts of the inner city known
respectively as the west and east ends. Highest of all,
in this respect, are Benwell, which is the site of a Community Development Project, Armstrong and Stephenson,
whose common boundary is straddled by the Cruddas Park
estate, and Elswick, which lies behind them at the crest
of the rise from the river. (27) In the east end, St
Anthony's and St Lawrence come within this group, while
Byker, which adjoins them, has rather fewer young families, since many have been moved already to other parts of
the city, or beyond, as was the case for the Longbenton

TABLE 52 Households with children aged 0-4 in Newcastle, 1971

Ward as in Figure 2	H'hlds with children aged under 15							H'hlds renting from		All h'hlds (%=100)
	0-4s only			0-4s & 5-14s	0-4s all		5-14s only	pt l'd	LA	
	1 no.	2+ no.	all %	no.	no.	%	%	%	%	no.
Benwell	242	162	13	310	714	23	14	52*	28	3,044
Stephenson	104	68	10	215	387	22	16	47*	40	1,735
Armstrong	170	121	10	239	530	19	14	39*	58*	2,848
St Lawrence	207	99	9	250	556	16	16	48*	43*	3,370
St Anthony's	236	131	9	287	654	16	14	40*	52*	3,999
Elswick	208	98	9	220	526	15	12	53*	13	3,524
Scotswood	187	117	7	415	719	17	18*	18	54*	4,124
Kenton	271	212	4	600	1,083	16	25*	3	69*	6,596
Walker	190	128	7	425	743	16	21*	7	88*	4,717
Walker Gate	240	125	8	303	668	14	19*	17	32	4,707
Blakelaw	133	114	5	423	670	13	20*	10	77*	4,849
Byker	90	53	8	96	239	13	10	41*	53*	1,802
Sandyford	204	87	8	212	503	13	11	49*	21	3,895
Westgate	174	86	8	147	407	13	13	56*	34	3,197
Arthur's Hill	144	92	7	264	500	13	16	30	20	3,825
Heaton	216	118	5	232	566	12	13	45*	9	4,777
Fenham	170	79	4	296	545	10	18*	10	44*	5,763
Dene	132	53	4	202	387	8	18*	12	33	4,807
Jesmond	196	91	5	182	469	8	8	60*	1	5,955
St Nicholas	38	15	5	35	88	8	10	26	72*	1,165
All (thousands)	3.6	2.0	7	5.4	11.0	14	16	30	42	78.7

Source: tabulations from 1971 Census small-area data.
wards above solid line: above CB average for % of h'holds with 0-4s
wards above broken line: also above CB average for % of h'holds with 0-4s only

*above average for whole CB

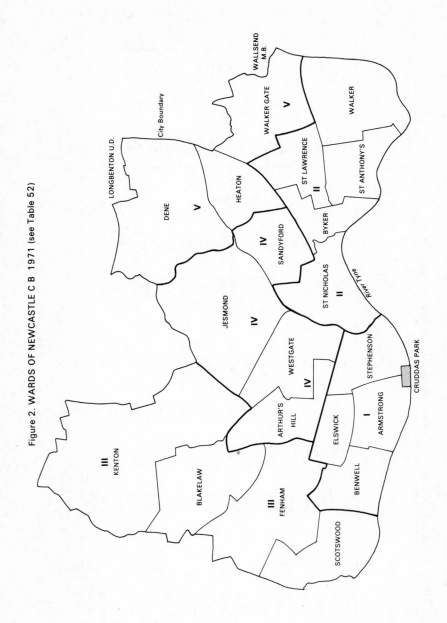

Figure 2. WARDS OF NEWCASTLE C B 1971 (see Table 52)

families included in Part one. (28) Both these parts of
the city are the site of past or prospective schemes of
local authority housing. There has been much redevelopment already and other areas are due for clearance or
revitalisation.

Scotswood and Kenton, in the west, and Walker in the
east, include the site of more established local authority
housing estates. Families here are larger, on average,
than elsewhere in the city and older children form a
higher proportion of the population.

The analysis shows, as one would expect, that families
with pre-school children tend to be most concentrated in
those areas where much of the responsibility for housing,
currently or in the future, rests with the local authority. The Council's interest in the provision of nursery
and other services for the under-fives, here and elsewhere
in the city, may serve to illustrate the general developments outlined earlier in the chapter. (29) But first it
is necessary to consider more precisely the record for
some of these services in England and Wales as a whole.

The statistical evidence in Tables 53-5 looks straightforward enough. But, ever since the Plowden and Seebohm
Committees estimated the percentage of the under-fives in
the country as a whole, for whom some provision was
notionally available, commentators have produced variations on these estimates, drawing attention to the am-
biguities, confusion of definition and omissions in the
data on which the calculations were based. (30) The distinction, for instance, between educational and other
facilities (as in Table 55 parts a and b), is not clear-
cut. Neither is the independent provision wholly devoid,
in all cases, of support from Exchequer funds. Moreover,
certain apparent increases are inflated by changes in the
rules governing registration, which have brought more establishments than hitherto to the notice of the appropriate department. (31)

The statistics presented here have been compiled from
those published by the Department of Education and Science
and the Department of Health and Social Security or the
equivalent, in each case, for the earlier years. It is
inappropriate, for this purpose, to repeat the debate
about these sources, or to enter into further discussion
of the ideological basis of each form of provision. The
following notes, with the references, should enable the
reader to obtain, from these data, a fair assessment of
the total known provision in early 1972 and to appreciate
both the enormous expansion that is implied by the new
national targets, and the local record, to be considered
presently, within Newcastle CB.

TABLE 53   Children aged 2-4 at school in England and Wales

		number on registers at January of:				
		1964	1966	1968	1970	1972
NURSERY SCHOOLS						
LA maintained	f	20,083	19,125	17,626	16,138	15,167
	p	6,184	9,044	12,716	17,779	23,998
Direct grant	f	578	515	432	458	384
	p	446	280	343	398	433
Independent recognised	f	220	193	174	189	162
	p	101	128	284	309	377
Independent other	f	1,797	1,408	1,094	1,092	1,131
	p	1,981	1,776	1,675	1,514	1,751
All nursery schools	f	22,678	21,241	19,326	17,877	16,844
	p	8,712	11,228	15,019	20,000	26,559
OTHER SCHOOLS						
LA maintained	*f	182,351	197,829	209,953	228,292	263,895
	p	.	.	16,857	28,520	48,257
Direct grant	f	240	282	270	219	225
	p	.	.	192	266	178
Independent recognised	f	4,332	4,906	4,649	5,514	5,792
	p	.	.	3,350	3,488	3,699
Independent other	f	11,279	11,980	11,194	10,324	9,412
	p	.	.	8,994	8,385	7,407
All other schools	f	198,202	214,997	226,066	244,349	279,324
	p	16,300	21,000	29,393	40,659	59,541
*include 'rising fives' (thousands):			134	141		162
Popn (thousands)						
	2-4	2,229	2,426	2,527	2,476	2,356
	0-4	4,009	4,168	4,155	4,007	3,920

Sources: see note 32
f: full-time
p: part-time

TABLE 54   Children aged 2-4 at school in England and Wales by age and by type of school, January 1972

		Number of children aged:			
		2 yrs	3 yrs	4 yrs	2-4 yrs
NURSERY SCHOOLS					
LA maintained	f	685	6,322	8,160	15,167
	p	1,112	12,486	10,400	23,998
Direct grant	f	20	174	190	384
	p	19	184	230	433
Independent	f	33	396	864	1,293
	p	155	989	984	2,128
All nursery schools	f	738	6,892	9,214	16,844
	p	1,286	13,659	11,614	26,559
OTHER SCHOOLS					
LA maintained	f	185	9,926	253,784*	263,895*
	p	371	17,708	30,178	48,257
Direct grant	f	-	2	223	225
	p	-	2	176	178
Independent	f	213	2,332	12,659	15,204
	p	599	4,403	6,104	11,106
All other schools	f	398	12,260	266,666*	279,324*
	p	970	22,113	36,458	59,541
All schools	f	1,136	19,152	275,880*	296,168*
	p	2,256	35,772	48,072	86,100
*include 161,806 'rising fives'					
Popn (thousands)		773	791	792	2,356

Source: see note 33
f: full-time
p: part-time

TABLE 55   Provision for the under-fives in England and Wales

(a) in day nurseries, private nurseries, with child-minders, etc.

	number of places (thousands), as at:					
	December			1969	March 1972 E & W	E only
	1963	1965	1967			
Day nurseries LA	21·7	21·4	21·2	21·1	23	f 23
Private (regd) Nurseries, etc.	31·0	54·9	109·1	203·1	296	{ f 23 p 262
Child-minders, etc.	20est.	25est.	42·7	70·5	90	{ f 55 p 33
All places	73est.	101est.	173	295	409	{ f 101 p 295

(b) in nursery and other schools

		number of pupils (thousands), aged 2-4 incl. at January				
		1964	1966	1968	1970	1972
Nursery schools LA	f	20·1	19·1	17·6	16·1	15·2
	p	6·2	9·0	12·7	17·8	24·0
other	f	2·6	2·1	1·7	1·7	1·7
	p	2·5	2·2	2·3	2·2	2·6
Other schools	f	198·2	215·0	226·1	244·3	279·3
	p	16·3	21·0	29·4	40·7	59·5
All pupils	f	221	236	245	262	296
	p	25	32	44	61	86
All places and pupils		319	369	462	618	791
Popn (thous.) aged 2-4		2,229	2,426	2,527	2,476	2,356
aged 0-4		4,009	4,168	4,155	4,007	3,920 – March 1971

Sources: see notes 44 and 32 and Table 53
f: full-time   p: part-time

Among the educational services, featured in Tables 53, 54 and 55b, nursery schools are separate establishments that are mainly intended for children under 5 years of age. (34) Other schools' provision for this age-group includes some nursery classes, each of which usually occupies a separate room within or annexed to a primary school. Each nursery school or class has at least one member of staff with an appropriate teaching qualification. Children aged under 3 are not generally admitted. Attendance may be full- or part-time. The number of 4-year-olds in 'other schools' is inflated by the presence of the 'rising fives', that is children who, where places are available, are admitted to infants' classes in maintained primary schools in advance of, but usually close to their fifth birthday. Local education authorities vary in their emphasis on full- or part-time nursery education, and in their policy regarding the 'rising fives'. The fact that these options are not always separated clearly, if at all, in the published figures, has given rise to much of the controversy over estimates of the national level of provision for this age-group. (35)

Both nursery and other schools are classified by the manner in which they are financed, and hence, by whether or not a charge is made for attendance. Maintained schools are financed by local education authorities, partly from local rates and partly from general grants from the Department of the Environment (formerly Ministry of Housing and Local Government). Direct grant schools are assisted from central government funds. All places in the former and many in the latter are free of charge. Maintained and direct grant schools are sometimes combined under the heading of 'grant-aided'. Independent nursery and other schools, being privately-run establishments, usually charge for attendance. Those in the tables, whether or not they are recognised as efficient, have been registered with the Department of Education and Science (or Ministry of Education), since they have a certain complement of pupils of compulsory school age. (36)

In Tables 53 and 54, pupils attending part-time have been separated out, wherever possible, from the published figures. (37) Several points may be made from these data with reference to the expansion already achieved through Urban Aid, and the wider plans that were introduced in early 1973. The widespread curtailment, in 1975, of the plans to expand a range of local authority services, including those for the under-fives, enhances the urgency of the message of this chapter. The analysis as presented here speaks for itself.

The proportion of children, aged 2-4, who were

receiving full or part-time schooling, remained at between
10 and 11 per cent until 1968 and increased thereafter to
just over 16 per cent in 1972. However, of those at
school, some 50 per cent to 1968 and 42 per cent in 1972
were 'rising fives'. If these are discounted, then, even
in 1972, the proportion at school was below 10 per cent of
all those aged 2-4. More pertinently, from Table 54, they
comprised under 1 per cent of 2-year-olds, some 7 per cent
of 3-year-olds and either 40 per cent or 20 per cent of 4-
year-olds, according to whether the 'rising fives' are included or omitted. These calculations include children in
direct grant and independent schools, but these are relatively few. The targets of maintained places for 50 per
cent of 3-year-olds and 90 per cent of 4-year-olds seem
remote, even though it is possible that the total numbers
in these age-groups will decline. (38)

Another aspect of policy that may be illustrated from
the table is the increasing emphasis on part-time schooling. In the maintained nursery schools, the ratio of
full-time to part-time provision has been inverted from
1968. The number of under-fives attending other maintained schools part-time has trebled between 1968 and
1972. In 1964 and 1965 a limited expansion of nursery
education was sanctioned by addenda to Circular 8/60. (39)
Local authorities who could comply with the requirements
for expanding their nursery programme were specifically
asked to consider the possibility of increasing the number
of part-time places, reserving full-time attendance for
children with special needs. (40) Both under the Urban
Aid programme, and in recent plans, the emphasis on part-
time attendance has been maintained. The 1973 White Paper
estimated the ultimate demand largely in these terms,
namely part-time nursery education for 35 per cent of 3-
year-olds and 75 per cent of 4-year-olds, leaving full-
time places for only 15 per cent of children in each
group. (41) Part-time, in this context, usually means
half-time, that is five mornings or afternoons a week.
The question of the children's opportunities for play outside school hours therefore remains important.

It is possible to take the analysis a stage further, in
the maintained sector. Circular 2/73 referred most of all
to places in nursery schools and in nursery classes attached to primary schools. Local authorities were in-
structed to plan, wherever possible, in terms of nursery
classes, because of the likely saving in building costs
and the further possibility that, in some areas, as the
primary school population declined, premises at primary
schools might become available for the use of the under-
fives. (42) Separate figures for nursery classes are not

given for every year. But the picture for 1972 can be pieced together from the notes to the published tables. (43)

TABLE 56   Children aged 2-4 in local authority maintained schools in England and Wales

Type of schooling	January 1972 (nearest thousand)		Changes since January 1971 (nearest hundred)	
	f-t	p-t	f-t	p-t
Nursery schools	15,000	24,000	−100	+ 3,300
Nursery classes	31,000	43,000	+500	+ 9,300
Both	46,000	67,000	+400	+12,500
Primary schools 'rising fives' others	162,000 71,000	− 5,000 }	+ 18,500 {	− + 1,500
All LA maintained schools	279,000	72,000	+ 18,900	+14,000

Table 56 depicts the situation at the start of the new expansion programme. The greatest proportionate increase over the previous year was in part-time places, and in all sectors. The increase in full-time attendance was largely due to the growing number of authorities admitting the rising fives to their primary schools. More recent changes may be expressed in these terms as the data become available. It is pertinent to note here that in 1972 only 5 per cent (113/2356) of children aged 2-4 were having the benefit of separate nursery education, in maintained nursery school or class.

Table 55a covers a still more varied set of services for the under-fives. These are not explicitly educational in the formal sense. Responsibility for them now rests, at central government level, with the Department of Health and Social Security (formerly Ministry of Health), and locally with social service departments. (44)

Day nurseries are a legacy of the war years, when they were set up to release mothers for work. Under section 22 of the National Health Service Act of 1946, responsibility for these establishments was lodged with local health authorities, or with voluntary bodies acting as agents for them. (45) Many day nurseries closed soon after the war, but some have remained to provide for children who, for

various reasons, are in special need of care during the
day. Though a small charge is made for attendance, waiting lists tend to be long. Children may be admitted from
as early as 6 months up to 5 years. Attention is given
most of all to their physical care and the staff are
qualified accordingly.

The number of day nurseries was halved during the
1950s, and has changed relatively little in the following
decade. In 1968 funds for expansion became available
under the first phase of the Urban Programme, and so,
since 1969, both nurseries and places have become slightly
more numerous. The Plowden Committee considered that the
day nursery was the proper place for children under 3
years of age who needed to be away from home during the
day, but that the more direct educational aims of the nursery school (or class) were appropriate for children aged
3 or 4. In fact, the committee advocated a unified system
of children's centres that would include nursery schools
(and classes), day nurseries and clinics. (46) Some
recent innovations for pre-school children are in line
with these ideas, for, under the Urban Programme, approval
has been given to expenditure in some areas, on combined
day nurseries and nursery schools. (47)

The other items in Table 55a include a wide range of
services, such as crèches on factory premises, private
nursery schools, exclusively for the under-fives, private
nurseries, playgroups, whether run by voluntary bodies or
by individuals, and arrangements for minding children,
during the day in private homes. (48) Playgroups may be
counted with private nurseries, if they are held in a hall
or on similar premises, or with child-minders if they meet
in the organiser's home. (49) Nurseries and child-minders
take children from a very early age. Most playgroups, on
the other hand, prefer not to admit them before the age of
2 or 3. (50)

The private services in Table 55a refer only to those
that were registered under the Nurseries and Child-Minders
Regulation Act. The Act was amended in 1968, following an
inquiry which suggested that local authorities did not
have the necessary powers to ensure reasonable standards
in private day-care. (51) By the new legislation, local
authorities' powers of control were increased. At the
same time, two official circulars gave guidance on the
application of the Act, and on the standards of care that
should be regarded as appropriate for this age-group. (52)
One immediate result of the new legislation was a sharp
rise in the number of both registered premises and persons. It was reported for 1969 that 50 per cent of the
increase in the former and 80 per cent of the rise in the

latter in the past year could be explained in these terms.
(53)

In 1973, Brian Jackson, director of the Child-Minding
Research Unit, argued that these measures had been intended to 'scaffold a framework for the admirable growth of
the pre-school playgroup movement, by ensuring minimal
physical standards for the care of middle-class children'.
One side-effect, he claimed, had been 'to drive still
further into the social jungle the vast army of illegal
child-minders', with some of whom children of working
mothers were left for long hours each day, in inadequate,
even distressing conditions. (54) Many of these persons
could not register, since, for example, their housing was
old and poor in quality and did not meet the Act's requirements for safety. (55) According to Jackson, illegal
child-minders have been ignored by many local authorities
and regarded with compassion by relatively few. (56) Current estimates suggest that they outnumber their registered counterparts by 14 to 1. (57) The number of children
in their care is put as high as 300,000, more than five
times the estimated 57,000 with registered minders.

The resort to child-minders, registered or not, has
grown along with the tendency for more mothers of young
children to go out to work. (58) Some local authorities
have started courses for their registered child-minders.
The Research unit is piloting schemes more directly to
assist the illegal minders and to encourage local authorities to change their approach to them. (59)

The provision in Table 55a falls considerably short of
the actual use of day services for the under-fives.
Nevertheless it is clear that, if the rising fives are
omitted from the numbers at school, the greater part of
the known (that is registered) pre-school provision in the
five years or so to 1972, was organised by private individuals or voluntary agencies. Some local authorities,
where accommodation in day nurseries is insufficient,
place children with special needs in private nurseries or
playgroups. (60) A stronger indication of the value of
these non-statutory services is the degree to which they
have been assisted from central government funds. (61) In
1972, substantial grants were made to three national organisations for the development of playgroups, especially
in the more needy areas. The Pre-School Playgroup Association, for example, with such assistance and with growing
public support, was able to report that the number of
places available has increased from 170,000 in 1970 to
over 250,000 in 1973. (62)

Still, in early 1972, all the places in Table 55a represented 1 in 6 of 2 to 4-year-olds, or more

realistically, 1 in 10 of all children under 5. Moreover,
attendance was mostly part-time, which usually meant for
fewer hours each week than was the case for part-time nursery schooling. Without labouring the national statistics
any further, it needs little imagination to appreciate
that, even when all these statutory and voluntary services
are extended, the task of ensuring that pre-school children have adequate opportunities for play in their spare
time will still be vast.

It is true that official provision for children's
leisure is unlikely to be needed, and may be unwelcome, in
areas where housing and the range of local amenities are
of a high standard or even just adequate. But, on the
evidence of the Newcastle data in Table 52 and a substantial literature on ecological variations in family size
and structure, it is reasonable to conclude that it is the
more restricted, or generally less favoured environments
that have the larger share of families with young children. (63) Moreover, these areas have been the most
poorly endowed with formal services, for the under-fives,
although in recent years the policy of positive discrimination has begun to redress the imbalance. There is evidence, both from the Plowden report and from van der
Eyken's analysis, that, in the late 1960s, the distribution of nursery schools among the regions and between individual local authorities could not be aligned with the
distribution of potential need. (64) And it has commonly
been supposed that the playgroup movement, with its re-
liance on private initiatives, has benefited middle-class
rather than working-class children. (65)

Table 57, which is based on the General Household
Survey, shows that, in 1971, slightly more of the children
attending playgroups than of those in nursery schools came
from homes where the head of the household was in non-
manual employment. (66) The difference, while rather too
small to support generalisations with a tolerable risk of
error, is probably understated, since day nurseries have
been grouped with playgroups and independent schools with
nursery schools. The data give stronger evidence of a
class difference, in these occupational terms, between the
children who were attending one or other of these establishments and those who were not. Put another way, while
19 per cent of all the under-fives in the 1971 sample were
at day nursery, playgroup, nursery school, etc., the proportion was 27 per cent for those of non-manual parents
and 14 per cent for the rest. An advance tabulation of
the survey findings for 1972 suggests that, in the intervening year, the prospects of nursery schooling had improved rather more for working-class children than for

TABLE 57   Occupational grouping of fathers of children under 5, England and Wales, 1971

Occupational category	At nursery school incl independent school for under-fives	At day nursery or playgroup	All others under 5	All children under 5
	%	%	%	%
NON-MANUAL				
Professional	8 ⎱	12 ⎱	5 ⎱	6
Employers and managers	23 ⎬ 48	17 ⎬ 52	12 ⎬ 32	14
Intermediate and junior non-manual	18 ⎰	23 ⎰	15 ⎰	16
MANUAL				
Skilled	33 ⎱	30 ⎱	44 ⎱	41
Semi-skilled	10 ⎬ 46	10 ⎬ 42	14 ⎬ 62	14
Unskilled	3 ⎰	2 ⎰	4 ⎰	4
OTHERS*	6	6	6	6
All	100	100	100	100
Number of children in sample	186	291	2,062	2,527

Source: General Household Survey 1971, note 66
*includes those not looking for paid employment;   Armed
 Forces are excluded

others. (67) The only (statistically) significant difference in the results for the two years is the rise in
attendance from 12 to 18 per cent among children whose
fathers (or household heads) were semi-skilled or
unskilled.

The effects of recent policy may be illustrated more
clearly at local level. Table 58 gives the distribution
of places in maintained nursery schools and classes, day
nurseries, registered private nurseries and playgroups
within parts of Newcastle CB. (68) The combinations of
wards, as in 1971, to which the areas refer, are shown in
Figure 2. (69) The analysis is based on the number of
places available in premises located in each area, not on
the home addresses of the children who attended. But the

TABLE 58   Geographical distribution of places in nursery schools and other services for the under-fives in Newcastle CB by end of 1973

Type of service	Area (as in Figure 2)					All
	I	II	III	IV	V	
	number of places*					
Nursery schools	250 (160)	80 (80)	–	–	–	330 (240)
Nursery classes	30 (30)	210 (180)	180 (120)	–	30	450 (330)
Day nurseries	50	100	50	50	–	250
Other nurseries and playgroups (regd)	130	70	201	341	132	874
All	460	460	431	391	162	1,904**
No. of children under 5 (thousands) in 1971	2·96	3·13	4·14	2·58	2·23	15·04
Places per 100 children	15	15	11	15	7	13
Play schemes	Number of schemes					
regular	3	4	7	4	–	18
summer	4	3	5	–	–	12
Households	% of all households in 1971					
with children under 5	19	15	14	11	11	14
tenants of:						
LA	33	63	61	14	24	41
private landlord	49	30	10	50	12	30
owner occupiers	18	7	29	36	64	28

Sources: see notes 68–74
* ( ) Urban Aid
**there were, too, approx. 2,000 others in primary school

two distributions are likely to be closer in terms of these large areas than they would be if individual wards were used. (70)

The areas are not entirely homogeneous, as comparison

with the tenure figures for separate wards, in Table 52,
will show. In area II, for instance, Walker and St
Nicholas have percentages of local authority tenants
similar to those in the wards to the west in area III.
But the grouping is realistic, given the location of the
various nursery schools, etc. and their potential catch-
ment areas. The data on tenure and population structure
have been compiled from the 1971 census. (71) The main
information has been assembled from council documents
which were considered shortly before, or immediately
after, Newcastle CB became part of a metropolitan district
of the new County of Tyne and Wear. The data here apply
only to projects that had been completed by the end of
1973. (72) Lists of nurseries and playgroups registered
under the Nurseries and Child-Minders Regulation Act were
supplied by the social service department. (73) Places
for the under-fives in primary schools are not included,
except for those in maintained nursery classes. In the
city, children are admitted to nursery schools from the
age of two, and to nursery classes from the age of three.
They may start at primary schools if their fifth birthday
falls at any time within the school year. In January 1973
there were 2,173 children under five at maintained primary
schools. The total includes nursery class children and
the rising fives. The number at maintained nursery
schools increased from 83 in January 1970 to 244 in
January 1973. (74)

Table 58 shows that the majority of places in maintained nursery schools and classes have been provided through
the Urban Aid programme. New nursery classes have been
associated with schools already granted EPA status. (75)
Prior to reorganisation, the education committee recommended that these measures for children and schools in deprived areas should be expanded, and that attention should
also be given to improvements in playgroups, playspace and
play schemes, to the work of playgroup advisers and to the
efforts of voluntary societies. (76)

The social service committee recorded its intention to
seek the help, in this regard, of the city's many voluntary associations and trusts and to offer in return all
possible encouragement and support. (77) In 1974 the department employed four playgroup therapists. Some measure
of assistance to the establishment of playgroups in more
needy areas is illustrated by the number of places recorded in area I.

Overall, of the items included in Table 58, while 70
per cent of maintained places, including all of those in
nursery schools, were in areas I and II, almost 40 per
cent of those in private establishments were in area IV,

where privately owned or rented housing was most prevalent, and which included, in Jesmond, a large professional
element in the population.

TABLE 59   Newcastle CB (end of 1973):   geographical distribution of places and of children under 5

area (as Table 58)
places, etc. per cent of total

Type of establishment	I %	II %	III %	IV %	V %	%	All no.
Statutory	32	38	22	5	3	100	1,030
Other	15	8	23	39	15	100	874
All places	24	24	23	21	8	100	1,904
Children under 5 (1971)	20	21	28	17	15	100	15,000
Places per 100 children under 5	15	15	11	15	7		13

Despite the recent progress and the plans for expansion, there are still no places of any kind for the great
majority of children.   In the inner areas, the question of
informal facilities for play remains important.   Evidence
of official provision is limited to the number of regular
(that is evening) and summer play schemes. (78)   In recent
years, the object of these schemes has been to provide
supervised, constructive activities for children, largely
from deprived areas.   They have been run, in many cases,
with the co-operation of voluntary organisations.   While
they are mainly intended for children of school age,
younger children may attend in most cases.   For this age-
group, however, they hardly begin to meet the need for a
continuous and day-time service.

Other interests, that could not be analysed in this
way, include those of the recreation committee in the organisation of adventure playgrounds and in the employment
of playleaders.   Both these items have been supported by
the Urban Programme.

The picture that has been drawn for Newcastle, while
inevitably crude and incomplete, conveys some idea of the
record of an authority that is sympathetic to the needs of
its young children, and whose organisation allows for co-
operation, both between the various departments that have
an interest in this matter, and with outside helpers.

The purpose of the whole discussion so far has been to
dispel any notion that the provision of play facilities
for the under-fives is a comparatively trivial matter. On
the national and local evidence, this is clearly not so.
Nor is the need for such provision likely to diminish
within the near future. Moreover, it must be stressed
that the adequacy of play arrangements, especially for
young children in multi-storey homes, whether high- or
low-rise, turns not so much on the amount of play space
per child as on the guarantee of supervision, however informal and unobtrusive. In this matter local needs must
be locally determined, and, in seeking both to assess and
to meet them, the involvement of parents and other voluntary helpers would seem to be essential.

LEGISLATION FOR PLAY

Legislation for play in this country has not received the
attention that has been accorded to it, for example, in
many countries of Western Europe. It is possible to list
around thirty Acts of Parliament, from 1859 onwards,
whereby facilities for children's recreation may be assisted from public funds. But the powers conveyed to local
authorities, by these measures, have been permissive
rather than mandatory. (79) Since the provision for recreation can involve several local departments, and since
other claims on local resources are often pressing, the
improvement of this particular local amenity has tended to
be rated as low priority.

   In Western Europe, Denmark's record is among the most
outstanding, not just for the origin of the adventure
playground, but also for the far-sighted legislation that
now applies to all building authorities. Requirements for
children's play were the subject of special clauses written into the 1939 City of Copenhagen Building Act. The
successful implementation of the Act and its survival
through years of war and austerity, have had results 'out
of all proportion to the simplicity of the original measures'. (80) Private play-spaces, mostly for pre-school
children, within safe and easy access from their homes,
are as common a feature of the environment as the more
public recreation areas or the popular adventure playgrounds. Now, for instance, mothers in flats can be confident that their children will have somewhere safe to
play. Local amenities can be improved by the transforma-
tion of unused or derelict sites.

   In this country, interest in the opportunities for
play, especially for the under-fives, has increased, in

the last decade or so, and has been augmented by the current concern about the widespread use of flats in public
housing schemes. (81)   Legislation for play in new housing
areas has been restricted, however, to recommendations for
the amount of space.   Only recently has any reference been
made to equipment.   The Parker-Morris report suggested
that, in local authority housing estates, space should be
allowed for children's recreation on the basis of 20-25
square feet per resident, excluding those in single or
two-person households, and that a certain expenditure
should be allocated to the surfacing and equipment of each
play area.   These standards were modified for inclusion in
Circular 36/67, whereby local authorities were recommended
to work on the basis of 15-20 square feet per bedspace, or
to a minimum ratio of 10 square feet, where, for example,
existing playgrounds were readily accessible in the immediate vicinity. (82)   These standards were superseded,
in 1972, by a circular to local authorities that followed
the Department of the Environment's study of children at
play.   For all schemes, regardless of their population
density, the new measures allow for a range of areas, with
minimum standards of equipment, according to the number of
child-bedspaces.   A special yardstick allowance is available to meet the extra expenditure involved. (83)

In practice, of course, standards of provision for play
vary between authorities.   Moreover, some financial help
for improvements or innovations in smaller areas of special need has been available through the Urban Aid
programme. (84)

In terms of general policy, the GLC is distinctive for
the importance that is attached to play facilities in new
schemes and on the older estates. (85)   In the former
case, space and facilities for unsupervised play are provided at least to the level recommended by Circular 79/72
and usually to the original more detailed standards of the
Parker-Morris committee.   The Council's general policy
goes further than the amount of space and equipment.   It
is sensitive to the needs of different age-groups, and,
for the under-fives, extends to support for playgroups,
play-schemes, and for the 'one-o-clock' clubs which have
evoked considerable interest elsewhere. (86)

The report of a survey of playground facilities in the
London borough of Lewisham re-emphasised the Parker-Morris
conclusions that the establishment of minimum standards of
space and equipment for play only begins to meet the problem, adding that the quality, allocation and accessibility
of play areas together with arrangements for caretaking,
management and supervision are at least as important as
space alone. (87)   As mentioned in Chapter 2, Hole and

Miller drew attention to these other aspects and to the need for variety of provision, especially for the younger children. (88)

For the under-fives, the most urgent need at present is to ensure that each child is able to play freely and safely in the place where he lives. Clearly this will not be served, in the short term, by legislation for more sophisticated standards to be applied in future housing projects. (89) It calls rather for measures that would require each local authority to initiate a review of the present situation, in areas where play is likely to be restricted, with the prospect of Exchequer support towards the cost of any schemes that result.

It is therefore suggested that each local authority should be asked, first of all, to convene a working group, in order to identify the areas where children's play is restricted, or hazardous. In some authorities, such groups may already have been formed in relation to formal services for pre-school children. Some authorities may have identified play-priority areas within the Urban Aid programme. (90) If such knowledge of potentially difficult areas does not already exist, it would seem desirable that the local councillors and members of voluntary organisations, with detailed local knowledge, should share in these initial discussions. But once the areas are chosen, it is important that, in each case, the parents of young children, other local residents, councillors and voluntary workers should be invited to share, with the appropriate officials, in drawing up a plan of action. (91) Though the needs of young children living in flats are likely to have first claim, it will not always be practicable to treat them as a distinct group. (92) Moreover, any discussion of play for the under-fives should be related to plans for nursery schooling and other forms of day-care. (93)

In the final sections, rather than combine the Tyneside findings with the various recommendations that have been made in other studies, some more general comments will be made with reference to the kind of procedure that has just been advocated.

COMMUNITY AND FAMILY NEEDS

The Seebohm report recommended that local social services should be geared to the needs of the community and that provision for children should be based on the circumstances of the family, and especially those of the mother. (94)

The community

The use of this term in the context of social planning may
entail an element of wistfulness or idealisation of
reality. (95) The implicit assumption, in this context,
is that those who share a common space or territory are
likely to hold certain interests in common, and to be
united by a sense of belonging. The Tyneside survey gave
little evidence of this. (96)

On the Cruddas Park estate social divisions among the
residents had built up over the years. For mothers in
the high flats, the block, rather than the estate was
the dominant social unit.

In Longbenton mothers felt more attached to the
inner area from which they had moved.

In Wallsend there was no sense of community at all.

In the case of Cruddas Park, if positive steps had been
taken to involve mothers from all parts of the estate in
help with activities for the children, some of the
barriers might have been broken down. In general, active
measures such as those that are envisaged here to improve
facilities for young children, can help to foster community spirit by appealing to a latent common interest.
The record of the playgroup movement gives evidence of
this, as do the examples of ventures in community education that have been part of the Educational Priority
action programme. (97)

For practical purposes, in this context, it is sufficient to recognise that these various parts of the
survey illustrate some contrasting environments that may
each require a different approach. (98)

Thus, Cruddas Park was a clearly demarcated inner-urban
estate of medium-high density.

The Longbenton families occupied part of a much
larger overspill development.

In Wallsend, the high and 4-storey flats were part
of a smaller estate on the fringe of the borough. Also
in Wallsend, the lower flats and maisonettes were scattered units, the latter in the older part of the town.

In Gateshead, the high blocks were separated from
each other by roads, shops and older property.

In each of the first three cases, the estate itself
could provide the basis for the discussion of children's
play. Elsewhere, blocks of the size of those in Gateshead, if children were still present, could be viable as
separate units. But in situations like those of the lower
flats and maisonettes in Wallsend, the recreational needs
of children in multi-storey housing could scarcely be considered apart from those of their neighbours in other

types of dwelling. It is likely that play-priority areas
would include some with a similar variety of building and
of tenure. (99)

Some of the main results varied more consistently by type
of dwelling than by type of locality. Some of these
relate to aspects of housing management and maintenance,
some to patterns of children's play, some to mothers' reactions to their situation. They have been fully discussed in Part one and some will be just mentioned here.
(100)

Management and maintenance

high flats	danger from windows, lifts, bal-conies, storage for coal and for prams
lower flats and maisonettes	danger from landings, stairs, bal-conies, problems of children's noise (exacerbated by the allocation of young families to the upper floors)
lower flats maisonettes and houses	dangers from traffic on estate or neighbourhood roads

Children's play

all multi-storey dwellings	importance of the 'threshold' as a place for informal play
high flats	similar patterns of use (and lack of use) of outdoor play-spaces; impor-tance of special areas for the under-fives, with seats where the mothers could watch their children and enjoy some company themselves
lower flats maisonettes and houses	tendency for children to play in the street

(In all dwellings mothers expressed their appreciation
of public open spaces where these were available.)

Mothers' reactions

high flats	adverse reactions associated with concern for their children
lower flats and maisonettes	dissatisfaction related to the strains of their own situation - e.g. lack of privacy, problems with neighbours

The mothers' circumstances

It has been argued that plans for nursery and related
facilities should be sensitive to the circumstances of the
mothers, as well as to their children's needs. This would
also apply to the arrangements for play in the children's
free time. Certain distinctive groups of mothers were
identified, on Tyneside, as follows:

Working mothers

The differences between Cruddas Park and Gateshead were
interesting in their context and a reminder that 'working mothers' are not a homogeneous group. (101) At the
time of the survey, arrangements for day-care were few
and little used. Now, however, the situation may be
different. When nursery centres are developed, for instance, children of mothers who have to work may spend
part of their day in nursery school, and the rest of
the mother's working time with childminders or in playgroups. This is not to say that such children will
have no further needs for play. And the improvement of
local opportunities may benefit childminders and playgroup leaders also. (102)

Mothers with more than one child under 5

These mothers were generally most vocal about their
problems, most worried about the effects of flat life
on their children and most forthcoming with suggestions
for improvement. The Seebohm report also singled them
out as having special needs. (103)

Mothers with just one child under 5

Within this group, the comparative newcomers in some
areas had special problems. (104) In general, where
the local authority is actually moving young families
out of flats, those with just one youngster may become
more isolated, being low on the transfer list. Their
special needs, if temporary, should not be overlooked.

The individual

Despite the similarities that have emerged, mothers'
views were seldom unanimous. Their differing assessment of their own responsibilities for their children's
care were evident in several contexts. (105) Opportunities should be provided for mothers to express
their own opinions.

A CASE FOR PARTICIPATION

The Labour Party has declared its resolve to 'encourage local authorities in a diversity of neighbourhood or community consultation'. (106) P.J. Dixon, who was Newcastle's Housing Manager when the Tyneside survey was being made, has recently expressed his support for a more advanced notion of participation, namely that future tenants should be involved in the design of their homes. (107) And it is not at all fanciful to regard the local amenities for leisure as part of home. He went on to mention the provision of play space among the topics for which consultation with current tenants would be especially appropriate. Holme and Massie have argued that, in developing a policy for play, local authorities should make sure that local residents are involved before decisions are made, rather than adhere to the old-style procedure of imposing facilities with no consultation. (108) If the government is to go along with the proposal that young families in flats, for whom no houses are available, should be compensated in some way, then it seems desirable that the families concerned should be invited to air their views, and to do so in public discussion, not by means of a questionnaire or interview with a council official. (109) In Newcastle, housing decisions regarding improvement or revitalisation are sensitive to the wishes of residents and to the differing responses evoked from one small area to another. (110) It would not be impracticable for such a localised procedure to be followed for children's play.

THE VOLUNTARY ORGANISATIONS

It has been seen already that services for the under-fives have depended substantially on voluntary effort. (111) In the present context, the role of the voluntary organisations with other lay helpers would be indispensable and catalytic. (112) This would involve them, for example, in publicising the venture especially among mothers with particular needs, in helping parents overcome any reluctance to articulate their own opinions, in organising volunteers from among the parents to help with any scheme that might be proposed, and in supplying workers from their own organisation to man more ambitious projects, such as a mobile playground, or 'playmobile'. (113)

Local authorities are sometimes better able to provide space and equipment than manpower. For the voluntary organisations the reverse may be the case. In short, a

process which, on paper, seems cumbersome and formal could
be enlivened by such intervention.

SUPERVISION

There is an undeniable need among the under-fives, especially those living in flats, for opportunities for supervised play out of doors and indoors. (114) The possibili-
ties will depend on local resources of manpower and space,
and for example on whether indoor accommodation, such as a
room on the ground floor of a block, can be set aside for
this purpose. Various options recur in the literature.
(115) Rather than list them here, it is tempting,
finally, to note that the supervision of children's play
space provides a schematic and practical way of linking
the general facilities for play with the playgroups, and
thence with the local constellation of provision, in
which it is hoped that the whole run of services for the
under-fives will eventually be co-ordinated. (116)

Notes

CHAPTER 1 BACKGROUND TO THE SURVEY

1 See Chapter 2 for references to the main studies that were available at the time, and some more recent ones.
2 See Chapter 8 and pp.175-6 for the extension of this concern to young children in lower flats and maisonettes.
3 Ministry of Housing and Local Government (MHLG), 'Families Living at High Density', unpublished report, 1963, see Chapter 2, p.13.
4 W.G. Bor, Deputy Planning Officer, LCC: remark at conference of the Town Planning Institute, 1960.
5 MHLG, 'Flats and Houses' (HMSO, London, 1958).
6 T. Burgess, Pre-School Education, 'New Society', no. 231, 2 March 1967.
7 J. Vaizey, 'Education for Tomorrow' (Penguin, Harmondsworth, 1962), p.36.
8 See pp.183ff.
9 Rt Hon. Henry Brooke in MHLG, 'Living in Flats' (HMSO, London, 1952).
10 The lack of consistency, in various parts of this book, in the definition of a 'high-rise' building and a 'high level' within such a building, will be apparent. It is partly due to the use of sources which employ different criteria. For instance, in the choice of Tyneside authorities, only those with build- ings of more than 5 storeys were included. The reason for this is now obscure. In Chapter 8, following the groupings used in certain series of official statis- tics, 5 storeys and over is classed as 'high-rise' (and see V. Hole, Housing in Social Research in E. Gittus ed., 'Key Variables in Social Research', vol.1 (Heinemann, London, 1972), p.60). It is also shown above in Chapter 8, pp.143ff, that, from 1956 to 1967,

extra subsidies were provided, under the Housing Subsidies Act of 1956, for each storey-height above the
6th.

   In the analysis of the survey data, families in the
high flats were classified according to whether they
were housed above the 5th floor, or lower. This was
done in order to compare with the results of the
London survey by J. Maizels (see Chapter 2, n.8).

11   Institute of Municipal Treasurers and Accountants
   (IMTA), 'Housing Statistics, 1965-66' (London, 1967).

CHAPTER 2   THE EVIDENCE AT THE TIME

1   For a critical and comparative review of 23 studies to
   1970, see J. Darke and R. Darke, 'Health and Environment: High Flats', University Working Paper 10
   (Centre for Environmental Studies, London, 1970). The
   most comprehensive studies, published since 1970, and
   to which reference is made in the notes to the chapter
   are: P. Jephcott with H. Robinson, 'Homes in High
   Flats' (Oliver & Boyd, Edinburgh, 1971); Department
   of the Environment (DOE), 'The Estate Outside the
   Dwelling', Design Bulletin 25 (HMSO, London, 1972);
   DOE, 'Children at Play', Design Bulletin 27 (HMSO,
   London, 1973).

2   See for example reference in 'The Times', 7 August
   1968, to Coventry's decision to build no more multi-
   storey blocks, and comment in 'The Times', 8 August
   1968.

3   A recent official circular to local authorities sets
   out new recommendations for equipped outdoor space for
   unsupervised play on future public housing schemes,
   with financial provision to meet the extra costs. See
   DOE Circular 79/72 and Welsh Office Circular 165/72
   (HMSO, London, August 1972).

4   N. Taylor, Flat Rejections, 'Sunday Times', 26
   November 1967.

5   Cf. Chapter 7, pp.88-91.

6   See Chapter 8, n.97 for a review of current building
   styles and their social implications.

7   Cf. DOE Design Bulletin 25 (n.1), where the
   attitude of respondents to the general design of the
   estate was found to be important.

8   J. Maizels, 'Two to Five in High Flats' (The Housing
   Centre, London, S.W.1, 1961).

9   Ibid., p.6.

10   As the survey was not based on a strictly random
   sample, formal statistical generalisations for this

whole age-group could not be made.

11 See Chapter 9, p.204 for some aspects of current policy in the Greater London area.

12 Cf. p.46.

13 See e.g. pp.14 and 88-91.

14 London School of Economics, 'Survey of Families Living High in New Blocks of Flats', interim report in Maizels, op. cit., pp.33f and pp.91-100 above.

15 Cf. pp.15-16 and 100.

16 p.16. The recognition of some of these factors was fundamental to the content and analysis of the Tyneside survey. See also Darke and Darke, op. cit., pp. 29, 30.

17 See Chapter 6.

18 MHLG, 'Families Living at High Density' (mimeo, 1963); and J. Ash, 'Families Living at High Density', 'Official Architecture and Planning', vol.29, 1966, pp.68-71; also MHLG, 'Families Living at High Density: A Study of Three Central Estates in Liverpool, Leeds and London', Design Bulletin 21 (HMSO, London, 1970). The references here are to the 1963 or 1966 publications.

19 Estate 'A' was in Liverpool and 'B' in Leeds.

20 The implicit assumption here has been called the 'phase hypothesis' in R.N. Morris and J. Mogey, 'The Sociology of Housing' (Routledge & Kegan Paul, London, 1965), pp.41-4ff.

21 See n.7 above.

22 See pp.88-91.

23 See Chapter 4.

24 See Chapter 6, pp.63-74, for discussion of these activities.

25 National Swedish Committee for Building Research, 'Effects of High Buildings on Families with Small Children', Report no.38, 1958, and see pp.69-72 above.

26 Cf. p.100.

27 See pp.109-13.

28 See n.7 above.

29 Cf. p.116, where 7/104 respondents in high flats are said to have experienced no problems at all - but for a variety of reasons.

30 Ash, op. cit., p.71.

31 W.V. Hole and A. Miller, Children's Play on Housing Estates, A Summary of Two B.R.S. Studies, 'Architects' Journal', vol.143, 1966.

32 Cf. DOE, op. cit., 1973.

33 See pp.65-8 and 74-5.

34 See pp.91-4.

35 See Chapter 9, p.204 with references also to DOE,

op. cit., 1973 and to A. Holme and P. Massie,
'Children's Play, A Study of Needs and Opportunities'
(Michael Joseph, London, 1970).

36   See various notes above.
37   Subsequently published as Jephcott with Robinson, op.
     cit.
38   A. Stevenson, E. Martin and J. O'Neill, 'High Living'
     (Melbourne University Press, 1967).
39   Ibid., p.1.
40   Ibid., p.16.
41   Ibid., p.144.
42   Ibid., p.135.

CHAPTER 3   THE SURVEY DESIGN

1   K. Mannheim, 'Ideology and Utopia', 1940, ref. in J.
    Rex, 'Key Problems of Sociological Theory' (Routledge
    & Kegan Paul, London, 1961), p.161.
2   Their names are given in the preface, with acknow-
    ledgment of their contribution to every stage of the
    research.
3   With the appreciated co-operation and advice of Mr P.
    Dixon, (then) Director of Housing for Newcastle CB,
    Mr J. Underwood, (then) Deputy Housing Manager for
    Gateshead CB, and Mr R. Taylor, (then) Head of the
    Housing Section for Wallsend MB.
4   See pp.14 and 16.
5   p.16.
6   See A.V. Cicourel, 'Method and Measurement in Socio-
    logy' (Free Press, London, 1964), p.79, where he
    states that the awareness of these commonsense cate-
    gories is vital to the effective use of interviewing.
7   Thanks are due to the Medical Officers of Health for
    Northumberland and for Newcastle CB for their co-
    operation.
8   Since the 'population' was so small, this was tech-
    nically a random sample with replacement. The number
    of distinct families to be visited was therefore
    rather smaller than the numbers given here, some being
    selected more than once.
9   See pp.12 and 15.
10 E. Mayo, 'The Social Problems of an Industrial Civili-
    zation' (Routledge & Kegan Paul, London, 1949), p.75,
    ref. in J. Madge, 'The Tools of Social Science'
    (Longmans, London, 1953), p.248.

CHAPTER 4 THE LOCAL SETTINGS

1 Since the survey was made, the completion of a new
road system has changed the centre of Gateshead, where
the interviews were conducted. In Newcastle, too,
there has been further redevelopment in the Cruddas
Park area. For stylistic convenience, past tense will
be used here in describing all the study areas, including those in Longbenton and Wallsend which are
little changed.
2 See p.14.
3 See pp.145-50 for construction costs and density of
the estate and Chapter 8, n.62, for T. Dan Smith's
eulogistic assessment of the plan.
4 See Figure 1.
5 Cf. n.2 and n.7 below.
6 Cf. Chapter 8, p.148 and n.61, where the density based
on approved plans for the construction of the various
parts of the estate, is estimated as 100-120 persons
per acre.
7 See Chapter 6, pp.65-7.
8 Victor Jupp reported on his visit as follows; an
adventure playground which was provided for 5- to 15-
year-olds by the Young Volunteer Force, in the summer
of 1969, in the neighbourhood Cambridge Street area,
attracted few children, if any, from those in the
Cruddas Park flats, by contrast to the greater interest shown by those in the maisonettes and houses.
Later, the Young Volunteer Force ran a similar scheme
on the adjoining Delaval estate, but the response from
Cruddas Park was small. The success of this venture
among the Delaval residents was attributed, by the
organisers, to the interest shown by the local
tenants' association. There was no such association
in Cruddas Park at the time, and without this unifying
organisation, the residents in Cruddas Park remained
apathetic to the scheme. The newly-formed Pre-School
Playgroups Association for Northumberland and Durham
was, by 1969, holding its meetings at the Cruddas Park
Community Centre. Yet no attempt had been made to organise playgroups on the estate, though the pre-school
population was still considerable. The warden of the
community centre remarked, at the time, that other
activities at the community centre seemed to attract
few of the residents from the high flats. Since then,
the Cruddas Park population has changed. Young families have been moving out from the flats and their
places taken by single persons and childless couples,
who often are more free and ready to share in

community activities. There is, for instance, a residents' association, with membership, according to
the warden, from all parts of the estate (and see, for
a review of the literature on these and other aspects
of participation, C.G. Pickvance, Voluntary Associations in E. Gittus ed., 'Key Variables in Social
Research', vol.2, forthcoming).

With regard to the earlier discouragements in
Cruddas Park it will be interesting to follow the
attempts of the organisers of the Community Development Project in Benwell immediately to the west of
Cruddas Park, to enhance the involvement of parents in
pre-school provision and in school events and activities (Benwell Community Project, Preliminary Report,
May 1973).

9   See pp.16-17.
10 See n.1.

CHAPTER 5   THE FAMILIES

1   N.B. Throughout the analysis of the survey results,
in this and later chapters, it is remembered that the
findings for the houses at Wallsend are based on a
sample amounting, finally, to 36/60 i.e. 3/5 of the
appropriate 'universe'. The nature of the universe is
so arbitrary, however, that the inclusion of sampling
errors for this group in each table would be un-
warranted. However, where the sample results differ
substantially from the rest, and where the contrast is
important to the argument, the margin of error due to
sampling has been allowed for before conclusions are
drawn. Amalgamation of this group with another, as in
Table 3b, is only made where the under-representation
of the Wallsend houses would have no distorting
effect.

2   For topics and items in the questionnaire, see sections A, B and part C, as on pp.25-6.

3   See p.42.

4   See pp.58-9.

5   Cf. Chapter 8, n.61, for the original specifications
of dwelling-size.

6   'Report of the Committee on Local Authority and Allied
Personal Services', Cmd 3703 (HMSO, London, 1968), pp.
60 and 220.

7   See p.11.

8   See p.15.

9   See Chapter 7, pp.88-91.

10 W.V. Hole and M.T. Pountney, 'Trends in Population

Housing and Occupancy Rates 1861-1961' (HMSO, London,
1971) Table 8, p.17 and K. Gales and P.H. Marks,
Twentieth Century Trends in the Work of Women in
England and Wales, 'Journal of the Royal Statistical
Society', Series A, vol.137(1), 1974, p.68.
11 See Chapter 6, p.69 and Chapter 7, p.82.
12 A. Stevenson, E. Martin and J. O'Neill, 'High Living'
(Melbourne University Press, 1967), pp.34-5.
13 See Table 4, p.43. One mother, in Cruddas Park, who
had lived there for all her married life, was omitted
from the cross-analysis with family structure.
14 See p.20.
15 J. Rex and R. Moore, 'Race, Community and Conflict'
(Oxford University Press, London, 1967). The theory
of housing classes has been much discussed and considerably elaborated since its introduction by Rex and
Moore. For a brief reference, see C. Filkin and D.
Weir, Locality in E. Gittus ed., 'Key Variables in
Social Research', vol.1 (Heinemann, London, 1972),
pp.112-14. The use of housing classes, here, has
deliberately been kept simple.
16 G. Popplestone, 'Reputation of Housing Areas in
Aberdeen', paper read to British Sociological Association Conference (Community Studies section), Reading,
1968.
17 See questionnaire, item 12f.
18 Time did not permit us to complement this study of
respondents' perceptions with an analysis of local
housing records.
19 See also Chapter 7, pp.109-15.
20 See Table 3, p.40 for the number of bedrooms.
21 See questionnaire, items 14b, c and 19.
22 See p.16.
23 See questionnaire, item 14b.
24 Elsewhere, when the response to this question was
'nowhere', the children concerned were under 2 years
old.
25 M. Willis, Private balconies in flats and maisonettes,
'Architects' Journal', 7 March 1957, vol.125.
26 Stevenson, Martin and O'Neill, op. cit., pp.64-5.
27 MHLG, 'Families Living at High Density' (mimeo), 1963,
p.63.
28 The numbers of families with prams (or push-chairs)
were slightly higher, in all areas, than the numbers
with a child of under 2 years old.

CHAPTER 6   THE UNDER-FIVES

1   See p.12.
2   See p.67.
3   See Chapter 5, p.42.
4   Neither was there any association, in Cruddas Park,
    between the use of the 'High Park' and the use of the
    estate playground (or its equivalent), or any sugges-
    tion that children went regularly to one rather than
    to the other.
5   See questionnaire, items 18 and 24.
6   See Chapter 9. It would have been more accurate to
    use 'day-care' rather than 'nursery' in this blanket
    designation. The latter term was considered to be
    more comprehensible to the respondents.
7   See Chapter 4, p.32 and n.8. See also Chapter 9 for
    later developments within Newcastle.
8   See Chapter 9, pp.197-8 and Table 58, p.200 for more
    recent estimates of the total provision nationally and
    locally.
9   It is interesting to note that, in Cruddas Park, 14/17
    who replied in this way also said that they had no
    difficulties in bringing up their children where they
    lived, although, when directly questioned about the
    local facilities for play they, like most respondents,
    had criticisms to make.
10 'Children and their Primary Schools', Central Advisory
    Council for Education, vol.1, Report (HMSO, London,
    1967), Chapter 9.
11 See Chapter 9, pp.183-97.
12 'Working Class Mothers and Pre-School Education' (East
    Newcastle Action Group, Newcastle, 1972).
13 P. Moss, J. Tizard and J. Crook, Families and Their
    Needs, 'New Society', 23 (546), 22 March 1973, pp.
    638-40.
14 See Chapter 2, p.12.
15 See questionnaire, item 23a, also Chapter 7, pp.98-100
    for comments on the risks incurred by children who
    played in these areas.
16 J. Maizels, 'Two to Five in High Flats' (The Housing
    Centre, London, S.W.1, 1961).
17 The answers to question 20b showed that 'neighbours'
    were not always regarded as those in the flats on the
    same landing, or in the houses next door. The answers
    reflected the pattern of the families' social con-
    tacts. The definition was left open to allow for
    this.
18 Children who were too young for active play are ex-
    cluded from the figures. Some children of course

played with siblings, or with other children older than themselves. But the question of isolation from the company of other unrelated children of the same age is of interest here.

CHAPTER 7   THE RESPONSE OF THE MOTHERS

1   See questionnaire, item 15.
2   Cf. p.48.
3   See questionnaire, item 16.
4   See questionnaire, item 27.
5   See p.71.
6   Cf. 'British Standard Code of Practice', C.P. 3, Ch. III, Sound Insulation and Noise Reduction, British Standards Institution, 1960.
7   See p.11.
8   See p.14.
9   A. Stevenson, E. Martin and J. O'Neill, 'High Living' (Melbourne University Press, 1967), pp.72-5.
10 See questionnaire, item 22.
11 See p.82.
12 See pp.54-7.
13 See questionnaire, item 23a.
14 Cf. Table 5, p.44.
15 Cf. V. Hole and A. Miller, Children's Play on Housing Estates, 'Architects' Journal', vol.143, 1966, pp. 1529-36, where a similar tendency was observed.
16 Ibid., p.1533.
17 See p.12, and Chapter 9, p.210.
18 Hole and Miller, op. cit.
19 See pp.67 and 74.
20 See pp.59-60.
21 'Journal' (Newcastle), 23 June 1967.
22 'Journal' (Newcastle), 29 August 1968.
23 'Evening Chronicle' (Newcastle), 6 July 1967.
24 'Spectrum' in 'Sunday Times', 19 May 1974.
25 'Journal' (Newcastle), 4 October 1968.
26 'Journal' (Newcastle), various reports in week commencing 15 July 1968.
27 See pp.76-7.
28 See pp.88-91.
29 See Chapter 4, n.8.
30 See questionnaire, items 29 and 30.
31 See pp.11 and 14.
32 See pp.81-2.
33 See p.57 and Table 34.
34 See p.89.
35 Cf. Table 35.

36   D.M. Fanning, Families in Flats, 'British Medical
     Journal', 1967, 4, pp.382-6.
37   See questionnaire, item 28.
38   See questionnaire, item 31.
39   Cf. pp.58-9, for discussion of the families' current
     use of their available space.
40   See p.107.
41   P. Townsend, Survey of Families Living High in New
     Blocks of Flats, interim report in J. Maizels, 'Two
     to Five in High Flats' (The Housing Centre, London,
     S.W.1, 1961).
42   MHLG, 'Families Living at High Density', 1963, p.19.
43   Stevenson, Martin and O'Neill, op. cit., pp.45, 137.
44   See Table 14, p.56.
45   Stevenson, Martin and O'Neill, op. cit., pp.36-7.
46   J. Rex, The Sociology of a Zone in Transition, in
     R.E. Pahl ed., 'Readings in Urban Sociology'
     (Pergamon Press, 1968), p.214.   J. Rex and R. Moore,
     'Race, Community and Conflict' (Oxford University
     Press, 1967).
47   See e.g. pp.54 and 86 above.
48   See p.107.
49   See questionnaire, item 32.
50   See pp.5-7 and 20-2.
51   See p.130.

CHAPTER 8   FLATS IN LOCAL AUTHORITY HOUSING: THE RECORD
OF THE 1960S

1   See for instance Tables 19, 22, 24, 25 and 32 and
    discussion.
2   'Children and their Primary Schools', Central Ad-
    visory Council for Education, vol.1, Report (HMSO,
    London, 1967).
3   A.H. Halsey ed., 'Educational Priority, Problems and
    Policies' (HMSO, London, 1972), Chapters 2 and 14.
4   See for instance T. Blackstone, 'A Fair Start' (Allen
    Lane, London, 1971), pp.72-3;   P. Jephcott, 'Homes in
    High Flats' (Oliver & Boyd, Edinburgh, 1971), Chapter
    9;   W. van der Eyken, 'The Pre-School Years' (Pen-
    guin, Harmondsworth, 1967), Chapter 4.
5   See especially sections dealing with noise, the
    various risks of accidents to young children while at
    play, and mothers' assessment of the effects, on
    themselves, of their present housing situation:
    Tables 27-32 and discussion.
6   See above pp.11-12, 16, and 21 for reasons for including
    them, Tables 19, 22, 24, 27-29, 31 and discussion,

for some matters that were of concern to them too.
7   Jephcott, op. cit.
8   H.A. Williams, 'True Resurrection' (Mitchell Beazley, London, 1972), p.66. For a sociological critique of the use of official statistics, see B. Hindess, 'The Use of Official Statistics in Sociology: A Critique of Positivism and Ethnomethodology' (Macmillan, London, 1973).
9   General Register Office (GRO) and Office of Population Censuses and Surveys (OPCS), 'Census of England and Wales: County Volumes', Durham and Northumberland, 1961, Tables 16 and 17, 1966, Table 9, 1971, Tables 19 and 20 – all include only households with at least one member present on census night.
10 Ibid., Table 2 and 'Registrar General's Statistical Review of England and Wales' for the census and intervening years.
11 V. Hole, 'A Study of Washington New Town', unpublished report for the Building Research Establishment, Dept of the Environment, 1973.
12 GRO, Census of England and Wales, 1966, 'Migration Summary Tables', Part II, Table 14B, for moves in the previous five years.
13 Cf. p.108.
14 P.A. Stone, 'Urban Development in Britain: Standards, Costs and Resources, 1964-2004', vol.1 Population Trends and Housing (Cambridge University Press, for National Institute of Economic and Social Research, 1970), p.286. In support of Stone, however, it must be noted that, whereas housing starts for local authorities, in the country as a whole, have fallen, the number of discretionary grants for the improvement of existing dwellings has increased. For notes on renovation v. replacement policies, see n. 105 below.
15 N. Dennis, Mass Housing and the Reformer's Myth, 'Planning Outlook', 6 (new series), Spring, 1969, p. 11.
16 P. Malpass, 'Professionalism in Architecture and the Design of Local Authority Houses', unpublished MA thesis (University of Newcastle upon Tyne, 1973), pp. 147-51.
17 See pp.85-8.
18 R. Jensen, 'High Density Living' (Whitefriars Press, London and Tonbridge, 1966), p.2.
19 Ibid., pp.2-5 and Malpass, op. cit., Chapter 3; A. Lipman, The Architectural Belief System and Social Behaviour, 'British Journal of Sociology', June 1969.
20 Jensen, op. cit., p.6.

21 Ibid., p.13.
22 R. Darke and J. Darke, Sheffield Revisited, 'Built
    Environment', November 1972, pp.558, 560.
23 J.B. Cullingworth, 'Town and Country Planning in
    Britain' (Allen & Unwin, London, 1964, 4th rev. ed.,
    1972), p.179.
24 GLC Development Plan, 'Statement and Report of
    Studies' (GLC, 1969), Chapter 8.
25 D.V. Donnison and D.C. Eversley eds, 'London, Urban
    Patterns, Problems and Policies' (Heinemann, London,
    1972), pp.42-3.
26 Van der Eyken, op. cit., pp.22-3.
27 Jephcott, op. cit., p.7.
28 Stone, op. cit., p.122.
29 MHLG, 'Housing Statistics, Great Britain' (HMSO,
    London), see under 'Notes and Definitions; 2, New
    Construction'. Reference also here to MHLG Circular
    76/65.
30 MHLG, 'Housing Statistics, Great Britain' (HMSO,
    London), (5) 1967 and DOE, 'Housing and Construction
    Statistics, Great Britain' (HMSO, London), (5) 1973.
    Note: Tables 39(a) and (b) include completions,
    starts and approvals for New Towns. Date of comple-
    tion: when dwellings were ready for occupation.
    Date of starts: when work began on laying the foun-
    dations. The time from start to completion was of
    the order of 12 months for houses, 17-19 months for
    flats, see e.g. 'Housing Statistics, Great Britain'
    (16) 1970, Table 5.
31 The Economic Planning Regions, as adopted in 1965,
    are as follows (see MHLG, op. cit., Notes and
    Definitions):
    Northern: Cumb., Durham, Northumb., Yorks N. Riding
    Yorks and Humberside: Lincs, Part of Lindsey, Yorks
                            E. and W. Ridings
    North-West: Cheshire, Lancs and High Peak of Derbys
    East Midlands: Derbys (rest), Leics, Lincs (part),
                    Northants, Notts, Rutland
    West Midlands: Heref, Salop, Staffs, Warwicks, Worcs
    East Anglia: Cambridgeshire (and Isle of Ely),
                    Hunts, Norfolk, E. and W. Suffolk
    South-Eastern (divisions for housing statistics):
     Beds, Essex, Herts
     Grtr London: area of GLC
     S-E Counties: Kent, Surrey, E. and W. Sussex
     S Counties: Berks, Bucks, Hants, IOWight, Oxon
    South-West: Cornwall (and Scilly Isles), Devon,
                    Dorset, Gloucs, Somerset, Wilts
    Wales: Wales and Monmouthshire

32 Cf. pp.160-7.
33 1964-8 figures include tenders for New Towns. For
    source see n.30 above.
34 See pp.142-4.
35 For a brief discussion of the productivity of the
    construction industry and the distribution of work
    between new residential and non-residential building
    and repairs and maintenance, all from 1966 to 1972,
    see R. Budd, The Real Needs for Housing, 'Built
    Environment', June 1973, pp.340-4; for an earlier,
    fuller discussion see Stone, op. cit., Chapter 14.
36 MHLG, 'Report of the Inquiry into the Collapse of
    Flats at Ronan Point, Canning Town' (London, HMSO,
    1968). The disaster occurred on 16 May 1968.
37 'The Times', 16 August 1968.
38 'Journal' (Newcastle), 16 August 1968.
39 See n.36 above for the requirements agreed by the
    Tribunal.
40 'The Times', 18 May 1968 (leader).
41 'Journal' (Newcastle), 14 August 1968.
42 See pp.157ff.
43 MHLG, 'Housing Statistics'; DOE, 'Housing and Con-
    struction Statistics' (as n.30), also see Notes and
    Definitions for the following:
    (i) Scheme: one for which separate contract, or
        direct labour estimate approved. One scheme may
        cover more than one site, alternatively a single
        site may be developed by several schemes.
    (ii) In the calculation of densities, as used here,
        the area for each scheme, is the acreage of land
        to be covered by housing (including $\frac{1}{2}$ width of
        boundary roads up to maximum of 20'); it ex-
        cludes land to be used for other purposes;
        persons, or designated bed spaces are the number
        of persons which the dwellings are designed to
        accommodate.
    For a discussion of various measures of density see
    V. Hole, Housing in Social Research, in E. Gittus
    ed., 'Key Variables in Social Research', vol.1
    (Heinemann, London, 1972), pp.72-4.
44 Stone, op. cit., pp.104f.
45 Ibid., also Hole (1972), p.73.
46 For data on the size of local authority schemes,
    approved in each year, see tables in MHLG, 'Housing
    Statistics' and DOE, 'Housing and Construction
    Statistics' as in n.30. It appears, from the tables,
    that from the early 1960s the percentage of dwellings
    in the larger schemes (i.e. comprising 250 dwellings
    or more) has tended to rise. See above pp.157ff. for

regional and local variations in flat construction.

47   P. Self, 'Cities in Flood, The Problems of Urban
Growth' (Faber, London, 1957), pp.44f. Also cf.
C.N. Craig, Factors Affecting Economy in Multi-Storey
Flat Design, 'Journal of the RIBA', April 1956.

48   MHLG, 'Homes for Today and Tomorrow' (HMSO, London,
1961).

49   MHLG, 'The Housing Cost Yardstick for Schemes at
Medium and High Densities' (HMSO, London, 1963), p.3.

50   Stone, op. cit., p.150.

51   Source for Table 42, as n.30 and see also 'Notes and
Definitions;   2, New Construction', for the various
components of cost.   Tables are given also for the
percentage of schemes negotiated by each type of contract, i.e. firm price (the majority), direct labour,
or contracts with fluctuation clauses.   Costings for
schemes negotiated by each method are not given
separately.   Table 42 includes all three types.

52   Stone, op. cit., Appendix 13.   MHLG and Welsh Office,
'Housing Subsidies Manual - The Housing Subsidies
Act, 1967' (HMSO, London, 1967).

53   Self, op. cit., p.49.

54   To take construction costs alone, however, is mis-
leading (see also p.148 and n.63 below).   It is unrealistic to assess costs without considering the
need for extra land occasioned by building high and
at high densities.   In 1963, for example, Stone
suggested that, in terms of the wider notion of cost,
10-16 storeys might be the optimum height range.
P.A. Stone, Housing, Town Development, Land and
Costs, 'Estates Gazette', 1963, p.59.

55   Stone (1970), p.239, where he notes the avoidance of
loss of population as a further inducement to local
authorities to develop central sites (given that expensive site subsidies are available), rather than
plan for overspill. Cf. J.B. Cullingworth, 'Housing
Needs and Planning Policy' (Routledge & Kegan Paul,
London, 1960), p.172, for a more tentative assessment
in favour of overspill.   For costs to the rate-payer,
see n.67 below.

56   The various elements of cost used in the analysis
follow the definitions given in 'Notes and Definitions' in MHLG, 'Housing Statistics' (n.30 above) and
in MHLG, 'The Housing Cost Yardstick' (n.49 above).
Table 43 constructed from 'Proceedings of Newcastle
upon Tyne City Council', Report of the Housing Committee on each scheme:
3 January 1962   maisonettes
21 March 1962   15-storey flats

6 June 1962   houses and 2-storey flats
For the houses and 2-storey flats, the superstructure
is separately costed at an average of £1,868 and
£1,705 respectively.

The number of bedrooms per dwelling, in the Table,
is the average for each group - no further detail
given.

The numbers of dwellings of each type, together
with those in the remaining high blocks, agree
closely with the numbers quoted on p.32.

57 See 'Proceedings of Newcastle upon Tyne City Council', 7 June 1961 and 20 June 1961 for discussion of
the revised costings, also 'Proceedings', 20 June
1962, for revisions to a proposal for multi-storey
flats in a neighbouring area of the City.

58 Ibid. The 'more recent scheme' referred to earlier
in this paragraph, is described in detail in Malpass,
op. cit., Chapter 8.

59 'Proceedings of the Newcastle upon Tyne City
Council', 20 June 1962.

60 The Chairman of the Housing Committee (T. Dan Smith),
in 'Proceedings of the Newcastle upon Tyne City
Council', 17 October 1962, referred to the Cruddas
Park flats as the 'cheapest of this quality produced
anywhere in he country'. The figure that he quoted
(£2,291 per flat, including foundations, external
works and garages) refers not to the two blocks in
Table 43, but to the remaining blocks, approved two
years earlier and re-costed in 1961. This analysis
was made before corruption charges were brought
against Mr Smith and some of his associates in the
North-East.

61 The numbers of bedrooms and persons in each type of
dwelling are given or estimated as follows:

table group	dwgs no.	bed-rooms per	per-sons per dwg	persons total	persons	area (T. 43)
A						
houses	48	2	4	192		
houses	93	3	5	465	} 752	16·8
2-s. flats	19	1	2	38		
2-s. flats	19	2	3	57		
B						
maisonettes	32	2	3	96	} 224	4·0
maisonettes	32	3	4	128		

table group	dwgs no.	bed-rooms per	per-sons per dwg	persons total	persons	area (T. 43)
C						
15-s. flats	4	½	1	4		
15-s. flats	58	1	2	116		
15-s. flats	116	2	4 (or 3)	464 (or 348)	594 (or 476)	2·0
15-s. flats	2	3	5 (or 4)	10 (or 8)		

No. of dwellings/acre [weighted: $A + B + 4C$] =
$(179 + 64 + 720)/16·8 + 4·0 + 8·0) = 963/28·8 = 33$
No. of persons/acre [weighted: $A + B + 4C$] =
$(752 + 224 + 2376)/28·8 = 3352/28·8 = 120$
or $(752 + 224 + 1904)/28·8 = 2880/28·8 = 100$

cf. also the distribution of persons/dwelling for the survey families in Table 3.

62 T. Dan Smith in 'Proceedings', 17 October 1962, reference to 'magnificent development of the site' ... 'we're going to build a park'.

63 As, e.g. Stone (1970), p.239.

64 See pp.83–5 and 101–3.

65 IMTA, 'Housing Management and Maintenance Statistics', published annually.

66 The costings presented to the City Council, for each scheme, were compiled on this assumption. By the Housing Act of 1961, the basic subsidy (excluding the special cases of housing for urgent industrial needs, and for town-development) became either £24 or £8, according to the local authority's level of expenditure. (See n.52 and p.143.)

67 The actual rent, at this time, was determined with relation to the total charges to the local authority's Housing Revenue Account, and was therefore not generally equivalent, for a particular scheme, to the actual charge incurred. The pattern of building by any local authority could therefore have implications for all its tenants. For instance, in the late 1950s, it was reported that council rents in Birmingham were to be increased from 1957, because a high percentage of new dwellings had to be multi-rise. See MHLG, 'Flats and Houses' (HMSO, London, 1958), p.173.

68 Hole (1972), pp.74–7, for a discussion of different measures of dwelling size.

69 See n.60.
70 MHLG, 'Homes for Today and Tomorrow' (HMSO, London, 1961), p.56; MHLG, 'The Housing Cost Yardstick Manual' (HMSO, London, 1963), p.3; 'Housing Subsidies Act 1967' (HMSO, London, 1967).
71 'Civil Appropriation Account' (Classes VI-XI), 1966-7 (HMSO, London, 5 February 1968).
72 For details, see MHLG and Welsh Office, 'Housing Subsidies Manual' (HMSO, London, 1967), especially p.14 for flats in blocks of 4 storeys or more.
73 MHLG, 'Circular 36/67' (HMSO, London, April 1967).
74 MHLG, 'Homes for Today and Tomorrow' (HMSO, London, 1961), p.28.
75 Ibid., pp.28-33, 52.
76 Ibid., p.56.
77 MHLG and Welsh Office, 'Housing Subsidies Manual' (HMSO, London, 1967), p.50, para.175.
78 For an attempt to construct a 'Constant Standards Cost Index' for traditionally-built one- or two-storey houses see MHLG, 'Housing Statistics', February 1970, Supplementary Tables, pp.73-4.
79 MHLG, 'Housing Statistics', February 1969, Supplementary Tables (III), p.71, also notes on Parker-Morris Standards, in the same volume.
80 MHLG, 'Homes for Today and Tomorrow' (HMSO, London, 1961).
81 N. Dennis, 'People and Planning' (Faber, London, 1970), pp.228-9.
82 The calculations are as follows, for
scheme I: dwgs A + B + C (Table 43): max. densities just under 80 persons per acre 3·7 persons per dwelling,
      II: dwgs A + B + 4C (Table 43): max. densities 120 persons per acre 3·5 persons per dwelling

Building costs per person

	I		II	
	costing £	yardstick £	costing £	yardstick £
Superstructure	562	388	623	539
Substructure and external works	131	102	161	90

Note: the 'maximum' no. of persons is taken (see n. 61), since the higher the density, the higher the overall yardstick figure.

Sources: costings (1962): figures as in Table 43
         yardstick (1963): MHLG, 'Housing Cost Yardstick', p.7 and p.4 for definitions.

83 In 1966 and 1967, 'high-rise' dwellings, i.e. in
    block of 5 storeys and over, comprised 47 per cent of
    all approvals for flats – tenders for GLC excluded
    (see Table 40(a) for 'industrialised' and 'tradi-
    tional' dwellings combined). In 1967 (cf. Table B),
    some 50 per cent of flats approved, other than those
    for GLC, incorporated all 6 Parker-Morris standards.
    It is unlikely that all high-rise were of this stan-
    dard. Moreover, while the percentage of flats of
    this quality more than trebled from 1964 (Table B),
    the percentage of flats in the high-rise category in-
    creased only from 42 to 47 per cent. It is unlikely
    that specifications for high-rise flats alone were
    brought up to standard.
84 See n.73.
85 MHLG, 'The Housing Cost Yardstick' (HMSO, London,
    1963), p.1.
86 Dennis (1970), pp.229, 239.
87 Housing Subsidies Act, 1967.
88 R. Budd, The Real Needs for Housing, 'Built Environ-
    ment', June 1973, p.341: 'It will have escaped the
    notice of few architects actively engaged in local
    authority housing that the fall in production coin-
    cides, in a simplistic sense, with the introduction
    of ... the housing cost yardstick.'
89 MHLG and Welsh Office, 'Housing Subsidies Manual'
    (HMSO, London, 1967), pp.49-50 and 53.
90 Ibid., where reference is made to a higher yardstick
    for schemes involving exceptional factors, as, for
    instance, abnormal site-conditions, the danger of
    subsidence, and special requirements of the setting.
    But (p.61), where loan-sanction was granted for ex-
    pensive schemes, the period of repayment was likely
    to be reduced to 10 years. For an example of the
    problems involved in such negotiations see Malpass,
    op. cit., Chapter 8 and especially pp.192-204.
91 Budd, op. cit., p.341 and Malpass, op. cit., p.202,
    for the application of a more recent 'fluctuations
    clause'.
92 Budd, op. cit., p.341; 'it has been said that local
    authorities have failed to come to terms with the
    yardstick, ... that there are few local authorities
    who are able quickly to calculate the benefits and
    effects of changes in density and occupancy factors
    on the waiting, clearance and transfer lists and
    that, because of this inability, (local authorities)
    maintain standard solutions irrespective of the needs
    and demands of the neighbourhood in which the
    development is to take place.'

93   See pp.140-2.
94   Hole (1972), p.73.
95   Cullingworth (1960), p.162.
96   Stone (1970), pp.102-10.
97   'Architectural Review', vol.142, no.849, November 1967;   theme: Housing and the Environment.
98   N. Taylor, The Failure of Housing, ibid., pp.341ff.
99   Ibid., p.344.
100 Ibid. and cf. pp.98-100, above.
101 J.R. Nicholls, The Townscape, 'Architectural Review', vol.142, no.849, November 1967.
102 'The Times', 15 January 1973, p.3.
103 M. McConville, High Society in 'Observer' (Review), 18 February 1968;   'Guardian', 2 March 1968 (correspondence);   J. Dobson, 'Up and Down the Low-Rise' in 'Guardian', 16 December 1971;   P. Hildrew, 'Trial and Error in Concrete' in 'Guardian', 8 August 1973: 'the new disasters of the council estates are proving to be the tower-blocks on their sides'.
104 See for instance D.V. Donnison, V. Chapman et al., 'Social Policy and Social Administration' (Allen & Unwin, London, 1965):   Chapter 9, 'High Flats in Finsbury', which illustrates some of the administrative problems affecting negotiations for large urban redevelopment schemes.   See also Malpass, op. cit., chart on p.205 and preceding discussion for the various interest groups and factors to be considered by the local authority architect.
105 The replacement v. renovation (or improvement) issue is essentially a matter for study at the local level, following, for instance, the accounts by N. Dennis and J. Davies of local debates on this issue and their consequences in the North-East.   See Dennis (1970), and 'Public Participation and Planners' Blight' (Faber, London, 1972) and J.G. Davies, 'The Evangelistic Bureaucrat' (Tavistock, London, 1972), Parts iii and iv.   At the macrolevel, Needleman, in 1965 argued in support of renovation policies; Sigsworth and Wilkinson, in 1967, took an opposing view.   See L. Needleman, 'The Economics of Housing' (Staples Press, London, 1965), E.M. Sigsworth and R.K. Wilkinson, Rebuilding or Renovation, 'Urban Studies' 4(2), 1967, pp.109-21.
     The Housing Acts of 1969 and 1971 increased financial support to local authorities for the improvement of existing dwellings.   From 1969, the number of discretionary improvement grants has increased sharply.   Their numbers may be compared with those of approved tenders for new dwellings (a fairer comparison than

with completions of new building):

Local authorities (and New Towns) in England and
Wales

Year	tenders approved for new dwellings	discretionary improvement grants awarded (thousands)
1961	104	10·7
1962	109	11·4
1963	125	10·5
1964	147	11·6
1965	162	12·1
1966	173	14·5
1967	170	20·4
1968	154	20·8
1969	112	22·5
1970	98	33·4
1971	97	57·3
1972	73	99·5

Source: CSO, 'Annual Abstract of Statistics' 1971-3
(HMSO, London).
N.B.   The 1971 Housing Act made special provision for
improvements in the development areas. From then on,
in some regions, improvement grants will have been
considerably in excess of tenders for new building.

106   The Conservatives' Housing Finance Act of 1972 and
the measures introduced pending its repeal by the
succeeding Labour government are likely to have a
profound effect on the course of local authority
housing in the 1970s. The Act was addressed to
fundamental problems in housing finance policy; while
some of the problems, especially the chaotic structure of housing subsidies by the beginning of the
1970s, were widely recognised, the plans for dealing
with these problems were highly controversial. The
succeeding Labour government, in 1974, was pledged,
at the outset, to repeal the 1972 Act (written answer
by the Secretary of State for the Environment, 11
April 1974).

   To simplify, so as to link with the discussion in
this chapter - by the 1972 Act, existing government
subsidies to local authorities were to be phased out,
and to be replaced by a series of 'bridging' subsidies, of varying duration, where, despite simul-
taneous measures to increase rents, the local Housing
Revenue Account was still in deficit, or where

expenditure from local revenue was excessively high
due, e.g. to heavy demands for new building, rising
costs, etc. Local authorities' autonomy in the de-
termination of rents, on a 'pooled' basis, and in the
contribution to the Housing Revenue Account from the
rate fund, was removed. Council rents were brought
within the 'fair rents' scheme and were likely to be
more closely related to the effective cost of the
dwellings - with implications for the tenants of the
relatively expensive high-rise schemes. A mandatory
system of rebates was intended to alleviate hardship
to tenants.

For the rationale behind these and other measures
introduced by the 1972 Act, see the White Paper, 'A
Fair Deal for Housing', Cmd 4728 (HMSO, 1971). For a
critique, see, e.g. R.A. Parker, 'The Housing Finance
Bill and Council Tenants', Poverty Pamphlet 9 (Child
Poverty Action Group, London, 1972) and J. Goudie,
'Councils and the Housing Finance Act', Young Fabian
Pamphlet 31 (Fabian Society, London, 1972), where it
is argued that the Housing Finance Act was designed
so as to reduce public investment in housing and to
do nothing to ensure that more council dwellings
would be built.

In 1974, the new Labour government froze rents and
suspended further increases due under the 1972 Act.
Interim proposals for rents, rebates and subsidies
were circulated for discussion by local housing
authorities. Before the parliamentary recess these
and other measures were included in the Housing,
Rents and Subsidies Bill which was given a formal
first reading. See 'Guardian', 26 July 1974.

Other aspects of housing policy are included in
the 1974 Housing Bill, currently before Parliament.

Moving the second reading of the Bill, the Secretary for the Environment explained the government's
intention to give priority to urban housing needs and
both to stimulate new building and to encourage the
take-up of improvement grants, while providing safeguards against their abuse. The role of Housing
Associations in supporting local authorities was also
to be enlarged.

See 'The Times' (leader), 23 April 1974;
'Guardian', 7 May 1974, p.32 and the Housing Bill
(HMSO, June 1974) [Bill 62]. The press reports refer
also to an emergency measure by which, in 1974/75,
£350 million was to be made available to local
authorities to enable them to build more accommodation for rent, to take over unsold private houses and

to buy flats from private landlords. At the same
time ('The Times', 23 April 1974, p.20), it was reported that the National Council of Building
Materials Producers was to appeal to the Minister of
Housing and Construction for action to stimulate
housing starts in the public sector, which had fallen
to their lowest figure since 1959.

All the above underlines the fact that the issues
discussed in this chapter, though complex enough, represent just one aspect of public housing policy.

107   DOE, 'Widening the Choice, The Next Steps in Housing'
(HMSO, London, April 1973), p.1.

108   Census data: Table 44 and n.109. General Household
Survey estimate: CSO, 'Social Trends' (3), 1972
(HMSO, London), Table 106.

109   Households: private households only.
Multi-dwelling buildings: buildings whether wholly
residential or not, containing more than one structurally separate dwelling (termed type III buildings
in the census tables).
Sources:
1961: Census of England and Wales, 1961
        'Housing Vol. Part I', Tables 4 and 6 for England
        and Wales, Region and Conurbation
        'County Reports', Northum. and Durham, Table 14
        for Newcastle and Gateshead respectively
1966: Census of England and Wales, 1966
        'County Reports', Northum. and Durham, Table 5 for
        Newcastle and Gateshead respectively
        'Housing Vol.', Table 7 for England and Wales,
        Region and Conurbation as in Table 44(a) and for
        the analysis, by tenure, of households with at
        least one person present, as in Table 44(b).

110   Cf. n.115 for an estimate of local authorities' contribution to the increase in 'flats', between 1966
and 1971, in England and Wales as a whole.

111   1961: Census of England and Wales, 1961, 'County
Vols', Northum. and Durham, Table 12.
1966 & 1971: IMTA, 'Housing Management and Maintenance Statistics', and see Table 51.

112   See Table 45, n.115, Table 51 and p.175.

113   Census of England and Wales, 1966, 'Housing Vol.',
Table 6, also Explanatory Notes and Definitions. For
the Economic Planning Regions, see n.31 above.

114   In the private sector, in 1966, according to census
data and definitions, the numbers of purpose-built
flats and of those resulting from structural conver-
sion were as follows:

	thousands	
	pb	c
England and Wales	463	303
Greater London	253	108
Rest of S-E	75	81
N Region	73	9
Rest of England and Wales	62	105

The traditional 2-storey Tyneside flats will account for a considerable number of the purpose-built flats in the Northern region. The way in which dwellings are defined as structurally separate will affect the number of conversions recorded.

115 The 'simple assumptions' are that:
   (i) 'flats' were similarly defined in the 1966 census and in the General Household Survey
   (ii) the 1971 estimate of 17 per cent for households would be closer to 15 per cent for dwellings
   (iii) no purpose-built flats were demolished or closed in the 5 years 1966-70 incl.
   (iv) in the public sector the number of flats that were not purpose-built was the same in 1971 as in 1966.

Then, given, as below, the numbers of dwellings completed in 1966-70 inc., by type and owner-group, and the total numbers demolished or closed, the number of dwellings in England and Wales by 1971 would be (thousands) 14,977 + 1,312 = 16,289, of which 15 per cent 'flats' = 2,442 thousand.

The following table may be constructed for 'flats' (1966 data from Table 45 or its source, n.113):

	No. of 'flats' (thousands)					
	pb		other		all	
	1966	1971	1966	1971	1966	1971
Owners:						
LAs or						
New Towns	755	1,122	17	17	772	1,139
Others	463	538	303	765	766	1,303
All	1,218	1,660	320	782	1,538	2,442

Thus, the increase between 1966 and 1971 of 904 thousand 'flats' would include:
purpose-built flats for LAs and New Towns: 367 thousand
purpose-built flats for all other owners: 75 thousand
balance, due on these assumptions to
   'conversions' in private sector: 462 thousand

i.e. 40 per cent of the increase in flats would be accounted for by new purpose-built dwellings for local authorities and New Towns. Nevertheless, on these assumptions, over 50 per cent of the increase would be the net result of conversions in the private sector.

New construction, in the five years 1966-70 incl. was as follows: (cf. all pb dwgs in 1966)

		thousands	%	thousands	%
for LAs or New Towns:	houses	358	22	3,145	22
for LAs or New Towns:	flats	367	22	755	5
for all other owners:	houses	859	52	10,294	70
for all other owners:	flats	75	5	463	3
		1,659	100	14,657	100

Sources: 1966 and 1971 counts as in Table 45; demolitions and completions, CSO, 'Annual Abstract of Statistics' 108 (HMSO, London, 1971), Tables 67 and 68.

116 Official data by region and by storey height are published for tenders approved in each year, not for completions (see n.118). In any event, given the time between approval and completion, the analysis of approvals is likely to be a fairer reflection of the impact of changes in housing policy.

117 CSO, 'Abstract of Regional Statistics', 1971 (HMSO, London, 1972). The regional groupings in Tables 47 and 48 correspond to the following approximate ratios, throughout the period, of completions for LAs and New Towns to all completions: Greater London 2 : 3; other regions in Table 47a 1 : 2 or a little less; regions in Table 47b 1 : 3 or less.

118 MHLG, 'Housing Statistics', GB (HMSO, London), April 1967, November 1968, February 1970, May 1971, February 1972. DOE, 'Housing and Construction Statistics', GB (HMSO, London), 2nd qtr 1972, Supplementary Table xvii for 1971 (provisional) figures. For notes on the date of approval, see notes to Table 38, above p.132.

119 Source of Table 49 and Appendix B: IMTA, 'Housing Statistics Part 2', 1971 (IMTA, London, 1972), Housing Revenue and Repairs Accounts.

120 See, for instance, n.104.

121 IMTA, 'Housing Management and Maintenance Statistics', available from 1966.

122 'Census of England and Wales', 1971, report for Greater London, part I, p.viii.

123 Ibid., County Reports.

124 R. Minns, Who Builds More?, 'New Society', vol.28 (603), 25 April 1974, pp.184-6.

125 Ibid. and cf. the conflicting results of other statistical attempts to relate local housing decisions to the political affiliation of local councils, e.g. N. Boaden and R. Alford, Sources of Diversity in English Local Government Decisions, 'Public Administration', Summer 1969; N. Boaden, 'Urban Policy-Making' (Cambridge University Press, 1971); R.J. Nicholson and N. Topham, The Determinants of Investment in Housing by Local Authorities: an Economic Approach, 'Journal of the Royal Statistical Society', Series A (134), Part 3, 1971, pp.273-320. Part of the difficulty in all of these studies, including that by Minns, lies in matching the period of political control to the time when the outcome of housing decisions might be inferred from the available indicators of 'performance'.

126 'Guardian', 23 August 1968.

127 Source as for Table 47(a), n.118 above.

128 The proportions living in local authority flats may be higher, in some cases, than shown in col. 6 of Table 50, and Table 51. This would apply if the dwellings owned by the local authority at the time and not built under the Housing Acts included some 'flats'.

129 Cols 4-6 have been derived by subtracting the 1966 from the 1971 IMTA figures for dwellings built under the Housing Acts and expressing each group by storey-height as a percentage of the total increase. For Newcastle and Gateshead the number of dwellings added in this period has been checked against statistics of completions by these authorities as given in the MHLG's published returns of 'Local Housing Statistics', which do not differentiate by type of dwelling.

130 'The Times', 14 June 1974, p.16.

131 Ibid., 25 May 1974, p.5, record of contribution by the Under-Secretary for the Environment to Parliamentary debate, 24 May 1974, and from subsequent correspondence with DOE.

CHAPTER 9 PLAY AND OTHER MEASURES FOR THE UNDER-FIVES

1 T. Blackstone, 'A Fair Start, The Provision of Pre-
School Education' (Allen Lane, London, 1971), Chapters 2-4; Blackstone's work is also of particular
theoretical interest, for she relates the interest in
nursery schooling to changes in the structure of the
family and in its role as a socialising agent. She
applies Smelser's model of structural differentiation
to the various aspects of these changes. W. van der
Eyken, 'The Pre-School Years' (Penguin, Harmondsworth, 1967, 2nd ed., 1969).

2 'Children and their Primary Schools', Central Advisory Council for Education, vol.1, Report (HMSO,
London, 1967); 'Report of the Committee on Local
Authority and Allied Personal Social Services', Cmd
3703 (HMSO, London, 1968), para.204; A.H. Halsey
ed., 'Educational Priority, Problems and Policies'
(HMSO, London, 1972). There have always been both
opponents and supporters of pre-schooling, for
various reasons, most of which were articulated by
the Tyneside mothers, see pp.71-2 above.

3 Cmnd 5174, 'Education, A Framework for Expansion',
December 1972 (HMSO, London), para.17; DES, 'Circular 2/73' (HMSO, London, 1973).

4 Ibid., especially Cmnd 5174, paras 27, 29.

5 The 1944 Education Act section 8(2)(b) required local
authorities 'to have regard to the need for securing
that provision is made for pupils who have not at-
tained the age of five years by the provision of nursery schools, or ... by the provision of nursery
classes in other schools'. These plans did not
materialise, however and Ministry of Education Circular 8/60, May 1960, asserted that 'there was no
change in the circumstances which had made it impossible to undertake any expansion in the provision
of nursery education'.
    For a documentary history of this and other as-
pects of education, from 1900-73, see W. van der
Eyken ed., 'Education, The Child and Society'
(Penguin, Harmondsworth, 1973).

6 Blackstone, op. cit., pp.75ff for a detailed discussion of the origin of the Association. For a
briefer account see, e.g. B. Crowe, 'The Playgroup
Movement' (Pre-School Playgroups Association, London
and Glasgow, 1971), Chapter 11.

7 Blackstone, op. cit., p.76 for the three objects of
the Association.

8 Halsey ed., op. cit., Chapter 14, especially pp.
182-3.

9   Both these matters are extremely complex. To get
    their full flavour, the reader should follow up the
    references that are given here, at least. Black-
    stone, op. cit., Chapter 2, discusses two strands of
    historical development. These are a middle-class
    strand, which is based on recognition of the value,
    to the child's development, of organised play outside
    the family, and is mainly dependent on parents' ini-
    tiatives (cf. the playgroups) and a working-class
    strand, philanthropically motivated towards meeting
    the needs of the 'infant poor'. Regarding the
    latter, she notes that, in 1907, a consultative
    Committee agreed that public provision of education
    in each area should reflect the degree of local need
    (e.g. the percentage of children in unsatisfactory
    homes) and that this principle has been an important
    factor, from 1908 to the 1950s, in the development of
    nursery schools (p.31 and see also Chapter 4). How-
    ever, from 1960, until the Plowden era, the 'needs of
    the poor' principle gave way to the ruling that in
    the 'freeze' following Circular 8/60, new nursery
    school places could only be provided in cases where
    admittance of the child to nursery school would re-
    lease the mother for teaching. Local authorities'
    claims would be considered if the number of such
    cases warranted it. See 'Addenda to Circular 8/60'
    (July 1964 and December 1965) and van der Eyken
    (1967), Chapter 7, for comment on this 'regressive
    policy'.

10 Blackstone, op. cit., pp.12-18; the distinction is
    not clear cut, however.

11 The Urban Programme was announced in July 1968. See
    'Circular 35/68' which was issued to the London and
    County Boroughs jointly by the Home Office, DES, and
    DHSS, inviting them to submit plans for a range of
    developments in areas of special social need. For
    the total expenditure approved under the various
    phases of the programme, see the annual reports of
    the departments concerned. Nursery schools, day nur-
    series and other services for the under-fives were to
    receive special attention. 'DHSS Annual Report,
    1972' (HMSO, London, 1973), para.9.35, for example,
    refers to the expansion of playgroups, particularly
    in 'deprived' areas, and to the appointment of play-
    group advisers by some local authorities. The
    National Adviser to the Pre-School Playgroups As-
    sociation, who was appointed with a grant first made
    to the Association by DES in 1966, has indicated
    some of the organisational difficulties that may

result, locally, from provision under the Urban Aid
scheme.   See Crowe, op. cit., pp.90-2;   Halsey ed.,
op. cit., p.184.

12   See pp.198-202, above.   Blackstone, op. cit., p.167.
A report in 'The Times', 6 February 1972 deplored the
lack of new nursery school places outside urban areas
of special need.   The ultimate objective of the expansion programme that was introduced in December
1972, and which is to be continued, with some modifications, by the present government, is a universal
system of nursery education.   The principle of positive discrimination is still to be applied in the
early stages, in the spirit of the Plowden and EPA
recommendations.   See Cmnd 5174, n.3 above and
'Labour's Programme for Britain' (Labour Party Annual
Conference, 1973).   Recent developments, in 1975,
have entailed at least a temporary halt in the expansion plans.

13   Halsey, op. cit., p.183, referred to the Plowden Committee's lukewarm acknowledgment of the playgroup
movement.   He ascribed this stance partly to the fact
that most of the Committee were professional educationalists who might undervalue, or even be sus-
picious of amateur intrusions into their field.   Such
feelings were detectable in the statement by the
National Union of Teachers, in December 1973, that
nursery schooling was the only acceptable form of
education for the under-fives.   The general secretary
of the Pre-School Playgroups Association reacted
strongly to the NUT's statement.   She took it as a
rebuff to the work of her Association - a work in
which many teachers were already involved, along with
parents, whose contribution the NUT seemed, to her,
to have seriously underestimated.   On the other hand,
the National Campaign for Nursery Education welcomed
the general tone of the White Paper (as in n.4 above)
and stressed that all the available knowledge and experience should be used in planning a varied service
for the under-fives, see 'Times Educational Supplement', 7 December 1973, p.13.

Nevertheless, uncertainties about the way ahead
for the playgroups and for their voluntary helpers
have prompted the Association seriously to examine
its future role, see 'Education Guardian', 2 April
1974, p.21 and 'New Society', 16 May 1974, p.384.

14   According to the White Paper (DES Cmnd 5174) diversity of provision was to be welcomed, so long as
standards in the education and care of young children
were not sacrificed.   More trained teachers would be

needed, if their complement in nursery school staff
was to grow from the ratio (then) of 1 in 3 to the
prospective 1 in 2. For nursery assistants, the
certificate for the National Nursery Examination
Board would be appropriate (see paras 23 and 31-2).
For discussion of training for workers with playgroups see Crowe, op. cit., Chapter 9 and Appendices,
and J. Lucas and V. McKennell, 'Penguin Book of Playgroups' (Penguin, Harmondsworth, 1974), Chapter 3 and
p.38.

The responsibility for providing such courses
rests with the local authorities' education departments (see also Labour Party, op. cit., pp.74f).
There is still no nationally recognised course for
playgroup leaders. Many mothers helping with playgroups have gone on to teacher training, but there
are others, with no formal qualification, who are un-
certain about their future standing. And some who
have taken a playgroup course, and who have considerable practical experience already, are unsure about
their acceptability as nursery staff ('Education
Guardian', 2 April 1974, p.21).

As suggested on p.210, some of the established
playgroup helpers might assist local mothers in
supervising the informal playtimes of children living
in flats and other restricted home environments.
Halsey, op. cit., pp.184f, while emphasising the need
to uphold standards, is anxious to preserve the involvement of parents and other volunteers, not least
for the valuable links that may thus be forged between home and school. He cites the experience of
EPA projects as examples of success in this field.

15 Van der Eyken (1967), p.81.
16 See pp.189-97.
17 A. Holme and P. Massie, 'Children's Play: A Study of
    Needs and Opportunities' (Michael Joseph, London,
    1970).
18 DOE, 'Children At Play', Design Bulletin 27 (HMSO,
    London, 1973). DOE, 'Circular 79/72' and Welsh
    Office, 'Circular 165/72' (HMSO, London, August
    1972).
19 MHLG, 'Circular 36/67' (HMSO, London, April 1967).
    MHLG, 'Homes for Today and Tomorrow' (HMSO, London,
    1961).
20 Central Advisory Council for Education, 'Children and
    their Primary Schools', vol.1, Report (HMSO, London,
    1967), p.126.
21 'Report of the Committee on Local Authority and
    Allied Personal Social Services', Cmd 3703 (HMSO,

London, 1968), paras 204-5.
22 M. Horrocks, Social Planning in New Communities,
    'Built Environment', November 1972, p.553.
23 See p.184.
24 Holme and Massie, op. cit., p.119.
25 Halsey ed., op. cit., p.181. DES, 'Circular 2/73'
    (HMSO, London, 1973).
26 1971 Census, compiled from Small Area (i.e. enumera-
    tion district) data for Households.
27 See Chapter 4, p.32. From the 1971 census data, it
    may be calculated that in all the high blocks at
    Cruddas Park, there were 41 households with children
    under 5, less than half the number (94) who were
    there at the time of the survey in 1967. In 1971, as
    in 1967, approximately 1 family in 2 with children
    under 5 had older children also. In the houses, the
    proportion of households with young children had not
    changed. The maisonettes could not be separately
    distinguished from the census data.
28 See Chapters 1 and 3.
29 See pp.183-6.
30 See for example van der Eyken (1967), Chapter 8 and
    also Blackstone, op. cit., Appendix 1.
31 See n.53.
32 Sources:
    PUPILS FULL/PART TIME
    1964, 1966, DES, 'Statistics of Education', Part 1,
    Table 6 (adjusted)
        for nursery schools, the numbers of part-time
        pupils are given separately in footnotes to the
        tables. They have been counted in the published
        figures as 0·5 pupil. The appropriate numbers
        have been deducted from the published counts as
        follows:
        n = published,   f = full-time,   p = part-time
            (composite)   (actual)   (actual)
        f = n - p/2
        for other schools the numbers attending part-time
        are not given for the separate categories;
        for the total of other schools the numbers attend-
        ing part-time have been calculated by subtracting
        the numbers of part-time pupils in nursery schools
        from the totals for part-time nursery education
        given for 1964 in: DHSS, 'Health and Personal
        Social Services Statistics', 1972, Tables 7-12.
    1968, DES, 'Statistics of Education', vol.1, Table 5
    (adjusted)
        for all categories of schools in this year, the
        numbers of part-time pupils are given in para.21,

Explanatory Notes. The composite figures in Table
5 have been adjusted as for 1964 and 1966 above.
1970, DES, 'Statistics of Education', vol.1, Table 5
(full-time), Table 8 (part-time)
1972, DES, 'Statistics of Education', vol.1, Table 5
(full-time), Table 9 (part-time)
RISING FIVES
1966, estimate quoted in van der Eyken (1967), p.83
1968, DES, 'Statistics of Education', vol.1, Explanatory Notes. Para.46 quotes their number as 16·93 per
cent of the 4-year-old age-group, i.e. 16·93 per cent
of 831,000 = 141,000, as shown.
1972, DES, 'Statistics of Education', vol.1, Introduction, p.ix.
POPULATION
2-4, from Education Tables as above for each year
0-4, DHSS, 'Health and Personal Social Services
Statistics' 1972, Table 1.2.

33   As for 1972, n.32.

34   For a useful summary of the various forms of provision see DOE, 'Design Bulletin' 27 (HMSO, London,
1973), Appendix III.

35   e.g. van der Eyken (1967), Chapter 8. His figures in
Table 2, p.86 do not all agree with the published
data;   e.g. he omits to note that the counts for
full-time grant-aided nursery schools include part-
time pupils divided by 2. Also the published tables
refer to the number of pupils, which is not necessarily the same as places;   they also include some
pupils aged 5 or more.
Reference is made to estimates of pre-school provision by the Plowden and Seebohm Committees. The
data in Tables 53-5 above have been carefully compiled from information that is freely available in
published form, so that the reader may construct his
own estimate for these earlier years, with due attention to the definitions of the various categories,
and also continue the series from more recent data.
It is important to note, in this context, that
educational opportunities for the under-fives will
vary according to the policy of their local authority
- both in regard to the rising-fives and to the age
when children are usually admitted to nursery school
or class (for Newcastle see pp.199-202).

36   See Blackstone, op. cit., p.85. Private nursery
schools with 5 or more children over 5 years of age
are required to register with the DES. Other private
nursery schools are registered with the DHSS, and
appear in Table 55a. The present government is

planning to 'give responsibility for all educational
provision for the pre-school child over the age of 3
to DES, whether the children are in nursery schools/
classes, day nurseries, playgroups, or with registered child-minders'. 'Labour's Programme for
Britain', Annual Conference 1973 (Labour Party,
Transport House, London), pp.74f. Cf. the Report of
the 'Committee on Local Authority and Allied Personal
Social Services', Cmd 3703 (HMSO, London, 1968),
paras 204-5. The majority Seebohm recommendations
were that responsibility for the under-fives should
be divided as it is now. Two members considered that
playgroups should come under the DES because of their
educational content. The present government would
seem to be extending this notion of education, except
for the youngest children, to other forms of day-
care.

37   As in n.32.

38   For most recent population projections see Office of
Population Censuses and Surveys, 'Population Projections no.4, 1973-2014' (HMSO, London, 1974).
    In France (1973) the proportions of children at
nursery school were as follows: aged 2 years - 33
per cent; 3 years - 72 per cent; 4 years - 92 per
cent; 5 years - virtually all. Expansion was
planned to improve the situation in the rural areas
(school starts at 6).
    In Sweden, where school starts at 7, 90 per cent
of 6-year-olds were already making use of pre-school
facilities. A bill currently before the Parliament
aimed to extend the play-school and day-nursery
facilities to all 6-year-olds, and as soon as
possible to 4 and 5-year-olds with special needs, and
eventually to younger age-groups also. 'Times
Educational Supplement', 23 November 1973, p.16.
    Here the TUC has criticised the absence of mention
of the 2-year-olds in the White Paper. The Council
was convinced that all children from the age of 2 can
benefit from nursery education. 'Guardian', 30
August 1973. For their numbers at nursery schooling
in 1972 see Table 54 and for other forms of day-care
for children at this early age, see pp.195-7 (and cf.
the record for France above). The playgroups do not
usually admit children so young, but it has been suggested that one outlet for their energies in a changing system would be to develop services for the
youngest children (Woman's Hour, 6 August 1974).

39   Addenda to M. of Edn Circular 8/60 dated July 1964
and December 1965.

40 Addendum 2 dated December 1965. Circular 8/60 has
    also drawn attention to the possibility of increasing
    numbers without extra cost by substituting part-time
    for full-time places.
41 20 per cent of full-time places was quoted, at the
    1973 Labour Party conference, as the target of the
    present government (source as n.36).
42 DES Circular 2/73, 'Nursery Education', 31 January
    1973. Educational advantages of nursery classes over
    nursery schools are also mentioned, 'namely that
    thereby a change of school at 5 is avoided and that
    educational development can be planned as a whole
    from when the child is 3 or 4 until he reaches the
    beginning of the junior- or middle-school course'.
43 Source of Table 56 - DES, 'Statistics of Education'
    1972, vol.1 (HMSO, London, 1973), Introduction pp.
    viii, ix, and see also Table 53.
44 See also n.36 above for proposals to transfer respon-
    sibility to DES. Sources of Table 55a:
    December 1963-9, DHSS, 'Health and Personal Social
        Service Statistics', 1972, Table 7.12.
    March 1972, England only: ibid., 1973, Table 7.8
        full and part-time figures only given here.
        England and Wales: CSO, 'Social Trends', 1973,
        Table 97.
45 For a concise description of each type of facility in
    Table 55a see Lucas and McKennell, op. cit., Chapter
    3. See also the annual reports of the appropriate
    central government departments, i.e. Ministry of
    Health to 1967, Dept of Health and Social Security
    thereafter (see DHSS, 'Annual Report', 1968, Cmnd
    4100, p.v).
46 Central Advisory Council for Education, 'Children and
    Their Primary Schools', vol.1, Report (HMSO, London,
    1967), pp.122-3.
47 For measures under the Urban Programme, see DHSS,
    'Annual Reports' starting with 1968, pp.12, 19.
    For the innovation mentioned here see DHSS, 'Annual
    Report', 1972, p.95.
48 As n.45.
49 Lucas and McKennell, op. cit., p.35.
50 The Pre-School Playgroups Association defines a play-
    group as 'a group of from six to thirty children aged
    $2\frac{1}{2}$ to 5 yrs who play together regularly daily or
    several sessions weekly', quoted in Blackstone, op.
    cit., p.76. The disparate age-groups that are
    catered for by the services in Table 55a make it im-
    possible to choose an accurate denominator for esti-
    mates of overall provision. The whole 0-4 group has

been used here for this purpose.

51 See DHSS, 'Annual Report', 1968, p.18.

52 DHSS, Circulars 36/68 and 37/68.

53 DHSS, 'Annual Report', 1969.

54 B. Jackson, The Childminders, 'New Society' 26 (582) 29 November 1973, p.522. He is especially concerned with the high proportion of West Indian children who are placed with illegal minders. He estimates that West Indian children aged under 5 number 120,000 and that two-thirds of their mothers go out to work. Moreover, in a large proportion of cases, the mother is the breadwinner, with no other financial support.

55 Ibid., p.522.

56 Ibid.

57 'Guardian', 23 July 1974, p.7.

58 Cf. p.46 above, which refers to the increase in the 'activity rate' for mothers with young children, in England and Wales, from 11 per cent in 1961 to 18 per cent in 1966. A sample analysis of the 1971 Census data puts the figure at 19 per cent – but this is for Great Britain, and so is not strictly comparable with the earlier estimate. CSO, 'Social Trends' (4), 1973, p.88.

59 In 1973 a project for training child-minders was organised in Birmingham (partly financed by Urban Aid). Though the scheme could only reach 20 out of the city's 800 registered minders, it was hoped that it would have a wider effect. 'Guardian', 25 July 1973, p.18. A similar scheme, based on an informal approach to training, has been successfully organised in Lewisham, 'Education Guardian', 14 May 1974, p.23. The Child-Minding Research and Development Unit is setting up a model scheme, intended to reach illegal minders also, in Yorks, W. Riding initially, and later possibly in Manchester. 'Guardian', 23 July 1974, p.7.

The high incidence of child-minding is also of urgent concern to the government's inter-departmental group on the under-fives (verbal communication from staff at DOE, July 1974).

60 They were encouraged to do so by DHSS, Circular 37/-68, and from the start of the Urban Programme by the HO, DES and DHSS joint Circular 35/68. The number of children so placed increased from 300 at December 1968 to some 3,000 by March 1972. In addition, some local authorities run their own part-time nursery groups, which currently provide over 2,000 places in all. DHSS, 'Annual Reports', 1968, p.18; 1969, p. 19; 1972, p.95.

61 Under the second phase of the Urban Programme,
   financial assistance was given to playgroups for the
   first time on a national scale. DHSS, 'Annual Reports', 1969, p.14 and 1972, p.95. See also Crowe,
   op. cit. and Lucas and McKennell, op. cit., pp.35-6
   for the record of support to the playgroup movement.
62 Crowe, op. cit., p.58 and Lucas and McKennell, op.
   cit., p.11.
63 See e.g. E. Gittus, Sociological Aspects of Urban
   Decay, in F. Medhurst and J. Parry Lewis, 'Urban
   Decay' (Macmillan, London, 1969), pp.27-35.
64 Central Advisory Council for Education, 'Children and
   Their Primary Schools', vol.1, Report (HMSO, London,
   1967), para.294. Van der Eyken (1967), Chapter 9.
   Also Blackstone, op. cit., Chapter 6, where, having
   analysed (separately for administrative counties and
   county boroughs) the relationships between the numbers of maintained and independent nursery places in
   1965 and a range of variables, including population
   characteristics and social conditions in each area,
   she concluded (p.119) that the associations were
   generally too weak to be interpreted as plausible
   measurable causes of the extent of provision. An exception was the relationship between independent
   places and the middle-class element in the population. For the maintained places, she stressed the
   importance of the attitudes and interests of local
   officials and politicians and their interpretation
   of the permissive powers conveyed to local authorities by the central government (pp.121-2). From the
   Plowden research (above), Blackstone concluded that
   attendance at nursery school or class did not appear
   to be related to any aspect of the child's home background any more than the extent of provision was related to local characteristics (p.119).
65 See p.184.
66 Office of Population Censuses and Surveys, Social
   Survey Division, 'The General Household Survey', Introductory report (HMSO, London, 1973), from Table
   7.11.
67 Ibid. and CSO, 'Social Trends' (4), 1973, Table 107
   (HMSO, London, 1973). By contrast to this, but for
   authorities, not households, a report for 'Where?'
   alleged that, in 1973, DES grants under the government's nursery building programme had benefited the
   higher-class areas rather more than the rest. Thus,
   among the English boroughs, all but one of the high-
   class areas, but only one of the low-class areas,
   achieved 25 per cent or more of their estimated needs

for places. The report's criterion for the proportion of nursery places was taken, somewhat question-
ably, as the proportion of males in the population
who were semi-skilled or unskilled. Report in 'Times
Educational Supplement', 7 December 1973, p.6.

68 The analysis was based on the wards as in 1971. The
ward boundaries have since been revised and other
formerly peripheral areas brought within the new
Metropolitan District. For the new areas, the Social
Services Department has produced a study of social
characteristics and the provision of services, including those for the under-fives (August 1974). The
results cannot be compared in detail with those here,
though their general emphasis is broadly similar.

69 See p.188. The groups are as follows: (see Table
52)
   I   Benwell, Stephenson, Armstrong, Elswick
   II St Anthony's, St Lawrence, St Nicholas, Byker,
       Walker
   III Scotswood, Blakelaw, Kenton, Fenham
   IV Arthur's Hill, Westgate, Jesmond, Sandyford
   V   Walker Gate, Heaton, Dene.

70 The disparity between the distributions cannot of
course be assessed, and, as was seen from the survey
in Cruddas Park (p.69), it is possible that some
children may travel a considerable distance to
attend.

71 Compiled from Small Area (enumeration district) data
for Population and Households.

72 This applies to the maintained provision. For the
private nurseries, etc. lists were supplied of the
registered provision in mid-1974. The number of
under-fives in the population may have changed since
1971 and calculations based on such out of date de-
nominators can convey only a general picture.

73 The lists applied only to private nurseries and playgroups taking 5 or more children. Child-minders were
not included. The assistance of the Social Services
Department is gratefully acknowledged.

74 Chartered Institute of Public Finance and Accounting,
Society of County Treasurers, 'Education Statistics',
1973.

75 County of Tyne and Wear, District A, Newcastle upon
Tyne. 'Report to Joint Consultative Committee' by
Education Working Group, April 1974, also informal
meeting of City Education Committee, 31 July 1973.

76 Ibid. and cf. pp.183-4 and n.4 above.

77 City Council of Newcastle upon Tyne. Budget 74/5,
paper considered at City Council meeting, 20 March
1974.

78 As n.75, discussion of play centres and summer play
    schemes. Provision of the former dates from 1918,
    following recommendations from the (then) Board of
    Education that 'play centres should be created to
    provide care and recreation for children out of
    school hours, especially those whose home conditions
    were unfavourable to happy and healthy development'.
    The same policy has governed the provision of summer
    play schemes, with some financial support from Urban
    Aid and with the co-operation of voluntary bodies.
        The recreation committee included, among future
    developments, the provision of more children's play-
    grounds, more adventure playgrounds and the employ-
    ment of more playleaders (n.77).

79 See e.g. Holme and Massie, op. cit., Appendix V,
    which also includes a list of voluntary organisations
    connected with play provision, also DOE, 'Children at
    Play', Design Bulletin 27 (HMSO, London, 1973),
    Appendix III, para.1.

80 D. Gilpin-Brown, Legislating for Play Provision,
    'Built Environment', August 1972, p.327.

81 Chapter 8, pp.175-6. While the emphasis here has
    been on children in local authority housing, the
    needs of children in the older areas command equal
    attention. The recent DOE survey includes a study of
    such areas (Chapter II) and Holme and Massie (Chap-
    ters 8 and 9) include a survey of two contrasting
    neighbourhoods, one relatively new and one old; see
    n.79.

82 Holme and Massie, op. cit., pp.291-2.

83 DOE, 'Circular 79/72' and Welsh Office, 'Circular
    165/72' (HMSO, London, 1972). The basic cost
    allowance is £18 per child-bedspace. Child-bedspaces
    are calculated as follows: total bedspaces (or
    designated popn) minus the sum of bedspaces in
    dwellings intended for old people, those in dwellings
    for 1 or 2 persons, and two bedspaces for every
    family dwelling. The smallest area should be
    equipped with at least one of a list of items. In
    addition, a seat or bench, suitable for adults,
    should be provided.

84 Holme and Massie, op. cit., pp.292-3, for some ex-
    amples before Urban Aid. Also, Urban Aid Programme,
    Local Government Grants (Social Need) Act, 1969, see
    DOE Design Bulletin 27, para.159.

85 The GLC's general standard of provision includes a
    number of 'client requirements' over and above those
    set out in DOE Circular 79/72. For example,
    toddlers' play spaces should be placed so that

mothers can watch the children from the windows. In providing for this age-group the main emphasis should be on usable grassed areas, including banks and mounds, paved areas, ramps for tricycles, etc. and simple equipment. The space should be enclosed by a protective barrier, with a gate not giving on to a road. See-saws and certain other items of equipment have been discontinued because of the risk of accident. Sandpits and paddling pools are also excluded because of misuse.

86 Besides supporting supervised playgroups, the GLC, through its Parks Department, has introduced one-o-clock clubs. Most of them are in parks, but some on housing estates. These clubs are open to all children under 5, there is no waiting list, no charge for admission and no register is kept. But each child or group of children must be accompanied by an adult. The clubs are all staffed and both indoor and outdoor facilities are provided. Their dual purpose is to enable the children to play and the adults to have somewhere to relax, have company and share, if they wish, in their children's activities. (See also DOE, 'Design Bulletin' 27, p.105. Cf. also Holme and Massie, op. cit., p.86.)

87 London Borough of Lewisham, Planning Dept, 'Playground Facilities', Research Report 1, 1972, p.3.

88 See pp.17-18.

89 Too much emphasis on standards in new projects may detract from the needs of children in the older areas. Cf. the analysis in Chapter 7, pp.85-8 above.

90 Urban Aid Programme, Local Government Grants (Social Need) Act, 1969. See DOE, 'Design Bulletin' 27, para.159.

91 See p.209 for discussion of participation in this context.

92 'First claim', that is, with reference to the DOE's current inquiry mentioned in Chapter 8, pp.175-6. The practical impossibility of maintaining a rigid separation is obvious, especially where blocks of low- or medium-rise flats are scattered through areas of older housing (as in the case of the Wallsend maisonettes - see p.206).

93 This conviction has prompted the general review of pre-school provision in the earlier part of this chapter.

94 Committee on Local Authority and Allied Personal Social Services, Cmd 3703 (HMSO, London, 1968), paras 210, 474-8.

95 For some sociological criticisms see C. Filkin and

D. Weir, Locality, in E. Gittus ed., 'Key Variables in Social Research', vol.1 (Heinemann, London, 1972), pp.119-20.

96   See Chapter 4.

97   n.94, paras 474-84, also Halsey ed., op. cit., Chapter 14 and E. Midwinter, 'Priority Education' (Penguin, Harmondsworth, 1972), pp.186f for an account of the Liverpool project.

98   For a useful, detailed discussion of the needs of children and their mothers in differing environments (including high flats areas), and with examples of the various attempts to meet these needs, with an emphasis on playgroups, see Crowe, op. cit., Chapter 6.

99   See nn.24-5.

100   See e.g. Chapter 5, pp.59-62; Chapter 6, pp.74-7; Chapter 7, pp.80-5, 88-91, 91-100 and 109-13.

101   See Chapter 5, pp.47-8.

102   The earlier references to non-registered childminders include expressions of alarm at the fact that many children are kept indoors all day, with no activities outside. In some cases this may have been for the simple reason that suitable and safe opportunities for play were non-existent. The distinction between play in a playgroup and supervised play out of doors is a very tenuous one - some playgroups make use of out-of-door facilities. See Lucas and McKennell, op. cit., p.233.

103   See Chapter 5, p.43 and n.6; Chapter 6, p.104; Chapter 7, pp.80, 82-3, 88, 90, 103 and 107.

104   See Chapter 5, pp.42, 50, 58; Chapter 7, pp.82-94.

105   See especially Chapter 6, p.72; Chapter 7, pp.85-8.

106   'Labour's Programme for Britain', Annual Conference, 1973 (Transport House, London, 1973), p.45 - 'local authorities to involve local tenants far more in the management of estates'. 'Labour Party Manifesto', October 1974, p.24.

107   P.J. Dixon, Council Houses - Theirs or Ours?, 'Housing', November 1973, pp.21-5. In the discussion, reference was made to the high degree of public involvement in the creation of multi-storey projects in Sheffield, and to its consequences in the level of appreciation and acceptance among the tenants. See above Chapter 8 (p.133). See also L. Hellman, Housing and Participation, 'Built Environment', July 1973, pp.328-31; D. Savill, Tenants' Participation in Management, 'Housing Review', January/February 1972, pp.12-15; T. Woolley, Tenants' Control in Housing, 'RIBA Journal', January 1974, pp.5-8;

N.J. Habraken, 'Supports' (Architectural Press, London, 1972).

108   Holme and Massie, op. cit., pp.116-17.

109   P. Jephcott, 'Homes in High Flats' (Oliver & Boyd, Edinburgh, 1971), pp.146-8, where she prefaces her case with the observation that multi-storey housing in Glasgow, for all its problems, is 'pregnant with opportunities for self-help'.

110   I am grateful to my colleague J.G. Davies, Chairman of Newcastle's Housing Review Sub-Committee, for information on this point. For an example of this micro-approach see City of Newcastle upon Tyne, Central Research Unit, 'Why People Wish to Stay - a study of attitudes to demolition and revitalization in a street in Newcastle', unpublished paper, 1974.

111   See pp.195-7.

112   'Report of the Committee on Local Authority and Allied Personal Social Services', Cmnd 3703 (HMSO, London, 1968), paras 477-84. Support is given to the view that one of the important functions of voluntary organisations should be to ensure a high degree of consumer participation and to help the spontaneous development of neighbourhood interests and activities in meeting needs - with the reservation that this function should be shared with the local authority's Social Services Department.

See also Holme and Massie, op. cit., pp.108-9, where the following distinction is made between the modes of voluntary participation in provision for children's play:

   (i) through nationally-based organisations, in an advisory and co-ordinating capacity (e.g. Pre-School Playgroups Assocn),

  (ii) through other 'external' organisations usually connected with specific schemes which they may have initiated (e.g. the Save the Children Fund, as mentioned on p.5 above),

(iii) through 'internal' groups which have sprung up or been generated within the communities themselves and whose members may include parents of the children who will be using the facilities.

There is of course some overlap between the last two categories. But it is mainly the promotion of the last mode that is of interest here. There are many instances, no doubt, where activities of this kind are quietly going on already. Those that have been most publicised include various ventures set up through the EPA projects (n.97) various groups in London, some in the more 'deprived' areas, see

'Guardian', 14 May 1970, p.11;   a good example,
though not confined in its activities to matters
affecting children, is the Notting Dale project, see
R. Mitton and E. Morrison, 'A Community Project in
Notting Dale' (Allen Lane, London, 1972), pp.166-71.
It is noted that 'people's participation ... does not
just happen, it has to be worked for', also that, in
striking the balance between 'provision' and 'community involvement', the role of the voluntary
workers can be crucial (see also pp.101-4, above).
The performance of such a role is indeed the princi-
pal object of the Northumberland and Tyneside Council
of Social Service, see 'Annual Report', 1973-4, p.1
and Preface, above.

113   The 'Playmobile' is now well known in EPA projects
and elsewhere. The idea seems to have been imported
from Australia. See A. Stevenson, E. Martin and J.
O'Neill, 'High Living' (Melbourne University Press,
1967), pp.90-1.

114   Holme and Massie, op. cit., pp.65-6, 86, and 123
where 'immediate action' is urged where there is no
opportunity for play in the home, for doorstep play,
or for the companionship of older children. DOE
Design Bulletin 27, 'Children at Play', pp.87-97,
also Chapter 2 above, p.12 and Chapter 7, pp.101f for
the Tyneside mothers' reactions.

115   e.g. references as in n.114 - both useful for their
bibliographies.

116   Cf. Halsey ed., op. cit., p.184, and see last para.
of n.14 above.

Bibliography

BOOKS AND ARTICLES

ASH, J., Families Living at High Density, 'Official Archi-
tecture and Planning', vol.29, 1966.
BLACKSTONE, T., 'A Fair Start, the Provision of Pre-School
Education' (Allen Lane, London, 1971).
BOADEN, N. and ALFORD, R., Sources of Diversity in English
Local Government Decisions, 'Public Administration',
Summer 1969.
BOADEN, N., 'Urban Policy Making' (Cambridge University
Press, 1971).
BUDD, R., The Real Needs for Housing, 'Built Environment',
June 1973.
BURGESS, T., Pre-School Education, 'New Society' 9 (231),
2 March 1967.
CICOUREL, A.V., 'Method and Measurement in Sociology'
(Free Press, London, 1964).
CRAIG, C.N., Factors Affecting Economy in Multi-Storey
Flat Design, 'Royal Institute of British Architects
Journal', vol.63(3), April 1956.
CROWE, B., 'The Playgroup Movement' (Pre-School Playgroups
Association, London and Glasgow, 1971).
CULLINGWORTH, J.B., 'Housing Needs and Planning Policy'
(Routledge & Kegan Paul, London, 1960).
CULLINGWORTH, J.B., 'Town and Country Planning in Britain'
(Allen & Unwin, London, 1964, revised 4th edn, 1972).
DARKE, J. and DARKE, R., Health and Environment, High
Flats, 'University Working Paper no. 10' (Centre for En-
vironmental Studies, London, 1970).
DARKE, J. and DARKE, R., Sheffield Revisited, 'Built En-
vironment', November 1972.
DAVIES, J.G., 'The Evangelistic Bureaucrat' (Tavistock,
London, 1972).
DENNIS, N., Mass Housing and The Reformer's Myth,

'Planning Outlook', no.6, new series, Spring 1969.
DENNIS, N., 'People and Planning' (Faber & Faber, London, 1970).
DENNIS, N., 'Public Participation and Planners' Blight' (Faber & Faber, London, 1972).
DIXON, P.J., Council Houses - Theirs or Ours?, 'Housing', November 1973.
DONNISON, D.V., CHAPMAN, V. et al., 'Social Policy and Social Administration' (Allen & Unwin, London, 1965).
DONNISON, D.V. and EVERSLEY, D.C. (eds), 'London, Urban Patterns, Problems and Policies' (Heinemann, London, 1972).
EYKEN, W. VAN DER, 'The Pre-School Years' (Penguin, Harmondsworth, 1967).
EYKEN, W. VAN DER (ed.), 'Education, The Child and Society' (Penguin, Harmondsworth, 1973).
FANNING, D.M., Families in Flats, 'British Medical Journal', vol.4, 1967.
FILKIN, C. and WEIR, D., Locality, in E. Gittus (ed.), 'Key Variables in Social Research', vol.1 (Heinemann, London, 1972).
GALES, K. and MARKS, P.H., Twentieth Century Trends in the Work of Women in England and Wales, 'Journal of the Royal Statistical Society', Series A, vol.137(1), 1974.
GILPIN-BROWN, D., Legislating for Play Provision, 'Built Environment', August 1972.
GITTUS, E., Sociological Aspects of Urban Decay, in F. Medhurst and J. Parry Lewis, 'Urban Decay' (Macmillan, London, 1969).
GOUDIE, J., Councils and the Housing Finance Act, 'Young Fabian Pamphlet', no.31 (Fabian Society, London, 1972).
HABRAKEN, N.J., 'Supports' (Architectural Press, 1972).
HALSEY, A.H. (ed.), 'Educational Priority, Problems and Policies' (HMSO, London, 1972).
HELLMAN, L., Housing and Participation, 'Built Environment', July 1973.
HINDESS, B., 'The Use of Official Statistics in Sociology: A Critique of Positivism and Ethnomethodology' (Macmillan, London, 1973).
HOLE, V., Housing in Social Research in E. Gittus (ed.), 'Key Variables in Social Research', vol.1 (Heinemann, London, 1972).
HOLE, V., 'A Study of Washington New Town', unpublished report for the Building Research Establishment (DOE, 1973).
HOLE, V. and MILLER, A., Children's Play on Housing Estates, A Summary of Two Building Research Station Studies, 'Architects' Journal', vol.143, 1966.
HOLE, V. and POUNTNEY, M., 'Trends in Population, Housing

254 Bibliography

and Occupancy Rates' (HMSO, London, 1971).
HOLME, A. and MASSIE, P., 'Children's Play, a Study of
Needs and Opportunities' (Michael Joseph, London, 1970).
HORROCKS, M., Social Planning in New Communities, 'Built
Environment', November 1972.
JACKSON, B., The Childminders, 'New Society' 26 (582), 29
November 1973.
JENSEN, R., 'High Density Living' (Whitefriars Press,
London and Tonbridge, 1966).
JEPHCOTT, P. and ROBINSON, H., 'Homes in High Flats'
(Oliver & Boyd, Edinburgh, 1971).
LIPMAN, A., The Architectural Belief System and Social
Behaviour, 'British Journal of Sociology', vol.XX(2),
1969.
LUCAS, J. and MCKENNELL, V., 'Penguin Book of Playgroups'
(Penguin, Harmondsworth, 1974).
MADGE, J., 'The Tools of Social Science' (Longmans, Green,
London, 1953).
MAIZELS, J., 'Two to Five in High Flats' (The Housing
Centre, London, 1961).
MALPASS, P., 'Professionalism in Architecture and the
Design of Local Authority Houses', MA thesis, University
of Newcastle upon Tyne, 1973.
MALPASS, P., Professionalism and the Role of Architects in
Local Authority Housing, 'Royal Institute of British
Architects Journal', vol.82(6), June 1975.
MANNHEIM, K., 'Ideology and Utopia: An Introduction to
the Sociology of Knowledge' (Routledge & Kegan Paul,
London, 1936, reprinted 1966).
MAYO, E., 'The Social Problems of an Industrial Civiliza-
tion' (Routledge & Kegan Paul, London, 1949).
MEDHURST, F. and PARRY LEWIS, J., 'Urban Decay' (Mac-
millan, London, 1969).
MIDWINTER, E., 'Priority Education' (Penguin, Harmonds-
worth, 1973).
MINNS, R., Who Builds More?, 'New Society', vol.28(603),
25 April 1974.
MITTON, R. and MORRISON, E., 'A Community Project in
Notting Dale' (Allen Lane, Penguin Press, 1972).
MORRIS, R.N. and MOGEY, J., 'The Sociology of Housing'
(Routledge & Kegan Paul, London, 1965).
MOSS, P., TIZARD, J. and CROOK, J., Families and Their
Needs, 'New Society', vol.23(546), 22 March 1973.
NEEDLEMAN, L., 'The Economics of Housing' (Staples Press,
London, 1965).
NICHOLLS, J.R., The Townscape, 'Architectural Review',
vol.142(849), November 1967.
NICHOLSON, R.J. and TOPHAM, N., The Determinants of In-
vestment in Housing by Local Authorities, 'Journal of the

Royal Statistical Society', Series A, vol.134(3), 1971.

PAHL, R.E. (ed.), 'Readings in Urban Sociology' (Pergamon Press, 1968).

PARKER, R.A., The Housing Finance Bill and Council Tenants, 'Poverty Pamphlet 9' (Child Poverty Action Group, London, 1972).

PICKVANCE, C.G., Voluntary Associations, in E. Gittus (ed.), 'Key Variables in Social Research', vol.2 (Heinemann, London, forthcoming).

POPPLESTONE, G., 'The Reputation of Housing Areas in Aberdeen', paper read to the Community Studies section of the British Sociological Association Conference, Reading, 1968.

REX, J., 'Key Problems in Sociological Theory' (Routledge & Kegan Paul, London, 1961).

REX, J. and MOORE, R., 'Race, Community and Conflict' (Oxford University Press, 1967).

SAVILL, D., Tenants' Participation in Management, 'Housing Review', January/February 1972.

SELF, P., 'Cities in Flood, The Problems of Urban Growth' (Faber & Faber, London, 1957).

SIGSWORTH, E.M. and WILKINSON, R.K., Rebuilding or Renovation, 'Urban Studies', vol.4(2), 1967.

STEVENSON, A., MARTIN, E. and O'NEILL, J., 'High Living' (Melbourne University Press, 1967).

STONE, P.A., Housing, Town Development, Land and Costs, 'The Estates Gazette', 1963, pp.52ff.

STONE, P.A., 'Urban Development in Britain: Standards Costs and Resources, 1964-2004', vol.1, 'Population Trends and Housing' (Cambridge University Press for National Institute of Economic and Social Research, 1970).

TAYLOR, N., The Failure of Housing, 'Architectural Review', vol.142(849), November 1967.

TOWNSEND, P., Survey of Families Living High in New Blocks of Flats, interim report in J. Maizels, 'Two to Five in High Flats' (The Housing Centre, London, 1961).

VAIZEY, J., 'Education for Tomorrow' (Penguin, Harmondsworth, 1962).

WILLIAMS, H.A., 'True Resurrection' (Mitchell Beazley, London, 1972).

WILLIS, M., Private Balconies in Flats and Maisonettes, 'Architects' Journal', vol.125, March 1957.

WOOLLEY, T., Tenants' Control in Housing, 'Royal Institute of British Architects Journal', vol.81(1), January 1974.

OFFICIAL PUBLICATIONS AND REPORTS
(Publisher: HMSO, London, unless stated otherwise)

BENWELL COMMUNITY PROJECT, 'Preliminary Report'
(Newcastle, May 1973).
BRITISH STANDARDS INSTITUTION, 'British Standard Code of
Practice' (BSI, London, 1960).
CENTRAL ADVISORY COUNCIL FOR EDUCATION, 'Children and
their Primary Schools' (the Plowden Report), vol.1, 1967.
CENTRAL STATISTICAL OFFICE, 'Abstract of Regional Statis-
tics', 1971.
CENTRAL STATISTICAL OFFICE, 'Annual Abstract of Statis-
tics', 1971-3.
CENTRAL STATISTICAL OFFICE, 'Social Trends', (3), 1972 and
(4), 1973.
CHARTERED INSTITUTE OF PUBLIC FINANCE AND ACCOUNTING,
SOCIETY OF COUNTY TREASURERS, 'Education Statistics', 1973
(the Institute, London, 1974), (and see IMTA).
CITY OF NEWCASTLE UPON TYNE, Proceedings of various coun-
cil meetings 1961, 1962, 1973 and 1974.
CIVIL APPROPRIATION ACCOUNT, Classes VI-XI, 1966-7, 5
February 1968.
COMMITTEE ON LOCAL AUTHORITY AND ALLIED PERSONAL SOCIAL
SERVICES (THE SEEBOHM COMMITTEE), 'Report', Cmnd 3703,
1968.
COUNTY OF TYNE AND WEAR, DISTRICT A, NEWCASTLE UPON TYNE,
'Education Report to Joint Consultative Committee', April
1974.
DEPARTMENT OF EDUCATION AND SCIENCE (DES), 'Statistics of
Education' various dates to 1972.
DES, 'Education, a Framework for Expansion', Cmnd 5174
(December 1972).
DES, Circular 2/73, 'Nursery Education' (31 January 1973).
DEPARTMENT OF THE ENVIRONMENT (DOE), Design Bulletin
25/72, 'The Estate Outside the Dwelling'.
DOE, Design Bulletin 27/73, 'Children at Play'.
DOE, Circular 79/72, 'Children's Play Space' (August
1972).
DOE, 'Housing and Construction Statistics Great Britain'
(1973).
DOE, 'Widening the Choice, The Next Steps in Housing'
(April 1973).
DOE, 'The Housing Bill', Bill 62 (June 1974).
DEPARTMENT OF HEALTH AND SOCIAL SECURITY (DHSS), Annual
Reports, various, 1968-1972.
DHSS, Circulars 36/68 and 37/68, on the application of the
Nurseries and Child-Minders Regulation Act, as amended
1968.
DHSS, Health and Personal Social Services Statistics, 1972
and 1973.

EAST NEWCASTLE ACTION GROUP, 'Working Class Mothers and Pre-School Education' (Newcastle, 1972).

GENERAL REGISTER OFFICE (GRO), or OFFICE OF POPULATION CENSUSES AND SURVEYS (OPCS) 1971 and later, Census of England and Wales.

County Reports, various, 1961, 1966, 1971.
Housing Volume, 1961 and 1966.
Migration Summary Tables, 1966.
Small area data for Newcastle, 1971.

OPCS, General Household Survey, Introductory Report (1973).

OPCS, Registrar General's Statistical Review of England and Wales, Population Tables, various.

OPCS, 'Population Projections no.4, 1973-2014' (1974).

GREATER LONDON COUNCIL Development Plan, 'Statement and Report of Studies' (GLC, 1969).

HOME OFFICE/DES/DHSS, Joint Circular 35/68 on the Urban Programme.

INSTITUTE OF MUNICIPAL TREASURERS AND ACCOUNTANTS (IMTA), 'Housing Statistics', 1965-6 (IMTA, London, 1967).

IMTA, 'Housing Management and Maintenance Statistics', various from 1966-71 (IMTA).

IMTA, 'Housing Statistics, Part 2, Housing Revenue and Repairs Accounts, 1971' (IMTA, 1972).

LABOUR PARTY, 'Labour's Programme for Britain' (Transport House, London, 1973).

LABOUR PARTY, 'Labour Party Manifesto' (Transport House, London, 1974).

·LONDON BOROUGH OF LEWISHAM, 'Playground Facilities', Research Report no.1 (Planning Department, Lewisham, 1972).

MINISTRY OF EDUCATION, Circular 8/60, on nursery education (May 1960), with Addenda (July 1964 and December 1965).

MINISTRY OF HOUSING AND LOCAL GOVERNMENT (MHLG), 'Local Housing Statistics', quarterly returns, various from 1966.

MHLG, 'Housing Statistics, Great Britain', various from April 1967 to February 1972.

MHLG, 'Living in Flats' (1952).

MHLG, 'Flats and Houses' (1958).

MHLG, 'Homes for Today and Tomorrow' (the Parker Morris Report) (1961).

MHLG, 'Families Living at High Density' (MHLG, mimeo, 1963).

MHLG, 'The Housing Cost Yardstick for Schemes at Medium and High Density' (1963).

MHLG, Circular 76/65, on the definition of industrialised building schemes.

MHLG, Circular 36/67, 'Housing Standards, Costs and Subsidies'.

MHLG, 'Housing Subsidies Manual – The Housing Subsidies Act 1967' (1967).

MHLG, 'Report of the Inquiry into the Collapse of Flats at Ronan Point, Canning Town' (1968).

MHLG, Design Bulletin 21/70, 'Families Living at High Density: A Study of Three Central Estates in Liverpool, Leeds and London'.

MHLG, 'A Fair Deal for Housing', Cmnd 4728 (1971).

NATIONAL SWEDISH COMMITTEE FOR BUILDING RESEARCH, 'Effects of High Buildings on Families with Young Children', Report no.38 (1958).

NORTHUMBERLAND AND TYNESIDE COUNCIL OF SOCIAL SERVICE, Annual Report (NTCSS, Newcastle, 1974).

Name index

General index

Routledge Social Science Series

Routledge & Kegan Paul   London and Boston

68–74 Carter Lane   London EC4V 5EL
9 Park Street   Boston   Mass 02108

Contents

*Authors wishing to submit manuscripts for any series in
this catalogue should send them to the Social Science Editor,
Routledge & Kegan Paul Ltd, 68–74 Carter Lane,
London EC4V 5EL*

●*Books so marked are available in paperback
All books are in Metric Demy 8vo format (216 × 138mm approx.)*

International Library of Sociology

General Editor John Rex

GENERAL SOCIOLOGY

Barnsley, J. H. The Social Reality of Ethics. *464 pp.*
Belshaw, Cyril. The Conditions of Social Performance. *An Exploratory Theory. 144 pp.*
Brown, Robert. Explanation in Social Science. *208 pp.*
● Rules and Laws in Sociology. *192 pp.*
Bruford, W. H. Chekhov and His Russia. *A Sociological Study. 244 pp.*
Cain, Maureen E. Society and the Policeman's Role. *326 pp.*
●**Fletcher, Colin.** Beneath the Surface. *An Account of Three Styles of Sociological Research. 221 pp.*
Gibson, Quentin. The Logic of Social Enquiry. *240 pp.*
Glucksmann, M. Structuralist Analysis in Contemporary Social Thought. *212 pp.*
Gurvitch, Georges. Sociology of Law. *Preface by Roscoe Pound. 264 pp.*
Hodge, H. A. Wilhelm Dilthey. *An Introduction. 184 pp.*
Homans, George C. Sentiments and Activities. *336 pp.*
Johnson, Harry M. Sociology: *a Systematic Introduction. Foreword by Robert K. Merton. 710 pp.*
●**Keat, Russell,** and **Urry, John.** Social Theory as Science. *278 pp.*
Mannheim, Karl. Essays on Sociology and Social Psychology. *Edited by Paul Keckskemeti. With Editorial Note by Adolph Lowe. 344 pp.*
Systematic Sociology: *An Introduction to the Study of Society. Edited by J. S. Erös and Professor W. A. C. Stewart. 220 pp.*
Martindale, Don. The Nature and Types of Sociological Theory. *292 pp.*
●**Maus, Heinz.** A Short History of Sociology. *234 pp.*
Mey, Harald. Field-Theory. *A Study of its Application in the Social Sciences. 352 pp.*
Myrdal, Gunnar. Value in Social Theory: *A Collection of Essays on Methodology. Edited by Paul Streeten. 332 pp.*
Ogburn, William F., and **Nimkoff, Meyer F.** A Handbook of Sociology. *Preface by Karl Mannheim. 656 pp. 46 figures. 35 tables.*
Parsons, Talcott, and **Smelser, Neil J.** Economy and Society: *A Study in the Integration of Economic and Social Theory. 362 pp.*
Podgórecki, Adam. Practical Social Sciences. *About 200 pp.*
●**Rex, John.** Key Problems of Sociological Theory. *220 pp.*
Discovering Sociology. *278 pp.*
Sociology and the Demystification of the Modern World. *282 pp.*
●**Rex, John** (Ed.) Approaches to Sociology. *Contributions by Peter Abell, Frank Bechhofer, Basil Bernstein, Ronald Fletcher, David Frisby, Miriam Glucksmann, Peter Lassman, Herminio Martins, John Rex, Roland Robertson, John Westergaard and Jock Young. 302 pp.*
Rigby, A. Alternative Realities. *352 pp.*

Roche, M. Phenomenology, Language and the Social Sciences. *374 pp.*
Sahay, A. Sociological Analysis. *220 pp.*
Strasser, Hermann. The Normative Structure of Sociology. *Conservative and Emancipatory Themes in Social Thought. About 340 pp.*
Urry, John. Reference Groups and the Theory of Revolution. *244 pp.*
Weinberg, E. Development of Sociology in the Soviet Union. *173 pp.*

FOREIGN CLASSICS OF SOCIOLOGY

●**Durkheim, Emile.** Suicide. *A Study in Sociology. Edited and with an Introduction by George Simpson. 404 pp.*
Professional Ethics and Civic Morals. *Translated by Cornelia Brookfield. 288 pp.*
●**Gerth, H. H.,** and **Mills, C. Wright.** From Max Weber: *Essays in Sociology. 502 pp.*
●**Tönnies, Ferdinand.** Community and Association. (*Gemeinschaft und Gesellschaft.) Translated and Supplemented by Charles P. Loomis. Foreword by Pitirim A. Sorokin. 334 pp.*

SOCIAL STRUCTURE

Andreski, Stanislav. Military Organization and Society. *Foreword by Professor A. R. Radcliffe-Brown. 226 pp. 1 folder.*
Coontz, Sydney H. Population Theories and the Economic Interpretation. *202 pp.*
Coser, Lewis. The Functions of Social Conflict. *204 pp.*
Dickie-Clark, H. F. Marginal Situation: *A Sociological Study of a Coloured Group. 240 pp. 11 tables.*
Glaser, Barney, and **Strauss, Anselm L.** Status Passage. *A Formal Theory. 208 pp.*
Glass, D. V. (Ed.) Social Mobility in Britain. *Contributions by J. Berent, T. Bottomore, R. C. Chambers, J. Floud, D. V. Glass, J. R. Hall, H. T. Himmelweit, R. K. Kelsall, F. M. Martin, C. A. Moser, R. Mukherjee, and W. Ziegel. 420 pp.*
Jones, Garth N. Planned Organizational Change: *An Exploratory Study Using an Empirical Approach. 268 pp.*
Kelsall, R. K. Higher Civil Servants in Britain: *From 1870 to the Present Day. 268 pp. 31 tables.*
König, René. The Community. *232 pp. Illustrated.*
●**Lawton, Denis.** Social Class, Language and Education. *192 pp.*
McLeish, John. The Theory of Social Change: *Four Views Considered. 128 pp.*
Marsh, David C. The Changing Social Structure of England and Wales, 1871-1961. *288 pp.*
●**Mouzelis, Nicos.** Organization and Bureaucracy. *An Analysis of Modern Theories. 240 pp.*
Mulkay, M. J. Functionalism, Exchange and Theoretical Strategy. *272 pp.*
Ossowski, Stanislaw. Class Structure in the Social Consciousness. *210 pp.*
●**Podgórecki, Adam.** Law and Society. *302 pp.*

SOCIOLOGY AND POLITICS

Acton, T. A. Gypsy Politics and Social Change. *316 pp.*

Clegg, Stuart. Power, Rule and Domination. *A Critical and Empirical Understanding of Power in Sociological Theory and Organisational Life. About 300 pp.*

Hechter, Michael. Internal Colonialism. *The Celtic Fringe in British National Development, 1536–1966. 361 pp.*

Hertz, Frederick. Nationality in History and Politics: *A Psychology and Sociology of National Sentiment and Nationalism. 432 pp.*

Kornhauser, William. The Politics of Mass Society. *272 pp. 20 tables.*

●**Kroes, R.** Soldiers and Students. *A Study of Right- and Left-wing Students. 174 pp.*

Laidler, Harry W. History of Socialism. *Social-Economic Movements: An Historical and Comparative Survey of Socialism, Communism, Co-operation, Utopianism; and other Systems of Reform and Reconstruction. 992 pp.*

Lasswell, H. D. Analysis of Political Behaviour. *324 pp.*

Mannheim, Karl. Freedom, Power and Democratic Planning. *Edited by Hans Gerth and Ernest K. Bramstedt. 424 pp.*

Mansur, Fatma. Process of Independence. *Foreword by A. H. Hanson. 208 pp.*

Martin, David A. Pacifism: *an Historical and Sociological Study. 262 pp.*

Myrdal, Gunnar. The Political Element in the Development of Economic Theory. *Translated from the German by Paul Streeten. 282 pp.*

Wootton, Graham. Workers, Unions and the State. *188 pp.*

FOREIGN AFFAIRS: THEIR SOCIAL, POLITICAL AND ECONOMIC FOUNDATIONS

Mayer, J. P. Political Thought in France from the Revolution to the Fifth Republic. *164 pp.*

CRIMINOLOGY

Ancel, Marc. Social Defence: *A Modern Approach to Criminal Problems. Foreword by Leon Radzinowicz. 240 pp.*

Cain, Maureen E. Society and the Policeman's Role. *326 pp.*

Cloward, Richard A., and **Ohlin, Lloyd E.** Delinquency and Opportunity: *A Theory of Delinquent Gangs. 248 pp.*

Downes, David M. The Delinquent Solution. *A Study in Subcultural Theory. 296 pp.*

Dunlop, A. B., and **McCabe, S.** Young Men in Detention Centres. *192 pp.*

Friedlander, Kate. The Psycho-Analytical Approach to Juvenile Delinquency: *Theory, Case Studies, Treatment. 320 pp.*

Glueck, Sheldon, and **Eleanor.** Family Environment and Delinquency. *With the statistical assistance of Rose W. Kneznek. 340 pp.*

Lopez-Rey, Manuel. Crime. *An Analytical Appraisal. 288 pp.*

Mannheim, Hermann. Comparative Criminology: *a Text Book. Two volumes. 442 pp. and 380 pp.*

Morris, Terence. The Criminal Area: *A Study in Social Ecology. Foreword by Hermann Mannheim. 232 pp. 25 tables. 4 maps.*

Rock, Paul. Making People Pay. *338 pp.*

●**Taylor, Ian, Walton, Paul,** and **Young, Jock.** The New Criminology. *For a Social Theory of Deviance. 325 pp.*

●**Taylor, Ian, Walton, Paul,** and **Young, Jock** (Eds). Critical Criminology. *268 pp.*

SOCIAL PSYCHOLOGY

Bagley, Christopher. The Social Psychology of the Epileptic Child. *320 pp.*

Barbu, Zevedei. Problems of Historical Psychology. *248 pp.*

Blackburn, Julian. Psychology and the Social Pattern. *184 pp.*

●**Brittan, Arthur.** Meanings and Situations. *224 pp.*

Carroll, J. Break-Out from the Crystal Palace. *200 pp.*

●**Fleming, C. M.** Adolescence: Its Social Psychology. *With an Introduction to recent findings from the fields of Anthropology, Physiology, Medicine, Psychometrics and Sociometry. 288 pp.*

● The Social Psychology of Education: *An Introduction and Guide to Its Study. 136 pp.*

●**Homans, George C.** The Human Group. *Foreword by Bernard DeVoto. Introduction by Robert K. Merton. 526 pp.*

● Social Behaviour: *its Elementary Forms. 416 pp.*

●**Klein, Josephine.** The Study of Groups. *226 pp. 31 figures. 5 tables.*

Linton, Ralph. The Cultural Background of Personality. *132 pp.*

●**Mayo, Elton.** The Social Problems of an Industrial Civilization. *With an appendix on the Political Problem. 180 pp.*

Ottaway, A. K. C. Learning Through Group Experience. *176 pp.*

Plummer, Ken. Sexual Stigma. *An Interactionist Account. 254 pp.*

Ridder, J. C. de. The Personality of the Urban African in South Africa. *A Thematic Apperception Test Study. 196 pp. 12 plates.*

●**Rose, Arnold M.** (Ed.) Human Behaviour and Social Processes: *an Interactionist Approach. Contributions by Arnold M. Rose, Ralph H. Turner, Anselm Strauss, Everett C. Hughes, E. Franklin Frazier, Howard S. Becker, et al. 696 pp.*

Smelser, Neil J. Theory of Collective Behaviour. *448 pp.*

Stephenson, Geoffrey M. The Development of Conscience. *128 pp.*

Young, Kimball. Handbook of Social Psychology. *658 pp. 16 figures. 10 tables.*

SOCIOLOGY OF THE FAMILY

Banks, J. A. Prosperity and Parenthood: *A Study of Family Planning among The Victorian Middle Classes. 262 pp.*

Bell, Colin R. Middle Class Families: *Social and Geographical Mobility. 224 pp.*

Burton, Lindy. Vulnerable Children. *272 pp.*

Gavron, Hannah. The Captive Wife: *Conflicts of Household Mothers. 190 pp.*

George, Victor, and **Wilding, Paul.** Motherless Families. *248 pp.*

Klein, Josephine. Samples from English Cultures.
1. Three Preliminary Studies and Aspects of Adult Life in England. *447 pp.*
2. Child-Rearing Practices and Index. *247 pp.*

Klein, Viola. Britain's Married Women Workers. *180 pp.*
The Feminine Character. *History of an Ideology. 244 pp.*

McWhinnie, Alexina M. Adopted Children. *How They Grow Up. 304 pp.*

● **Morgan, D. H. J.** Social Theory and the Family. *About 320 pp.*

● **Myrdal, Alva,** and **Klein, Viola.** Women's Two Roles: *Home and Work.* *238 pp. 27 tables.*

Parsons, Talcott, and **Bales, Robert F.** Family: Socialization and Inter-action Process. *In collaboration with James Olds, Morris Zelditch and Philip E. Slater. 456 pp. 50 figures and tables.*

SOCIAL SERVICES

Bastide, Roger. The Sociology of Mental Disorder. *Translated from the French by Jean McNeil. 260 pp.*

Carlebach, Julius. Caring For Children in Trouble. *266 pp.*

George, Victor. Foster Care. *Theory and Practice. 234 pp.*
Social Security: *Beveridge and After. 258 pp.*

George, V., and **Wilding, P.** Motherless Families. *248 pp.*

●**Goetschius, George W.** Working with Community Groups. *256 pp.*

Goetschius, George W., and **Tash, Joan.** Working with Unattached Youth. *416 pp.*

Hall, M. P., and **Howes, I. V.** The Church in Social Work. *A Study of Moral Welfare Work undertaken by the Church of England. 320 pp.*

Heywood, Jean S. Children in Care: *the Development of the Service for the Deprived Child. 264 pp.*

Hoenig, J., and **Hamilton, Marian W.** The De-Segregation of the Mentally Ill. *284 pp.*

Jones, Kathleen. Mental Health and Social Policy, 1845-1959. *264 pp.*

King, Roy D., Raynes, Norma V., and **Tizard, Jack.** Patterns of Residential Care. *356 pp.*

Leigh, John. Young People and Leisure. *256 pp.*

●**Mays, John.** (Ed.) Penelope Hall's Social Services of England and Wales. *About 324 pp.*

Morris, Mary. Voluntary Work and the Welfare State. *300 pp.*

Morris, Pauline. Put Away: *A Sociological Study of Institutions for the Mentally Retarded. 364 pp.*

Nokes, P. L. The Professional Task in Welfare Practice. *152 pp.*

Timms, Noel. Psychiatric Social Work in Great Britain (1939-1962). *280 pp.*

● Social Casework: *Principles and Practice. 256 pp.*

Young, A. F. Social Services in British Industry. *272 pp.*

Young, A. F., and **Ashton, E. T.** British Social Work in the Nineteenth Century. *288 pp.*

SOCIOLOGY OF EDUCATION

Banks, Olive. Parity and Prestige in English Secondary Education: a Study in Educational Sociology. *272 pp.*

Bentwich, Joseph. Education in Israel. *224 pp. 8 pp. plates.*

●**Blyth, W. A. L.** English Primary Education. *A Sociological Description.*
1. Schools. *232 pp.*
2. Background. *168 pp.*

Collier, K. G. The Social Purposes of Education: *Personal and Social Values in Education. 268 pp.*

Dale, R. R., and **Griffith, S.** Down Stream: *Failure in the Grammar School. 108 pp.*

Dore, R. P. Education in Tokugawa Japan. *356 pp. 9 pp. plates.*

Evans, K. M. Sociometry and Education. *158 pp.*

●**Ford, Julienne.** Social Class and the Comprehensive School. *192 pp.*

Foster, P. J. Education and Social Change in Ghana. *336 pp. 3 maps.*

Fraser, W. R. Education and Society in Modern France. *150 pp.*

Grace, Gerald R. Role Conflict and the Teacher. *150 pp.*

Hans, Nicholas. New Trends in Education in the Eighteenth Century. *278 pp. 19 tables.*

● Comparative Education: *A Study of Educational Factors and Traditions. 360 pp.*

●**Hargreaves, David.** Interpersonal Relations and Education. *432 pp.*

● Social Relations in a Secondary School. *240 pp.*

Holmes, Brian. Problems in Education. *A Comparative Approach. 336 pp.*

King, Ronald. Values and Involvement in a Grammar School. *164 pp.*
School Organization and Pupil Involvement. *A Study of Secondary Schools.*

●**Mannheim, Karl,** and **Stewart, W. A. C.** An Introduction to the Sociology of Education. *206 pp.*

Morris, Raymond N. The Sixth Form and College Entrance. *231 pp.*

●**Musgrove, F.** Youth and the Social Order. *176 pp.*

●**Ottaway, A. K. C.** Education and Society: An Introduction to the Sociology of Education. *With an Introduction by W. O. Lester Smith. 212 pp.*

Peers, Robert. Adult Education: *A Comparative Study. 398 pp.*

Pritchard, D. G. Education and the Handicapped: *1760 to 1960. 258 pp.*

Richardson, Helen. Adolescent Girls in Approved Schools. *308 pp.*

Stratta, Erica. The Education of Borstal Boys. *A Study of their Educational Experiences prior to, and during, Borstal Training. 256 pp.*

Taylor, P. H., Reid, W. A., and **Holley, B. J.** The English Sixth Form. *A Case Study in Curriculum Research. 200 pp.*

SOCIOLOGY OF CULTURE

Eppel, E. M., and **M.** Adolescents and Morality: *A Study of some Moral Values and Dilemmas of Working Adolescents in the Context of a changing Climate of Opinion. Foreword by W. J. H. Sprott. 268 pp. 39 tables.*

●**Fromm, Erich.** The Fear of Freedom. *286 pp.*
● The Sane Society. *400 pp.*
Mannheim, Karl. Essays on the Sociology of Culture. *Edited by Ernst Mannheim in co-operation with Paul Kecskemeti. Editorial Note by Adolph Lowe. 280 pp.*
Weber, Alfred. Farewell to European History: *or The Conquest of Nihilism. Translated from the German by R. F. C. Hull. 224 pp.*

SOCIOLOGY OF RELIGION

Argyle, Michael and **Beit-Hallahmi, Benjamin.** The Social Psychology of Religion. *About 256 pp.*
Nelson, G. K. Spiritualism and Society. *313 pp.*
Stark, Werner. The Sociology of Religion. *A Study of Christendom.*
Volume I. *Established Religion. 248 pp.*
Volume II. *Sectarian Religion. 368 pp.*
Volume III. *The Universal Church. 464 pp.*
Volume IV. *Types of Religious Man. 352 pp.*
Volume V. *Types of Religious Culture. 464 pp.*
Turner, B. S. Weber and Islam. *216 pp.*
Watt, W. Montgomery. Islam and the Integration of Society. *320 pp.*

SOCIOLOGY OF ART AND LITERATURE

Jarvie, Ian C. Towards a Sociology of the Cinema. *A Comparative Essay on the Structure and Functioning of a Major Entertainment Industry. 405 pp.*
Rust, Frances S. Dance in Society. *An Analysis of the Relationships between the Social Dance and Society in England from the Middle Ages to the Present Day. 256 pp. 8 pp. of plates.*
Schücking, L. L. The Sociology of Literary Taste. *112 pp.*
Wolff, Janet. Hermeneutic Philosophy and the Sociology of Art. *150 pp.*

SOCIOLOGY OF KNOWLEDGE

Diesing, P. Patterns of Discovery in the Social Sciences. *262 pp.*
●**Douglas, J. D.** (Ed.) Understanding Everyday Life. *370 pp.*
●**Hamilton, P.** Knowledge and Social Structure. *174 pp.*
Jarvie, I. C. Concepts and Society. *232 pp.*
Mannheim, Karl. Essays on the Sociology of Knowledge. *Edited by Paul Kecskemeti. Editorial Note by Adolph Lowe. 353 pp.*
Remmling, Gunter W. The Sociology of Karl Mannheim. *With a Bibliographical Guide to the Sociology of Knowledge, Ideological Analysis, and Social Planning. 255 pp.*

9

Remmling, Gunter W. (Ed.) Towards the Sociology of Knowledge. *Origin and Development of a Sociological Thought Style. 463 pp.*

Stark, Werner. The Sociology of Knowledge: *An Essay in Aid of a Deeper Understanding of the History of Ideas. 384 pp.*

URBAN SOCIOLOGY

Ashworth, William. The Genesis of Modern British Town Planning: *A Study in Economic and Social History of the Nineteenth and Twentieth Centuries. 288 pp.*

Cullingworth, J. B. Housing Needs and Planning Policy: *A Restatement of the Problems of Housing Need and 'Overspill' in England and Wales. 232 pp. 44 tables. 8 maps.*

Dickinson, Robert E. City and Region: *A Geographical Interpretation 608 pp. 125 figures.*

The West European City: *A Geographical Interpretation. 600 pp. 129 maps. 29 plates.*

● The City Region in Western Europe. *320 pp. Maps.*

Humphreys, Alexander J. New Dubliners: *Urbanization and the Irish Family. Foreword by George C. Homans. 304 pp.*

Jackson, Brian. Working Class Community: *Some General Notions raised by a Series of Studies in Northern England. 192 pp.*

Jennings, Hilda. Societies in the Making: *a Study of Development and Redevelopment within a County Borough. Foreword by D. A. Clark. 286 pp.*

●**Mann, P. H.** An Approach to Urban Sociology. *240 pp.*

Morris, R. N., and **Mogey, J.** The Sociology of Housing. *Studies at Berinsfield. 232 pp. 4 pp. plates.*

Rosser, C., and **Harris, C.** The Family and Social Change. *A Study of Family and Kinship in a South Wales Town. 352 pp. 8 maps.*

●**Stacey, Margaret, Batsone, Eric, Bell, Colin,** and **Thurcott, Anne.** Power, Persistence and Change. *A Second Study of Banbury. 196 pp.*

RURAL SOCIOLOGY

Chambers, R. J. H. Settlement Schemes in Tropical Africa: *A Selective Study. 268 pp.*

Haswell, M. R. The Economics of Development in Village India. *120 pp.*

Littlejohn, James. Westrigg: *the Sociology of a Cheviot Parish. 172 pp. 5 figures.*

Mayer, Adrian C. Peasants in the Pacific. *A Study of Fiji Indian Rural Society. 248 pp. 20 plates.*

Williams, W. M. The Sociology of an English Village: *Gosforth. 272 pp. 12 figures. 13 tables.*

SOCIOLOGY OF INDUSTRY AND DISTRIBUTION

Anderson, Nels. Work and Leisure. *280 pp.*

●**Blau, Peter M.,** and **Scott, W. Richard.** Formal Organizations: *a Comparative approach. Introduction and Additional Bibliography by J. H. Smith. 326 pp.*

Dunkerley, David. The Foreman. *Aspects of Task and Structure. 192 pp.*

Eldridge, J. E. T. Industrial Disputes. *Essays in the Sociology of Industrial Relations. 288 pp.*

Hetzler, Stanley. Applied Measures for Promoting Technological Growth. *352 pp.*

Technological Growth and Social Change. *Achieving Modernization. 269 pp.*

Hollowell, Peter G. The Lorry Driver. *272 pp.*

Jefferys, Margot, *with the assistance of Winifred Moss.* Mobility in the Labour Market: *Employment Changes in Battersea and Dagenham. Preface by Barbara Wootton. 186 pp. 51 tables.*

Millerson, Geoffrey. The Qualifying Associations: *a Study in Professionalization. 320 pp.*

●**Oxaal, I., Barnett, T.,** and **Booth, D.** (Eds). Beyond the Sociology of Development. *Economy and Society in Latin America and Africa. 295 pp.*

Smelser, Neil J. Social Change in the Industrial Revolution: *An Application of Theory to the Lancashire Cotton Industry, 1770–1840. 468 pp. 12 figures. 14 tables.*

Williams, Gertrude. Recruitment to Skilled Trades. *240 pp.*

Young, A. F. Industrial Injuries Insurance: *an Examination of British Policy. 192 pp.*

DOCUMENTARY

Schlesinger, Rudolf (Ed.) Changing Attitudes in Soviet Russia.
2. The Nationalities Problem and Soviet Administration. *Selected Readings on the Development of Soviet Nationalities Policies. Introduced by the editor. Translated by W. W. Gottlieb. 324 pp.*

ANTHROPOLOGY

Ammar, Hamed. Growing up in an Egyptian Village: *Silwa, Province of Aswan. 336 pp.*

Brandel-Syrier, Mia. Reeftown Elite. *A Study of Social Mobility in a Modern African Community on the Reef. 376 pp.*

Crook, David, and **Isabel.** Revolution in a Chinese Village: *Ten Mile Inn. 230 pp. 8 plates. 1 map.*

Dickie-Clark, H. F. The Marginal Situation. *A Sociological Study of a Coloured Group. 236 pp.*

Dube, S. C. Indian Village. *Foreword by Morris Edward Opler. 276 pp. 4 plates.*

India's Changing Villages: *Human Factors in Community Development.* *260 pp. 8 plates. 1 map.*

Firth, Raymond. Malay Fishermen. *Their Peasant Economy. 420 pp. 17 pp. plates.*

Firth, R., Hubert, J., and **Forge, A.** Families and their Relatives. *Kinship in a Middle-Class Sector of London: An Anthropological Study. 456 pp.*

Gulliver, P. H. Social Control in an African Society: a Study of the Arusha, Agricultural Masai of Northern Tanganyika. *320 pp. 8 plates. 10 figures.*

Family Herds. *288 pp.*

Ishwaran, K. Shivapur. *A South Indian Village. 216 pp.*

Tradition and Economy in Village India: *An Interactionist Approach. Foreword by Conrad Arensburg. 176 pp.*

Jarvie, Ian C. The Revolution in Anthropology. *268 pp.*

Little, Kenneth L. Mende of Sierra Leone. *308 pp. and folder.*

Negroes in Britain. *With a New Introduction and Contemporary Study by Leonard Bloom. 320 pp.*

Lowie, Robert H. Social Organization. *494 pp.*

Peasants in the Pacific. *A Study of Fiji Indian Rural Society. 248 pp.*

Smith, Raymond T. The Negro Family in British Guiana: *Family Structure and Social Status in the Villages. With a Foreword by Meyer Fortes. 314 pp. 8 plates. 1 figure. 4 maps.*

SOCIOLOGY AND PHILOSOPHY

Barnsley, John H. The Social Reality of Ethics. *A Comparative Analysis of Moral Codes. 448 pp.*

Diesing, Paul. Patterns of Discovery in the Social Sciences. *362 pp.*

●**Douglas, Jack D.** (Ed.) Understanding Everyday Life. *Toward the Reconstruction of Sociological Knowledge. Contributions by Alan F. Blum. Aaron W. Cicourel, Norman K. Denzin, Jack D. Douglas, John Heeren, Peter McHugh, Peter K. Manning, Melvin Power, Matthew Speier, Roy Turner, D. Lawrence Wieder, Thomas P. Wilson and Don H. Zimmerman. 370 pp.*

Jarvie, Ian C. Concepts and Society. *216 pp.*

●**Pelz, Werner.** The Scope of Understanding in Sociology. *Towards a more radical reorientation in the social humanistic sciences. 283 pp.*

Roche, Maurice. Phenomenology, Language and the Social Sciences. *371 pp.*

Sahay, Arun. Sociological Analysis. *212 pp.*

Sklair, Leslie. The Sociology of Progress. *320 pp.*

International Library of Anthropology

General Editor Adam Kuper

Brown, Paula. The Chimbu. *A Study of Change in the New Guinea Highlands. 151 pp.*

Hamnett, Ian. Chieftainship and Legitimacy. *An Anthropological Study of Executive Law in Lesotho. 163 pp.*
Hanson, F. Allan. Meaning in Culture. *127 pp.*
Lloyd, P. C. Power and Independence. *Urban Africans' Perception of Social Inequality. 264 pp.*
Pettigrew, Joyce. Robber Noblemen. *A Study of the Political System of the Sikh Jats. 284 pp.*
Street, Brian V. The Savage in Literature. *Representations of 'Primitive' Society in English Fiction, 1858–1920. 207 pp.*
Van Den Berghe, Pierre L. Power and Privilege at an African University. *278 pp.*

International Library of Social Policy

General Editor Kathleen Jones

Bayley, M. Mental Handicap and Community Care. *426 pp.*
Butler, J. R. Family Doctors and Public Policy. *208 pp.*
Davies, Martin. Prisoners of Society. *Attitudes and Aftercare. 204 pp.*
Holman, Robert. Trading in Children. *A Study of Private Fostering. 355 pp.*
Jones, Kathleen. History of the Mental Health Service. *428 pp.*
   Opening the Door. *A Study of New Policies for the Mentally Handicapped. 260 pp.*
Thomas, J. E. The English Prison Officer since 1850: *A Study in Conflict. 258 pp.*
Walton, R. G. Women in Social Work. *303 pp.*
Woodward, J. To Do the Sick No Harm. *A Study of the British Voluntary Hospital System to 1875. 221 pp.*

International Library of Welfare and Philosophy

General Editors Noel Timms and David Watson

● **Plant, Raymond.** Community and Ideology. *104 pp.*

Primary Socialization, Language and Education

General Editor Basil Bernstein

Bernstein, Basil. Class, Codes and Control. *3 volumes.*
   1. *Theoretical Studies Towards a Sociology of Language. 254 pp.*
   2. *Applied Studies Towards a Sociology of Language. 377 pp.*
   3. *Towards a Theory of Educational Transmission. 167 pp.*
Brandis, W., and **Bernstein, B.** Selection and Control. *176 pp.*
Brandis, Walter, and **Henderson, Dorothy.** Social Class, Language and Communication. *288 pp.*

Cook-Gumperz, Jenny. Social Control and Socialization. *A Study of Class Differences in the Language of Maternal Control. 290 pp.*

●**Gahagan, D. M.,** and **G. A.** Talk Reform. *Exploration in Language for Infant School Children. 160 pp.*

Robinson, W. P., and **Rackstraw, Susan D. A.** A Question of Answers. *2 volumes. 192 pp. and 180 pp.*

Turner, Geoffrey J., and **Mohan, Bernard A.** A Linguistic Description and Computer Programme for Children's Speech. *208 pp.*

Reports of the Institute of Community Studies

Cartwright, Ann. Human Relations and Hospital Care. *272 pp.*

● Parents and Family Planning Services. *306 pp.*

Patients and their Doctors. *A Study of General Practice. 304 pp.*

Dench, Geoff. Maltese in London. *A Case-study in the Erosion of Ethnic Consciousness. 302 pp.*

●**Jackson, Brian.** Streaming: *an Education System in Miniature. 168 pp.*

Jackson, Brian, and **Marsden, Dennis.** Education and the Working Class: *Some General Themes raised by a Study of 88 Working-class Children in a Northern Industrial City. 268 pp. 2 folders.*

Marris, Peter. The Experience of Higher Education. *232 pp. 27 tables.*

Loss and Change. *192 pp.*

Marris, Peter, and **Rein, Martin.** Dilemmas of Social Reform. *Poverty and Community Action in the United States. 256 pp.*

Marris, Peter, and **Somerset, Anthony.** African Businessmen. *A Study of Entrepreneurship and Development in Kenya. 256 pp.*

Mills, Richard. Young Outsiders: *a Study in Alternative Communities. 216 pp.*

Runciman, W. G. Relative Deprivation and Social Justice. *A Study of Attitudes to Social Inequality in Twentieth-Century England. 352 pp.*

Willmott, Peter. Adolescent Boys in East London. *230 pp.*

Willmott, Peter, and **Young, Michael.** Family and Class in a London Suburb. *202 pp. 47 tables.*

Young, Michael. Innovation and Research in Education. *192 pp.*

●**Young, Michael,** and **McGeeney, Patrick.** Learning Begins at Home. *A Study of a Junior School and its Parents. 128 pp.*

Young, Michael, and **Willmott, Peter.** Family and Kinship in East London. *Foreword by Richard M. Titmuss. 252 pp. 39 tables.*

The Symmetrical Family. *410 pp.*

Reports of the Institute for Social Studies in Medical Care

Cartwright, Ann, Hockey, Lisbeth, and **Anderson, John L.** Life Before Death. *310 pp.*

Dunnell, Karen, and **Cartwright, Ann.** Medicine Takers, Prescribers and Hoarders. *190 pp.*

Medicine, Illness and Society

General Editor W. M. Williams

Robinson, David. The Process of Becoming Ill. *142 pp.*
Stacey, Margaret, *et al.* Hospitals, Children and Their Families. *The Report of a Pilot Study. 202 pp.*
Stimson, G. V., and **Webb, B.** Going to See the Doctor. *The Consultation Process in General Practice. 155 pp.*

Monographs in Social Theory

General Editor Arthur Brittan

● **Barnes, B.** Scientific Knowledge and Sociological Theory. *192 pp.*
Bauman, Zygmunt. Culture as Praxis. *204 pp.*
● **Dixon, Keith.** Sociological Theory. *Pretence and Possibility. 142 pp.*
Meltzer, B. N., Petras, J. W., and **Reynolds, L. T.** Symbolic Interactionism. *Genesis, Varieties and Criticisms. 144 pp.*
● **Smith, Anthony D.** The Concept of Social Change. *A Critique of the Functionalist Theory of Social Change. 208 pp.*

Routledge Social Science Journals

The British Journal of Sociology. *Managing Editor – Angus Stewart; Associate Editor – Michael Hill. Vol. 1, No. 1 – March 1950 and Quarterly. Roy. 8vo. All back issues available. An international journal publishing original papers in the field of sociology and related areas.*
Community Work. *Edited by David Jones and Marjorie Mayo. 1973. Published annually.*
Economy and Society. *Vol. 1, No. 1. February 1972 and Quarterly. Metric Roy. 8vo. A journal for all social scientists covering sociology, philosophy, anthropology, economics and history. Back numbers available.*
Religion. *Journal of Religion and Religions. Chairman of Editorial Board, Ninian Smart. Vol. 1, No. 1, Spring 1971. A journal with an interdisciplinary approach to the study of the phenomena of religion.*
Year Book of Social Policy in Britain, The. *Edited by Kathleen Jones. 1971. Published annually.*

Printed in Great Britain by Unwin Brothers Limited
The Gresham Press Old Woking Surrey
A member of the Staples Printing Group

June 1975